Making Social Sciences More Scientific

Making Social Sciences More Scientific

The Need for Predictive Models

Rein Taagepera

OXFORD
UNIVERSITY PRESS

OXFORD
UNIVERSITY PRESS

Great Clarendon Street, Oxford OX2 6DP

Oxford University Press is a department of the University of Oxford.
It furthers the University's objective of excellence in research, scholarship,
and education by publishing worldwide in

Oxford New York

Auckland Cape Town Dar es Salaam Hong Kong Karachi
Kuala Lumpur Madrid Melbourne Mexico City Nairobi
New Delhi Shanghai Taipei Toronto

With offices in

Argentina Austria Brazil Chile Czech Republic France Greece
Guatemala Hungary Italy Japan Poland Portugal Singapore
South Korea Switzerland Thailand Turkey Ukraine Vietnam

Oxford is a registered trade mark of Oxford University Press
in the UK and in certain other countries

Published in the United States
by Oxford University Press Inc., New York

British Library Cataloguing in Publication Data

Data available

Library of Congress Cataloging-in-Publication Data

Taagepera, Rein.
Making social sciences more scientific : the need for predictive
models / Rein Taagepera.
p. cm.
ISBN 978–0–19–953466–1
1. Social sciences–Research. 2. Social sciences–Fieldwork.
3. Social sciences–Methodology. 4. Sociology–Methodology.
5. Sociology–Research. I. Title.
H62.T22 2008
300.72–dc22   2008015441

Typeset by SPI Publisher Services, Pondicherry, India
Printed in Great Britain
on acid-free paper by
Biddles Ltd., King's Lynn, Norfolk

ISBN 978–0–19–953466–1

1 3 5 7 9 10 8 6 4 2

Foreword: Statistical Versus Scientific Inferences

Psychology is one of the heavier consumers of statistics. Presumably, the reason is that psychologists have become convinced that they are greatly aided in making correct scientific inferences by casting their decision-making into the framework of statistical inference. In my view, we have witnessed a form of mass deception of the sort typified by the story of the emperor with no clothes.

Statistical inference techniques are good for what they were developed for, mostly making decisions about the probable success of agriculture, industrial, and drug interventions, but they are not especially appropriate to scientific inference which, in the final analysis, is trying to model what is going on, not merely to decide if one variable affects another. What has happened is that many psychologists have forced themselves into thinking in a way dictated by inferential statistics, not by the problems they really wish or should wish to solve. The real question rarely is whether a correlation differs significantly, but usually slightly, from zero (such a conclusion is so weak and so unsurprising to be mostly of little interest), but whether it deviates from unity by an amount that could be explained by errors of measurement, including nonlinearities in the scales used. Similarly, one rarely cares whether there is a significant interaction term; one wants to know whether by suitable transformations it is possible or not to get rid of it altogether (e.g., it cannot be removed when the data are crossed). The demonstration of an interaction is hardly a result to be proud of, since it simply means that we still do not understand the nature and composition of the independent factors that underlie the dependent variable.

Model builders find inferential statistics of remarkably limited value. In part, this is because the statistics for most models have not been worked out; to do so is usually hard work, and by the time it might be completed, interest in the model is likely to have vanished. A second reason is that often model builders are trying to select between models or classes of models, and they much prefer to ascertain where they differ maximally and to exploit this experimentally. This is not easy to do, but when done it is usually far more convincing than a fancy statistical test.

Let me make clear several things I am not saying when I question the use of statistical inference in scientific work. First, I do not mean to suggest that model builders should ignore basic probability theory and the theory of stochastic processes; quite the contrary, they must know this material well. Second, my objection is only to a part of statistics; in particular, it does not apply to the area devoted to the estimation of parameters. This is an area of great use to psychologists, and increasingly statisticians have emphasized it over inference. And third, I do not want to imply that psychologists should become less quantitative and systematic in the handling of data. I would urge more careful analyses of data, especially ones in which the attempt is to reveal the mathematical structure to be found in the data.

R. Duncan Luce (1989)

Preface

After completing my Ph.D. in physics, I became interested in social sciences. I had published in nuclear physics (Taagepera and Nurmia 1961) and solid state (Taagepera et al. 1961; Taagepera and Williams 1966), and some of my graphs were even reprinted (Hyde et al. 1964: 256–8; Segré 1964: 278). As I shifted to political science and related fields, at the University of California, Irvine, I still continued to apply the model-building and testing skills learned in physics.

The transition was successful. *Seats and Votes* (Taagepera and Shugart 1989), in particular, received the 1999 George Hallett Award, given to books still relevant for electoral studies 10 years after publication. The book became part of semi-obligatory citations in the field. It was less obligatory to actually read it, however, and even less so to understand it. Felicitous phrases were quoted, but our quantitative results were largely overlooked. Something was amiss.

Moreover, publishing new results was becoming more of a hassle. When faced with quantitatively predictive logical models, journal referees would insist on pointless statistical analyses and, once I put them in, asked to scrap the logical models as pointless. It gradually dawned on me that we differed not only on methodology for reaching results but also on the very meaning of "results."

Coming from physics, I took predictive ability as a major criterion of meaningful results. In social sciences, in contrast, unambiguous prediction—that could prove right or wrong—was discounted in favor of statistical "models" that could go this way or that way, depending on what factors one included and which statistical approach one used. Social scientists still talked about "falsifiability" of models as a criterion, but they increasingly used canned computer programs to test loose, merely directional "models" that had a 50–50 chance of being right just by chance.

At first, I did not object. Let many flowers bloom. Purely statistical data processing can be of some value. I expected that predictions based on logical considerations, such as those in *Seats and Votes*, would demonstrate the usefulness of quantitative logical models. But this is not how it works out, once the very meaning of "results" is corrupted so as to discount predictive ability. Slowly, I came to realize that this was a core problem not only in political science but also within the entire social science community.

Computers could have been a boon to social sciences, but they turned out to be a curse in disguise, by enabling people with little understanding of scientific process to grind out reams of numbers parading as "results", to be printed—and never used again. Bad money was driving out the good, although it came with a price. Society at large still valued predictive ability. It gave quantitative social scientists even less credence than to qualitative historians, philosophers, and journalists. Compared to the latter, quantitative social scientists seemed no better at prediction—they were just more boring.

Giving good example visibly did not suffice. It became most evident in June 2004 as I observed a student at the University of Tartu present another mindless linear regression exercise, this time haughtily dismissing a quantitatively predictive logical model I had published, even while that model accounted for 75% of the variation in the output variable. Right there, I sketched the following test.

Given synthetic data that fitted the universal law of gravitation near-perfectly, how many social scientists would discover the underlying regularity? See Chapter 2 for the blatantly negative outcome. Like nearly all regularities in physics, the gravitation law is nonlinear. If there were such law-like social regularities, purely statistics-oriented social science would seem unable to pin them down even in the absence of random scatter!

This was the starting point of a paper at a methodology workshop in Liège, Belgium: "Beyond Regression: The Need for Logical Models" (Taagepera 2005*a*). Inspired by a list of important physics equations pointed out by Josep Colomer, I located a number of differences in the mathematical formats usual in physical and social sciences (see Chapter 5) as well as in the meaning of "results"(see Chapter 7).

Upon that, Benoît Rihoux invited me to form a panel on "Predictive vs. Postdictive Models" at the Third Conference of the European Consortium for Political Research. Unusual for a methodology panel, the large room in Budapest was packed as Stephen Coleman (2005), Josep Colomer and Clara Riba (2005), and I (Taagepera 2005*b*) gave papers. While we discussed publishing possibilities during a "postmortem" meeting in the cafeteria of Corvinus University, Bernard Grofman, a discussant at the panel, suggested the title "Why Political Science Is Not Scientific Enough". This is how the symposium was presented in *European Political Science* (Coleman 2007; Colomer 2007; Grofman 2007; Taagepera 2007*a*, *b*).

It turned out that quite a few people had misgivings about the excessive use and misuse of statistical approaches in social sciences. Duncan Luce told me about his struggles when trying to go beyond naïve linear regression (see Chapter 1). James McGregor (1993) and King et al. (2000) in political science and Aage Sørensen (1998) and Peter Hedström (2004) in sociology had voiced concerns. Geoffrey Loftus (1991) protested against the "tyranny of hypothesis testing." Gigerenzer et al. (2004) exposed the "null hypothesis ritual." Bernhard Kittel (2006) showed that different statistical approaches to the very same data could make factors look highly significant in opposite directions. "A Crazy Methodology?" was his title (see Chapter 7).

Writing a book on *Predicting Party Sizes* (Taagepera 2007*c*) for the Oxford University Press presented me with a dilemma. Previous experience with *Seats and Votes* showed that if I wanted to be not only cited but also understood, I had to explain the predictive model methodology in appreciable detail. The title emphasized "Predicting," but the broad methodology did not fit in. It made the book too bulky. More importantly, the need for predictive models extends far beyond electoral and party systems, or even political science. This is why *Making Social Sciences More Scientific: The Need for Predictive Models* became a separate book. While many of the illustrative examples deal with politics, the general methodology applies to all social sciences.

Methodological issues risk being perceived as dull. I have tried to enliven the approach by having many short chapters, some with provocative titles. Some mathematically more demanding sections are left to chapter appendices. To facilitate the use as a textbook, the gist of chapters is presented in special introductory sections that try to be less abstract than the usual abstracts of research articles.

Will this book help start a paradigm shift in social science methodology? I hope so, because the alternative is a Ptolemaic dead end. Those social scientists whose quantitative skills are restricted to push-button regression will put up considerable resistance when they discover that quantitatively predictive logical models require something that cannot be reduced to canned computer programs. Yes, these models require creative thinking, even while mathematical demands as such often do not go beyond high-school algebra. Creative thinking is what science is about. This is why the shift may start precisely among those social scientists who best understand the mathematics underlying the statistical approaches. Among them, unease with limitations of purely statistical methods is increasing. We shall see.

Many people have wittingly or unwittingly contributed to this book in significant ways. I list them in alphabetical order, with apologies to those whom I may have forgotten. They are Mirjam Allik (who also finalized most of the figures), Rune Holmgaard Andersen, Lloyd Anderson, Daniel Bochsler, Stephen Coleman, Josep Colomer, Lorenzo De Sio, Angela Lee Duckworth, John Ensch, John Gerring, Bernard Grofman, Oliver Heath, Bernhard Kittel, Arend Lijphart, Maarja Lühiste, Rikho Nymmik, Clara Riba, Benoît Rihoux, David Samuels, Matthew Shugart, Allan Sikk, Werner Stahel, Mare Taagepera, Margit Tavits, Liina-Mai Tooding, Sakura Yamasaki, and the monthly *Akadeemia* (Estonia). Elizabeth Suffling, Louise Sprake, Natasha Forrest, Gunabala Saladi, Abhirami Ravikumar, and Maggie Shade at Oxford University Press have edited the book into technically superb form. My greatest thanks go to Duncan Luce who graciously agreed to have an excerpt of his published as Foreword to this book, and who also pinned down various weak aspects of my draft. The remaining shortcomings are of course my own.

Rein Taagepera

Contents

Contents

List of Figures

List of Tables

Part I

The Limitations of Descriptive Methodology

1

Why Social Sciences Are Not Scientific Enough

- This book is about going *beyond* regression and other statistical approaches. It is also about improving their use. It is not about "replacing" or "dumping" them.
- Science is not only about the empirical "What is?" but also very much about the conceptual "How *should* it be on logical grounds?"
- Statistical approaches are essentially descriptive, while quantitatively formulated logical models are predictive in an explanatory way. I use "descriptive" and "predictive" as shorthand for these two approaches.
- Social scientists have overemphasized statistical data analysis, often limiting their logical models to prediction of the *direction* of effect, oblivious of its quantitative extent.
- A better balance of methods is possible and will make social sciences more relevant to society.
- Quantitatively predictive logical models need not involve more complex mathematics than regression analysis. But they do require active thinking about how things connect. They cannot be abdicated to canned computer programs.

Social sciences have made great strides during the last 100 years, but now a cancer is eating at the scientific study of society and politics—excessive and ritualized dependence on statistical data analysis in general and linear regression in particular. Note that cancer cells are our own cells, not alien invaders. They just proliferate into places where they have no business to be and crowd out more useful cells. *Descriptive* statistical data analysis, too, is welcome at its proper place, but it has crowded out the quantitatively *explanatory* approaches at those stages of research where logical thinking is called for. It is time to restore some balance, so as to bring to completion research that presently all too often stops before reaching the payoff stage.

From psychology to political science, pressure is heavy to apply simplistic statistical approaches, such as linear regression and its *probit* and *logit* extensions, to any and all problems, to the exclusion of quantitative approaches based on logic. Duncan Luce, one of the foremost mathematical psychologists, told me about his struggle to publish an article by Folk and Luce (1987). The authors evaluated a data plot (fig. 3 in their published version) and decided that the nature of the problem called for log-linear analysis (table 2 in the published version). The editors, however, most likely on the advice of reviewers, insisted on replacing it by straight linear analysis (table 1 of Folk and Luce 1987). The best the authors could do was to fight for permission to retain their own analysis along with the linear, even while they considered the latter pointless.

Luce (1988) has protested against "mindless hypothesis testing in lieu of doing good research: measuring effects, constructive substantive theories of some depth, and developing probability models and statistical procedures suited to these theories." James McGregor (1993) in political science and Aage Sørensen (1998) in sociology have stressed that applying only statistical methods to any and all problems is not the way to go. Sociologist James Coleman (1964, 1981) strongly proposed the use of substantive rather than statistical models, but in Peter Hedström's opinion (2004) often did not apply his own precepts, yielding to the rising hegemony of statistical analysis. I have met similar pressures in political science.

The result is that social sciences are not as scientific as they could be. It is not that the methods presently used are erroneous—they are just overdone. Imagine members of a formerly isolated tribe who suddenly run across a metal tool—a screwdriver. They are so impressed with it that they use it not only on screws but also to chisel and to cut. If pointed out that other people use other tools for those purposes, they respond that other people, too, use screwdrivers, which proves their value. They argue that the materials they use differ from those of other people and are uniquely suitable for screwdrivers. If the cut is scraggy, it just shows they are working with extraordinarily difficult materials. They are absolutely right in claiming that there is nothing wrong with the tool. But plenty is wrong with how they are using it. Abraham Maslow (1966: 15–16) put it more succinctly: "It is tempting, if the only tool you have is a hammer, to treat everything as if it were a nail."

Actually, those proficient in statistics are not happy either about the superficial ritual ways to which statistics is reduced in much of social sciences. A recent editorial in the *Journal of the Royal Statistical Society* (Longford 2005) deems much of contemporary statistics-based research a "junkyard of unsubstantiated confidence," because of false positives. Ronald Fisher (1956: 42) felt that it was unreasonable to reject hypotheses at a fixed level of significance; rather, a scientific worker ideally "gives his mind to each particular case in the light of his evidence and his ideas." Geoffrey Loftus wrote of "the tyranny of hypothesis testing in the social sciences" (1991) and tried to reduce the mindless reporting of p-, t- or F-values after becoming editor of *Memory & Cognition* (1993)— apparently to little avail. Gigerenzer et al. (2004) feel that not much would be lost if there were no null hypothesis testing. So the cancer of ritualized statistics crowds out not only methods other than statistical but also more thoughtful uses of statistics.

I have no quarrel with purely qualitative studies of society. But essentially qualitative studies should not feel obliged to insert ritualized quantitativeness that often looks like a blind man pinning a tail on a cardboard donkey. If some people wish to take the word "science" in social science seriously, they better do science.

The direct purpose of this book is to offer methods that go beyond statistics, but it also deals with better ways to use statistics. Social sciences have been overusing a limited range of statistical methods, much to the exclusion of everything else. By doing so, an essential link in the scientific method has been largely neglected, ignored, and dismissed.

Omitting One-Half of the Scientific Method

Science stands on two legs. One leg consists of systematic inquiry of "What *is*?" This question is answered by data collection and statistical analysis that leads to empirical data fits that could be called descriptive models. The second leg consists of an equally systematic inquiry of "How *should* it be on logical grounds?" This question requires building *logically consistent and quantitatively specific models* that reflect the subject matter. These are explanatory models.

One does not get very far hopping on one leg. If we omit "What *is*?" we are left with mythology, religion, and maybe art. If we omit

"How *should* it be?", we are left with stark empiricism. It could lead to Tycho Brahe's description of planetary paths but not to Johannes Kepler's elliptical model. It could lead to the Linnean nomenclature of plants but not to Darwinian evolution. Such empiricism has been the main path of contemporary social science research. My goal is to restore to social sciences its second leg. Explanation must complement description.

All this requires qualifications. "Should be" (on logical grounds) is distinct from "ought to be" (on moral grounds). One is subject to verification, the other may not be. Also, legs will not stand if left unconnected. It does not suffice that some scholars ask "What is?" while others ask "How should it be?" They also must intercommunicate. Science is a continuous dialogue, a spiral that rises with the synergy of "What is?" and "How should it be?" It means that construction of explanatory models can in principle precede systematic data collection, and in quite a few cases does so. Even religion does not completely avoid the question "What is?" It just addresses it less systematically than science. Sooner or later, *systematic* inquiry involves a quantitative element. This addition does not abolish the need for systematic qualitative thought. To the contrary, it requires qualitative rigor.

When it comes to models, note the stress on *quantitativeness*. Predicting merely the *direction* does not suffice. Every toddler tests the fact that objects fall downwards, but it does not make him or her a scientist. The science of gravity began when Galileo asked: *"How fast* do objects fall?"* soon followed by Isaac Newton's *"Why* do they fall precisely like that?"* Social sciences certainly have reached their Tycho Brahe (1546–1601) point—painstaking collecting of data. But have they reached their Johannes Kepler (1571–1630) point? Kepler broke with the belief that all heavenly motions are circular. Statistical modelers fool themselves if they think they are more Kepler than Brahe, just because they call statistical data fits "empirical models."

Neglecting the explanatory half of the scientific method hurts today's social sciences severely. Valuable research stops in its tracks, just short of reaching fruition, because the authors are satisfied to publish pages of regression coefficients (or worse, only R^2), without asking: "Are these coefficient values larger or smaller than I would have expected? What kind of interaction do they hint at?" This is incomplete science.

Such science is also unimpressive for outsiders, sociopolitical decision-makers included. How much attention do politicians pay to political science or other social sciences? We all know. Of course, there was a time when engineers did not have to pay attention to physics, nor physicians

Table 1.1. Predictive vs. descriptive models

Main question	Nature	Core method	Mathematical format	Direct output	Indirect output
How?	Descriptive	Statistical data analysis	Generic statistical	Nonfalsifiable postdiction	Limited-scope postdiction-based prediction
Why?	Explanatory	Logical considerations	Subject-specific conceptualization	Prediction falsifiable upon testing	Broader substantiated prediction

to biology. Science becomes useful to practitioners only when it has reached a somewhat advanced stage of development. The question is: Do social sciences contribute to society and politics all they can, at their present stage? The answer is "no," if social scientists refuse to espouse a major part of scientific thinking.

It does not mean that we must start from scratch. We are well prepared for a "Brahe-to-Kepler" breakthrough. Social scientists have accumulated enormous databases, and statistical analysis has helped to detect major connections and clarify the underlying concepts. Thanks to this accumulation, we could now vastly expand our understanding of society and politics with relatively little effort, once we realize that one further step is needed and often possible—adding quantitatively predictive logical modeling to the existing essentially descriptive findings.

Description and Prediction

A major goal of science is to explain in a way that can lead to substantiated prediction. Such an explanation consists of "This *should* be so, *because*, logically...." In contrast, there is no explanation in "This *is* so, and that's it." Table 1.1 presents the basic contrasts in the two approaches. It owes much to Peter Hedström (2004) and needs more detailed specifications in chapters that follow.

Descriptive models arise from the question "*How* do things interact?" The core method is statistical analysis of existing data, picking among generic statistical formats. The direct output consists of equations that describe how variables interrelate statistically, on the basis of input data. Strictly speaking, these equations apply only to the cases that entered the statistical analysis in the first place. They are "postdictive" in that one is "predicting" the past as seen in the data (Coleman 2007). They are not subject to falsification, given that they merely describe what is. If the sample analyzed can be considered representative of a wider universe, then a limited-scope prediction could legitimately be proposed. The question remains: On what basis can a descriptive model be considered applicable outside the data-set it was based on? Unless a logical explanation is supplied, such prediction is based on postdiction plus an act of faith. Whenever new data are added, the regression equation shifts somewhat, leading to a slightly different prediction.

To say that statistical approaches are essentially descriptive is at once too narrow and too broad. They are more than just descriptive in allowing us to predict outcomes for cases outside the initial data-set, as long as we feel (on whatever grounds) that these cases are of the same type. On the other hand, statistical approaches are less than fully descriptive of the data-set supplied because they only respond to questions we have the presence of mind to ask.

Statistical approaches do not talk back to us. If we run a linear regression on a curved data cloud, most computer programs do not print out "You really should consider curvature." When we omit a factor that logically should enter but is swamped out by random noise, the program does not whisper "Choose a subset where it could emerge!" When the researcher fails to ask relevant questions, the statistical approach produces an incomplete description, which might even be misleading. Characterizing statistical approaches as "essentially descriptive" tries to even out their expanding into prediction in some ways, yet falling short of even adequate description in other ways. From where can we get the questions to be posed in the course of statistical analysis? This is where the conceptual "How *should* it be on logical grounds?" enters.

Explanatory models arise from questions such as "*Why* do things interact the way they do?" or even "*How* should we expect them to interact, without knowing how they actually do?" The core method is consideration of logical connections and constraints. Their conceptualization imposes mathematical formats that are specific to the given subject. The direct output consists of predictive equations that could prove false upon testing with data. Given that prediction is substantiated on logical grounds, successful testing with even limited data allows for prediction in a broader range. Such prediction is relatively stable when new data with extended range are added.

Quantitatively formulated logical models are essentially predictive in an explanatory way. Prediction can follow from other approaches too, such as adequate description or nonquantitative logic. Still, predictive ability marks a major contrast between quantitative logical models and the core of statistical approaches. Therefore, this book uses "descriptive" and "predictive" as shorthand.

The Laws of Physics Were Discovered Without Statistical Hypothesis Testing

Stephen Coleman (2007) compares the role of statistical analysis in medical research, economics, and physics. Medical research has used statistics more extensively than many social sciences, and with more controls and replication. Yet, now it is finding an alarming rate of "false positives," where statistically "significant" differences are not confirmed upon replication. Advances in econometrics have not led to better theories, and Popper's idea of theory falsification has run into major roadblocks.

"It bears repeating that the laws of physics were discovered without statistical hypothesis testing" (Coleman 2007). Indeed, physicists do what psychologists have found comes naturally to humans. When trying to explain events, people start with causal models, rather than acting like "naive social scientists" by drawing inferences from observed covariation (Ahn et al. 1995, Coleman 2005). Coleman argues that we must develop causal models that make definitive predictions—predictions that clearly test and differentiate between alternative theories. Chapter 7 returns to this issue.

Solid predictive laws are few in social sciences. Is it because there are few to be found or because our standard methods lead us astray? A simple test with data that fit the universal law of gravitation (described in Chapter 2) intimates that quite a few predictive models may beg to be found, if only we were conditioned to look for them.

Reversing the Roles of Scientist and Statistician

The purely statistical approach reverses the usual roles of scientist and statistician, as stressed by Hedström (2004), echoing Aage Sørensen:

The proper division [of labor] should be one in which sociological theory suggests a mathematical model of a social process and statistics provides the tools to estimate the model, not, as is common today, that statistics provides models that sociologists use as ad hoc models of social processes. (Hedström 2004)

Properly, the social scientist should start with some idea about the social process at hand. The researcher should try to express this process as a quantitative model that connects the variables involved in a substantive way, most often leading to algebraic equations. The social scientist also supplies the data. It is then up to the statistician to propose the proper way to transform the data into a form suitable for testing, to test the model, and to determine the numerical values of open parameters, if there are any. The goal is not "hypothesis testing" in a narrow sense of statistical data analysis but verifying a substantive model (cf. Coleman 1981: 5). This is what *should* be.

In the purely descriptive approach, however, the social scientist abandons to the statistician the choice of the model. Instead of looking into the nature and constraints of the specific social situation, the statistician does what statisticians are supposed to do: choose a generic statistical format (ordinary least squares, *probit*, *logit*, ...) that most fits the general statistical configuration of the data. Social framework is out of the picture. Often, the social scientist himself plays at being an amateur statistician. It can make it even worse because some methodological safeguards a professional statistician would apply are omitted. The basic flaw remains: conceptual model building has been abdicated. It must be brought back because describing the world is only one part of science. It must also be *explained*.

Thus, the goals of the statistician and the scientist are both legitimate but they often diverge. What is the endpoint for the statistician may be only a starting point for the scientist, who asks: What can I do with this result in a wider context?

We Can Do Better than That

Social sciences must advance in two directions. First, they must go beyond statistical approaches, into model building. Second, they must clean up their use of statistics, by reducing misapplications of its method as well as misinterpretations of its results. Many social scientists have been building models and using statistics in appropriate ways, but they have been a minority. My evaluation applies to the predominant current in social sciences.

Any science remains incomplete if it limits itself to a descriptive "This is" and does not ask "*Why* is it the way it is?" One cannot just throw all conceivable factors into a grand regression equation. Passive descriptive thinking is made easy by computerization and canned statistical programs. It has enabled mindless number crunching to be published, while impeding creative predictive thinking. But it comes with a price. Most numbers published in social sciences are dead on arrival: Once printed, they are never used for anything (as documented in Chapter 7).

Omitting one-half of the scientific method might not be of concern if social sciences nonetheless enjoyed high prestige in society and among decision-makers in particular. We know how it actually is. Physical sciences get respect because they have produced usable results ever since they emerged from under the shadow of alchemy and astrology. They have done so by making full use of predictive models. Social scientists can continue to stick to a restricted set of methods, publish in a not very cumulative way, have little impact on the real world, and suffer from physics envy. But we can also do better than that.

Quantitatively predictive logical models have proven themselves in natural sciences and can help in social sciences. Statistical methods still enter. Along with qualitative insights, they serve a purpose in exploratory inquiry at the one end of research, preparing ground for constructing logical models, and they later serve in testing them. But in between, science needs the type of explanation that can lead to more specific prediction than "if x is up then y is down."

Social sciences may be ripe for a breakthrough toward broader and more productive methods. It is a matter of widening the tool kit. We can build on present achievements by incorporating more of the approaches proven in natural sciences. Does it mean junking what has been done up to now? No. Examples presented in this book (especially Chapters 4 and 16) suggest that much of the existing descriptive research could be put on firmer predictive grounds with relatively little new effort. It is not a question of starting from scratch but bringing to fruition existing research. True, it will require more emphasis on thinking, of the type that cannot be abdicated to computers. Addiction to canned statistical programs must be reined in, and social scientists must break with the belief that most social relationships are linear. It can be done.

The next three chapters document a serious limitation of the descriptive method and offer a quick idea of what the predictive models are about. Thereafter, Chapters 5–7 elaborate on the critique of one-sided dependence on descriptive methods. It is the one-sidedness that is criticized, not the inherent value of such methods when properly applied. Chapters

8–13 present in more detail some approaches to building quantitatively predictive logical models—and some successes in using them. Finally, Chapters 14–18 bring about a synthesis of predictive and descriptive approaches.

Appendix to Chapter 1

Previous Attempts to Make Social Science More of a Science

A tension sometimes surfaces between qualitative and quantitative approaches to studying society in a broad sense. I stand squarely in the middle, witness four of my books which include no quantitative analysis (Taagepera 1984, 1993, 1999a; Misiunas and Taagepera 1993) and two others that do (Taagepera and Shugart 1989; Taagepera 2007c). There are many ways to do good social scholarship, and they differ in more than one basic aspect. Bernard Grofman (2007) has presented a $2 \times 2 \times 2$ breakdown for political studies, which may apply more broadly: analytic and quantitative versus humanistic and interpretive; empirical versus normative; and theoretical versus applied. He finds examples for each of the resulting eight cells.

I have no quarrel with any of them, even while the approach stressed in this particular book is empirical, quantitative, and theoretical (with some application in institutional engineering). All sorts of approaches to the study of society can be carried out well or poorly. My point is that if some people wish to take the word "sciences" in social sciences seriously and focus on empirical, quantitative, and theoretical aspects, they better make the most of it. And yes, I expect it to lead to major breakthroughs. Regarding prospects of breakthroughs following other approaches, I simply take no stand.

Purposeful attempts to make social science more of a "genuine" science in the image of natural sciences have occurred over at least two centuries. Grofman (2007) reviews the successive tides in American political science. They all ebbed, which may seem to bid ill for my present attempt. I will soon point out a major difference that gives hope. Of course, the previous ebbs hardly were complete—there was some lasting effect. The use of statistics was introduced, and fact was separated from value. Behavioral and game theoretical models added new perspectives, even while they did not turn out to be solutions to everything. They all came to be included into "political science as usual" (Grofman 2007).

Among social sciences, political science has sought methodological or conceptual inspiration from and through other social sciences, mainly sociology, economics, and social psychology. Statistics has been an outside field from which all social sciences have drawn. Biology and chemistry have offered less inspiration, apart from evolutionary game theory. As the oldest among natural sciences, physics has appealed to some social scientists ever since Auguste Comte, but it also has meant many naïve attempts to apply superficial analogies—which have discredited such an approach. Hence, my drawing on physics will raise hackles, and should do so. In response, it is time to point out a major difference.

Typical attempts to make any or all social sciences more scientific have mainly pointed out promising avenues to be followed in the future: Let us discuss methodology, get together a sufficient mass of researchers (and grants), and great findings will follow. When the actual findings prove modest, great expectations turn into great disappointment so that even the findings achieved may be unduly discounted. In my case, in contrast, results came first and methodological argument last. Over decades, I have devised and tested a number of relationships, often interlocked, based on logical considerations (see Chapters 10 and 11). They qualify as laws in the strict scientific sense of not only presenting a quantitative relationship but also a theoretical model to explain why such a relationship should prevail.

There is no vague promise here. I refrained from offering a methodology until I had enough proof that it not only *can* produce but actually *has* produced some results in some subfields of social sciences. Are these results sufficiently broad to offer the methodology for consideration over a wider range? This is discussed in Chapter 17. Methods with some results should be taken more seriously than methods offered with promise only. This is so, in particular, when the present methods lead to limited results.

2

Can Social Science Approaches Find the Law of Gravitation?

- When a number of social scientists were given synthetic data that fitted the universal law of gravitation with negligible error, they all missed the underlying pattern.
- Yet they found results satisfactory and complete by the current social science norms: high R^2 and high degree of significance of input factors.
- The design of this experiment can be criticized, but it still should give us pause. If some social phenomena existed that were of the form most prevalent in physics, then the quantitative methods currently dominant in social sciences might not suffice to discover them.

Statistical approaches such as regression apply quite widely. Regardless of where the numerical data come from and what they represent, regression analysis almost always can be carried out. The degree of fit to some simple generic relationship (most often linear) can always be expressed, and statistical significance can be estimated.

Much of the statistical analysis published in social science journals could be carried out without knowing what the given set of numbers is about. It helps, of course, to know both the subject matter and statistical methods, so as to choose the most promising among the panoply of statistical approaches, but canned programs enable one to carry out basic multilinear regression quite automatically. Quite a few published studies go no further.

Applied physics and engineering also use statistical analysis extensively, but there it comes on top of basic laws that mostly are not linear. Even when the broad pattern is curved, linear analysis can be applied over sufficiently short ranges. Indeed, even a circle can be approximated by a straight line if the segment is sufficiently short. But what is a sufficiently short range? Linear approximations can be applied properly only when the broad nonlinear picture is known. If such broader relationships existed in the social realm and if some of them were of the form most prevalent in physics, could linear analysis or anything else in the usual tool kit of social scientists discover them? If not, then all we do might be playing around with descriptive approximations to unknown laws.

James McGregor's Question

In his "Procrustus and the Regression Model," James McGregor (1993) raised the possibility of restrictive methods in political science. His approach was to take random data that fitted three laws of nature perfectly and analyze these data by linear regression. He concluded that the underlying laws did not become apparent. The laws considered were the following. Galileo's law of falling objects expresses distance (d) fallen from a rest position as function of time (t): $d = at^2$, where a is a constant. Boyle's ideal gas law, $V = RT/P$, connects volume (V) to absolute temperature (T) and pressure (P), R being a constant. Newton's law of gravitation expresses the force of gravitational attraction (F) between two bodies in terms of the masses of these bodies (M and m) and the distance (r) between them: $F = GMm/r^2$, G being the universal constant of gravitation. As is the case with most variables in physics, the factors in these equations do not add or subtract—they rather multiply and divide. (Chapter 5 expands on this major difference, compared to social science practices.)

A most unsettling aspect for McGregor (1993) was that, by the usual social science criteria, linear analysis seemed to work just fine! Indeed, R^2 was .52 for gases and as high as .97 for falling objects. Such values would make social scientists quite happy. For them, nothing would point to the need to go any further, even while they would miss the essential.

It could be claimed that some other social scientists might have used further methods McGregor omitted. For falling objects, all that was needed was to take the square of the input variable, something social scientists are familiar with—except that once linear analysis yielded an R^2 of .97, there would hardly be any incentive to go any further. Gases and gravitation involve division, an operation less familiar to social scientists. Still, it is conceivable that some more sophisticated statistical methods could figure it out. Of course, taking logarithms of all the variables, prior to linear regression, would clinch it. But would social scientists automatically include such an option?

A more open-ended test would be to submit such data to a number of social scientists proficient in data analysis. Ask them to analyze these data, using whatever methods they consider suitable, and see whether they can discover the underlying pattern. This is what I did with the law of gravitation. The objective was to see what social scientists would do with the data and how the results would compare with the actual relationship.

Those engaged in natural sciences may legitimately protest that such blind analysis is not the way science proceeds. One has to know what the data are about, so that raw data can first be transformed according to some logical constructs, before statistical analysis is applied. In particular, before linear regression is used, data must be converted into a form where all the inputs logically enter in linear way, which may or may not be easy.

Yes, logical model-building should precede statistical analysis. However, the hard fact is that this is not general practice in social sciences. Here, regression tends to be applied as if all raw inputs did enter linearly. When products, logarithms, or squares of some variables are also thrown in, this tends to be done on the basis of statistical configuration of the data— or just to see what happens, without a substantive model to justify it. Therefore, offering unidentified data to social scientists and asking them to try to elucidate the relationships among the variables arguably does not unduly restrict the methodological range of what they would do with identified social data.

The Universal Law of Gravitation

My test was based on the aforementioned universal law of gravitation: $F = GMm/r^2$, one of the three laws used by McGregor (1993). This law is one of the most basic in classical physics. Replacing the masses M and m by two electric charges, the same equation (with a different constant) also expresses the force of attraction or repulsion between two electrically charged bodies. Its multiplicative format is typical in physics. It is also typical that the law involves one—and only one!—constant, determined experimentally. The numerical value of this constant of gravitation depends on the units of force, mass, and distance used. It is calculated by reversing the previous equation: $G = Fr^2/Mm$, and plugging in known masses, distance, and force. It is a universal constant. This means that, for any combination of masses, distance, and force, the same value of G has been found to apply, within the range of experimental error.

At the time this law was discovered, several centuries ago, the statistical methods on which today's social scientists so heavily depend hardly existed, not to mention computers that enable us to apply these methods with great speed. With our present tools, it should be much easier to detect such an underlying pattern, when one is given data where random fluctuation does not mask the pattern too heavily. So, if I generated some data to fit an equation of the form $y = Gx_1x_3/x_2^2$ almost perfectly and submitted it for analysis by social scientists, would they discover the underlying pattern?

For the purposes of such a test, the format of the law of gravitation had the following desirable features. It involves three input variables. When only two variables are multiplied, any program that automatically tests for the standard "interactive" term $(x_i x_j)$ could easily detect the relationship. The equation also involves a division—an operation that will be seen to be absent from the social scientists' toolbox (Chapter 5). Given that many regressions in social research involve at least three input variables, a three-variable law should otherwise present no excessively complex challenge.

The Test

The proposed data-set included 25 values of 3 input variables labeled x_1, x_2, and x_3, all selected essentially randomly by picking the last 2 digits of successive entries in a telephone book, excluding 00 and 01. The corresponding values of the output variable, labeled y, were calculated from $y = 980x_1x_3/x_2^2$, with 2-digit precision. In other words, force was coded as y, masses (or electric charges) were coded as x_1 and x_3, respectively, and distance r was coded as x_2. The constant was chosen such as to keep y larger than 1 in all cases. Table 2.1 shows the resulting synthetic data.

To repeat, the data for x are essentially random numbers ranging from 2 to 99. The values of y come from $y = 980x_1x_3/x_2^2$, with values rounded off to integers. The resulting error is within $\pm0.2\%$, except for Case F (2%). Apart from this rounding-off error, I introduced no distortions so as to simulate random error. Thus, the underlying pattern was easy to detect, compared to usual measurement data. Moreover, the pattern involved only multiplication, division, and exponents. If one had the idea of taking the logarithms of all the variables, the result would be

Table 2.1. Synthetic data where $y = 980 x_1 x_3 / x_2^2$

	x_1	x_2	x_3	Y
A	89	36	45	3,028
B	77	50	69	2,083
C	35	65	36	292
D	7	53	61	149
E	2	33	66	119
F	8	95	27	23
G	25	99	96	240
H	55	92	24	153
I	27	10	67	17,728
J	83	59	85	1,986
K	19	82	81	224
L	19	39	78	955
M	69	30	16	1,202
N	69	65	31	496
O	18	54	84	508
P	87	52	57	1,797
Q	32	72	98	593
R	8	37	49	281
S	58	23	3	322
T	48	41	50	1,399
U	80	92	74	685
V	24	35	33	634
W	28	65	79	513
X	37	35	36	1,066
Y	56	18	10	1,694

$\log y = \log 980 + \log x_1 - 2 \log x_2 + \log x_3$, so that linear regression of logarithms would fit almost perfectly ($R^2 = .99$). In this sense, discovery of the underlying relationship was made easy. Relationships that involve addition on top of multiplication and exponents, plus some error, would be much harder to ferret out by regression or any other statistical approach.

On the other hand, finding the underlying relationship was made more difficult by the relatively narrow range of input data—only from 2 to 99, for all three variables. With more extended ranges, systematic relationships become more evident and R^2 tends to improve. However, in contrast to experimental sciences, in social sciences, we all too often face precisely this limitation: We may be restricted to tantalizingly narrow ranges of input variables, with no ways to widen them.

These numbers were sent to 38 social scientists, mainly in political science, with the following wording: "Attached is an Excel data file for 25 cases. Included are three input variables (x_1, x_2, x_3) and one output variable (y). I have my ideas about the way the 'y' might be connected to the x-es, but I do not want to influence you by telling you what the variables are. Try to make sense out of this possible relationship."

The eight individuals or pairs who graciously responded ranged from advanced Ph.D. students to senior professors, mainly in comparative politics, but also in economics. Appendix 2 shows three responses (some of them shortened), indicating statistical skills clearly beyond basic canned OLS analysis. One extremely sophisticated approach cannot be described for fear of identifying the author. Most other respondents indicated briefly that they tried various multiple regression type approaches, with no clear-cut results. Oral comments indicate that quite a few more researchers tried their hand at the data but did not respond in view of inconclusive results.

The Negative Outcome

No respondent discovered the pattern of the law of gravitation. Yet, very high correlations were found, especially when one eliminated some presumed "outliers" (that fully fit the actual law!). Depending on the approach, R^2 ran mainly from .70 to .90. It surpassed .98 in one approach that eliminated outliers. This may be the most unsettling aspect of the test, given that an R^2 as high as .70 is most social scientists' dream and would preclude further inquiry. McGregor's concerns (1993) are confirmed.

By the current social science norms, the results were satisfactory and complete. Every respondent correctly found that y increases with increasing x_1 and x_3, while decreasing with increasing x_2. All input factors looked significant, and R^2 was high. Yet they all missed the underlying pattern. (The sample excluded students who actively work with me on quantitatively predictive logical models; one of them, with a civil engineering background, did find the relationship.)

McGregor (1993) pointed out that, unless logical model-building precedes statistical analysis, the latter may lead to two types of error. (1) One may miss a very real nonlinear relationship by assuming a linear or otherwise inadequate format that leads to low R^2 and low statistical significance. (2) Conversely, a high R^2 may result from an essentially linear approach, lulling us into complacent satisfaction while missing the essential. The latter was the case here. High levels of statistical significance may go hand in hand with little conceptual significance and vice versa, as will be discussed in detail later on (Chapter 4). The respondents reported

19

a profusion of coefficient values, quite different from each other. Given such dispersal, none of them could be firm steppingstones for further research—they are doomed to remain endpoints (as expanded on in Chapter 7).

Does it mean that today's social scientists could not discover an inverse square law, if it applied to some social phenomenon, even when random error is practically zero? Several reservations can be voiced. The sample of social scientists was small and nonrandom. The number of responses was low. By restricting input data to the range 2–99, I inadvertently suggested that these might be percentages. Without this impression, some respondents might conceivably have been goaded into trying some other methods. So, in retrospect, I should have multiplied all the random inputs by 3, which would not have altered the output. It just so happened that one of the random outputs (case I in Table 2.1) was much higher than the rest, justifying its deletion as a suspicious outlier. In hindsight, maybe I should have doctored the random sample so as to have several high outputs.

The use of blind data is debatable. One of the respondents later felt that I was misleading them by presenting error-free data as real data, by not stating that they were generated by a formula, and by implying that they were of a political nature (simply by my being a political scientist). Yes, if I had said "These data, including what look like outliers, fit a formula exactly," then an R^2 of .90 would not have stopped the inquiry. But the planets did not tell Kepler either: "Our motion actually fits a pretty simple formula. Just try to find it."

Even with these reservations, the starkly negative outcome should make us pause. If some social phenomena did follow quantitative laws of the format most frequent in physics (as shown in Chapter 5), then the quantitative methods currently dominant in social sciences just might not suffice to discover them.

Does It Matter?

This is *not* a critical experiment—too much in its design can be questioned. It cannot be concluded that social sciences flunk the gravitation test. At most, the test might serve as a warning light.

But even if the present dominant methodology should flunk a test with a better design, does it matter? It depends on whether relationships with a multiplicative format can occur in the social realm. Few such laws are known. Is it because there are none to be found or because our standard methods lead us astray? If there are none, because of deep differences in the nature of physical and social phenomena, then the potential failure reported here is of no consequence. But if they can occur, then the negative outcome of the gravitation test could mean that we might have missed out on significant social relationships as well. Chapters 10 and 11 present a number of well-tested quantitatively predictive logical models for sociopolitical phenomena. Most of them do follow the multiplication–division–exponent format of the law of gravitation. Hence, this format does occur in the social realm. Chapter 14 asks whether these relationships could have been discovered by statistical analysis. It will be seen that a most basic input factor would not emerge as significant, from raw data, not to mention finding the logical shape of the relationship.

College students seem to undervalue social sciences "as legitimate scientific enterprises," compared to physical sciences (Hill 2004). To improve the standing of social sciences, Hill's approach is to debunk presumable myths about the solidity of physical sciences. To which Ozminkowski (2005) replies: "However, pointing to the weaknesses of 'the other guy' does not help in building respect for social sciences."

When, given the same data, one discipline offers a predictive law of nature, while the other offers descriptive regression coefficients and R^2, the reception is likely to be different not only among college students but also among the public at large and sociopolitical decision-makers. Is this the best social sciences can do? Are they doomed to remain eternally immature disciplines (cf. Oren 2005; Strakes 2005; Hill 2005)? I do not think so. The next two chapters offer some guidelines for constructing predictive models, followed by a specific example.

Appendix to Chapter 2

Typical Analyses of Gravitation-Like Data Offered by Social Scientists

Response A

I first ran a correlation matrix between all four variables and then a multivariate regression. Then I tried creating composite variables by multiplying pairs of dependent variables to see if including these new variables in a multivariate regression would improve predictive power or fit. Then, I looked for *max* and *min* values on each independent variable to see what is happening at the extremes. My next step, if I had had the time, would have been to create a small 3 way cross-table, with polychotomous categories on each of the x variables (high, medium, low) and mean y values in the cells.

Response B

We looked at Tukey's exploratory data guides and observed that the value of y has a positive relation on x_1, x_3, and negative on x_2, the relation is decreasingly increasing, and there is one anomalous extreme value (I). We thus chose the logarithm of y, for which we found the following relation: $\ln y = 5.95 + 0.028x_1 - 0.038x_2 + 0.024x_3$ with $R^2 = .76$.

Variant: If the extreme I value is eliminated, we have some improvement, with $R^2 = .83$. Alternative: We could also choose the squared root of y, which produces the following: $(y)^{1/2} = 17.67 + 0.36x_1 - 0.30x_2 + 0.19x_3$ with $R^2 = .43$, which is not very good. Only if the value I is eliminated, then for the latter relation, $R^2 = .80$, which is good but still not as good as the logarithmic relation under the same condition.

[My comment: This analysis came close. The respondent did take the logarithm of y, because of its wide range, but not of the input variables. If one wanted to use the results of this analysis to calculate y directly from the input data, the reported expression $\ln y = 5.95 + 0.028x_1 - 0.038x_2 + 0.024x_3$ corresponds to $y = 384(1.028)^{x_1}(1.024)^{x_3}(1.039)^{x_2}$. This expression is far more complex than the actual $y = 980x_1x_3/x_2^2$, and it would take a real fancy logic to justify such a relationship, compared to multiplication and division and simple exponents.]

Response C

Controlling for case number 9 [case I in Table 2.1]: reg y x_1 x_2 x_3 case 9

Source	SS	df	MS			
Modal	283855969	4	70963992.1	Number of obs =		25
Residual	3575223.44	20	178761.172	F(4, 20 =		396.98
				Prob > F =		0.0000
Total	287431192	24	11976299.7	R-squared =		0.9876
				Adj R-squared =		0.9851
				Root MSE =		422.80

Y	Coef.	Std. Err.	t	P>|t|	[95% Conf. Interval]	
x1	20.86665	3.180685	6.56	0.000	14.23186	27.50145
x2	−15.84126	4.070628	−3.89	0.001	−24.33244	−7.350077
x3	9.416735	3.563831	2.64	0.016	1.982713	16.85076
case9	16371.25	480.729	34.06	0.000	15368.47	17374.04
_cons	320.389	295.9571	1.08	0.291	−296.5168	938.1947

[Adjusted R^2 ranging from .707 to .877 were obtained when excluding number 9; or normalizing y (natural logs), while controlling, not controlling, or excluding case 9.]

3

How to Construct Predictive Models: Simplicity and Nonabsurdity

---

- Predictive models should be as simple as one can get away with. This parsimony is what "Occam's razor" is about.
- Predictive models must not predict absurdities even under extreme circumstances.
- As Sherlock Holmes put it: Eliminate the impossible, and only one possible outcome may remain. This goes for science, too. Show how things *cannot* be related, and only one acceptable form of relationship may remain—or very few.
- Quantitative predictions are more valuable than merely directional ones.
- Agreement with a quantitatively predictive model is not tied to R^2.
- All too many variables are interdependent rather than "independent" or "dependent." So it is safer to talk about input and output variables under the given circumstances.

The purpose of this book is to help social sciences to become more of an exact science. This term does not mean that every result is given with three decimals. Exact science rather means striving to be *as exact as possible*, under the given conditions—and specifying the likely range of error. In the beginning, this range of possible error may be huge. It is acceptable if there is some basis for gradually improving our measurements and conceptual models.

Nothing would stifle such advance more than advice to give up on quantitative approaches just because our first measurements involve a wide range of fluctuation or our conceptual model does not agree with the measurements. A three-decimal precision will never be reached, if one refuses to work out problems approximately, at first. Exact science means being as exact as possible *at the given stage* of research and thus making it possible to be more exact in the future. This applies not only to measurements but also to conceptual approaches. How should we start? Start with a story.

Galileo and the Peasant of Tuscany

A peasant near Florence was told that a scholar named Galileo is trying to determine how various objects fall. "Those learned men really know how to make simple things complicated," the peasant said. "I could have told him offhand that things fall downwards."

It was hard to explain to him that all he knew was *directionality* of the motion, and that there was more to know. In mathematical language, the peasant was satisfied with the knowledge that $dx/dt < 0$, when we count x from the center of the Earth and t is time. In contrast, Galileo wanted to figure out the entire functional form $x = f(t)$, and for all bodies.

Galileo basically found that an object dropped from a height x_0 falls as $x = x_0 - (g/2)t^2$, where g is a positive number. This equation tells us, indeed, that $dx/dt = -gt$ is negative, confirming the peasant's insight. But it tells us much more. Galileo soon determined that the value of g is pretty much the same for all objects in all places. It is basically a worldwide constant on the surface of the Earth.

When the peasant was told that Galileo's work enables us to measure the gravitational pull of the Earth, he yawned. When told that this way we can predict how soon things dropped from the tower of Pisa reach the ground, he said: "So what? I already knew they reach the ground pretty quickly. Who needs more?" Then the peasant grinned slyly: "By the way, if this thing is a feather, it may never fall, until it's out of sight. So this fellow Galileo's finding is not only useless but doesn't even always work. So much for your constant of gravity!"

Before one could tell him about second approximations that deal with air friction and all that, he was off to have some wine at the local tavern. It could as well have been a faculty club for those social scientists who stop their work at the very point where Galileo's began: They test a *directional* prediction and are oblivious of the functional form. They verify the sign of dy/dx, and do not see the need to determine $y = f(x)$. I have culled the peasant's wisdom from journal reviewers' responses to my efforts to go beyond directionality.

To be sure, the directionality of social relationships is not always as obvious as that of a falling lead ball. In social data, the analogues of lead balls are often outnumbered by the analogues of feathers, flies, and flat leaves, which do not follow the simple equation $x = x_0 - (g/2)t^2$. Thus, it is sometimes a genuine social science achievement to show that x actually does affect y, and in a certain direction.

The problem is that, in the course of the effort to determine directionality, the need to proceed to the Galilean level all too often gets forgotten. It does not suffice to show that more food leads to more sense of well-being or that more votes lead to more seats. Like Galileo, one has to ask: "How much more?" or "How many more?"

Once one goes quantitative, an inquiry may talk back to you and say: "You are asking the wrong question!" Initially one may ask: "How fast do falling objects fall?" Quantitative inquiry will soon tell you that the speed of a falling object is not constant but increases the longer it falls. So the corrected question becomes "With what *acceleration* do objects fall?"

Galileo found a nonlinear relationship. He would have been on the wrong track, if he had blithely assumed that all relationships $y = f(x)$ are linear: $x = a + by$. This is an assumption all too many social scientists take as an article of faith. More often than not, such an assumption is on shaky logical grounds (as explained in Chapter 8). We live in a largely multiplicative world.

Directional Versus Quantitative Predictions

All predictions are not equally precise. A vague prediction is easier to verify, but it also is less useful. In particular, we must distinguish between directional and quantitative predictions. The latter offers a specific function $y = f(x)$, which enables us to calculate the values of y for any given values of x. In contrast, the directional prediction (dy/dx positive or negative) leaves the values of y widely open. A test by regression may confirm a directionally predictive hypothesis regarding the effect of x, but the regression equation is postdictive regarding the other components of $y = f(x)$. It might or might not offer a starting point for developing a predictive model on logical grounds, but it is not yet a predictive model by itself, except in the limited directional sense.

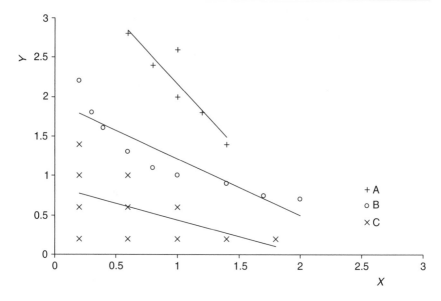

Figure 3.1. Best linear fits to different patterns that all satisfy the directional prediction $dy/dx < 0$

Figure 3.1 illustrates the observation that the directional prediction $dy/dx < 0$ is all too easy to satisfy. The hunch ("hypothesis") may be that y decreases with increasing x. All three data-sets satisfy this loose directional prediction. Indeed, one-half of the lines we draw at random would satisfy it.

Yet the three data-sets send quite different messages. Data-sets A and B correspond to very different slopes and intercepts. Furthermore, pattern B is clearly curved, so that the linear fit misrepresents reality severely, even while R^2 remains quite high. The data-set C fills in a triangular space. Pretending that it is a linear pattern also misrepresents reality.

A further difficulty arises when only positive values (and zero) have meaning for x and y. Indeed, quite a few variables of interest to social scientists cannot possibly take negative values. For sufficiently high values of x, the regression lines for all three data-sets would lead to negative values of y—which is an absurd proposition when y cannot conceptually go negative.

Now suppose that, for some logical reason, we feel that y might be inversely proportional to x. This means predicting $y = k/x$, where k is a positive constant of unknown numerical value. Figure 3.2 shows the corresponding family of curves, produced by assigning various different

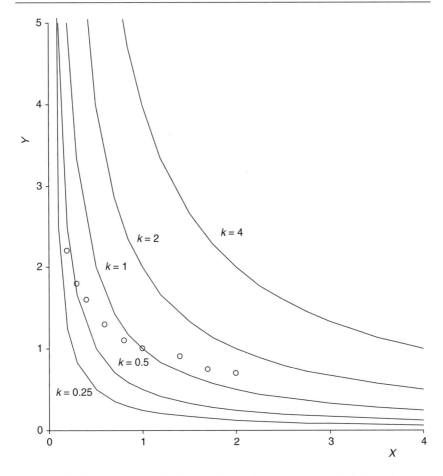

Figure 3.2. Curves for quantitative model $y = k/x$, and an unsatisfactory data-set

values to k. Note that these curves do not predict negative y for any positive x, and thus avoid absurdity. They all fit the directional prediction of negative slope ($dy/dx < 0$), given that $y = k/x$ leads to $dy/dx = -k/x^2$, but they demand much more. Could the previous data-sets A, B, and C in Figure 3.1 satisfy $y = k/x$?

It can be checked that pattern A, although it looks straight, actually roughly agrees with the model (with $k = 2$), over the short range of data. The curved pattern B may look close to the family $y = k/x$, but when shown transposed to Figure 3.2, it clearly diverges. Indeed, this data-set would require that k in $y = k/x$ be 0.5 at low x but around 1.5 at high x. It might fit better with $y = k/x^{0.5}$. (The general two-parameter

27

family, $y = k/x^a$, is discussed in Chapter 8.) The highly dispersed pattern C actually fits (with $k = 0.25$), albeit with a low correlation coefficient of around $R^2 = .25$.

The first message is that data-sets that easily satisfy the directional prediction need not satisfy a more specific functional prediction. Actually, I constructed patterns A and C so that they would roughly fit $y = k/x$. Most randomly picked patterns would not fit.

A second message is that agreement with a quantitatively predictive model is not tied to R^2. Indeed, it is precisely the very lack of scatter in pattern B that leads to its clear disagreement with the model $y = k/x$. If it were more diffuse, like C, it might have the benefit of the doubt. For descriptive data fits, the correlation coefficient is the only measure of goodness. For quantitatively predictive models, in contrast, even a diffuse agreement with the predicted functional shape is better than a clean pattern of a wrong shape. This is a feature to which we will return (Chapters 4 and 6).

Finally, note that linear fits ($y = a + bx$) involve two adjustable coefficients (a and b). In contrast, $y = k/x$ (that might fit the sets A and C) involves only one (k). This expression is more parsimonious. We get more bang for less buck.

Quantitatively Predictive Logical Models

This is the time to specify what I mean by "quantitatively predictive logical models." Why do we need such a long specification? All predictive logical models are not quantitative—they can be merely directional. Today's social sciences are full of such vague predictions. Conversely, all quantitatively predictive models are not based on logical considerations— regression equations can be used for quantitative prediction, albeit with grave reservations. Today's social sciences are full of such "empirical models" where every new regression produces a different equation and hence a different prediction.

When this book talks of the need for predictive models, it has in mind predictive models that are both quantitatively predictive and based on logical considerations—like the law of gravitation. It does not imply that their predictions are precise, as further known or unknown factors may enter. The path of gliding feathers cannot be predicted on the basis of law of gravity alone. Predictions based on such models always carry the qualification *ceteris paribus*—everything else remaining the same, or "in the absence of other factors." They differ from statistically based descriptive models in that we can know under which conditions the logical models can or cannot apply. Indeed, Galileo showed that when air is pumped out, feathers do fall like stones. We can also combine different simple models in a logical way so as to predict under more complex conditions.

Quantitatively predictive logical models include all models that can be introduced without input of numerical data, based solely on broader general notions. This is a more specific term than "theoretical" or "formal" models, but broader than "substantive models," as used by Sørensen (1998) and Hedström (2004). This is so because the logical considerations used may be much broader than specifically sociological or psychological. At times, I feel more comfortable talking about conceptual models, instead of logical models, without making a clear distinction.

Simplicity and Avoidance of Absurdity

Even when convinced of the need to go beyond descriptive methods, how do we go about in constructing quantitatively predictive logical models? The inconvenient truth one has to face is that one has to shed reliance on canned computer programs that make dependence on statistical methods so painless (and often correspondingly fruitless). One has to think. One has to consider broad conceptual constraints and the specific social framework of the problem on hand, which differs for each problem. Nonetheless, the following broad guidelines can be offered:

1. Predictive models should be as simple as one can get away with (parsimony).
2. Predictive models must not predict absurdities.

The following advice might be called the *Sherlock Holmes principle*: Eliminate the impossible, and only one possible outcome may remain. This goes for science as well as for solving murder cases. Show how things *cannot* be related, and only one acceptable form of relationship may remain—or very few. How does one develop an eye for detecting the impossible? It often means consciously making note of things that one has taken so much for granted that one does not see them. Later chapters offer specific examples and, by doing so, help developing such skills.

Occam's razor tells us to eliminate from consideration all that is not essential to the issue. This notion of parsimony goes back many centuries and was essential for development of physical sciences, to the point where physical scientists use it automatically, without mentioning it. They first go after the most general and only gradually flesh it out with more details. In contrast, computer-addicted social scientists all too often throw into their regressions whatever variables they can imagine. "The more, the merrier" has tended to supplant Occam's razor, once the latter has been given lip service in the introductory course on the scientific method. Does a colleague suggest another variable? "OK, I'll put it in the regression." This is the verbatim response I jotted down at a conference, January 14, 2005, where the respondent had entered all his variables linearly. If it were a physics conference, the reaction might be "OK, I'll try to work it into the model."

This is a point where the statistician's and the scientist's goals diverge. From the statistical point of view, it often makes sense to add variables, as it improves parameters such as unadjusted R^2. From the scientific point of view, Occam's razor helps to pin down the essential, before further factors are gradually introduced. When introduced too early, such factors muddle up the basic relationships.

Some social science journal referees aggressively push the statistician's approach on their colleagues, insisting that further factors be introduced. This is the wrong way to go. Factors that do not impose themselves logically and affect prediction only to a minor degree should be omitted. In different ways, Occam's razor and the Sherlock Holmes principle involve the same idea: Predictive models should be as simple as one can get away with.

A complementary requirement is that predictive models must not predict absurdities. In particular, if, for a conceptually possible value of x, the model predicts a conceptually impossible value of y, the model must be modified. As the number of teachers increases, illiteracy goes down. One may try a downward-sloped linear model, and it may fit actual data just beautifully. But at a very high number of teachers it will predict negative illiteracy! This is the problem pointed out in Figure 3.1. Such an implication is conceptually unacceptable, even if the number of teachers at which the absurdity appears is "unrealistically" huge. The model must be modified. Avoidance of absurdities is an aspect of the Sherlock Holmes principle: eliminate the impossible. This issue is revisited in Chapter 5.

Contradiction is one aspect of absurdity. Logical models must avoid internal contradictions. Mathematician Richard Hamming (1980) has argued that Galileo might have determined that all bodies must fall at the same speed (in the absence of friction and other forces) by reasoning, even before testing it experimentally. The existing wisdom was that heavier bodies fall faster. But if one connects fairly small and hence light stones with string or glue, how would they know that now they must fall faster? When do two pieces become a single one? The only noncontradictory conclusion is that speed cannot depend on the weight as such.

Similar thought experiments have played a major role in natural sciences. Galileo *could* have reached the right conclusion this way. We have no hard evidence that he consciously did, because he had the luxury of another option—experimentation. Of course, he would not have started to experiment unless he had some doubts in the first place, but he could experiment relatively easily. But what about those social disciplines where experimentation is difficult? Should we not place even more emphasis on using our brain power? Logical models have to be tested, but it is so much easier to find a suitable test once one knows what one is looking for.

Most Variables Are Interdependent, Not "Independent" or "Dependent"

It makes more sense to talk of input and output variables under the given circumstances rather than inherently "independent" and "dependent" variables, because all too many variables are *interdependent*. Causal direction may vary. Sometimes the existing number of teachers affects literacy, and sometimes existing literacy affects the number of teachers. An existing party system may strongly affect the choice of electoral system, but later the electoral system preserves the party system. The terms "input" and "output variables" indicate their respective roles in the moment's context, without passing judgment on some inherent dependence or independence.

Ideal Gas Law and Engineering Freshmen

To continue with model building methodology in the abstract would suit people who already have a feel for what it means. But quantitatively predictive logical models are novel to many social scientists, so their use needs substantive illustration. Therefore, the next chapter addresses a specific problem: electoral volatility. A more abstract presentation of model building methodology continues later on (Chapter 8).

A warning is due. The reader may at first have great reservations about the approach proposed in the next chapter, be it for volatility or for any other social science issue. I can empathize because I remember my first exposure to logical models. It came in Walberg Building of Chemical Engineering, University of Toronto. We were 84 freshmen. The professor presented a simple model that led to the aforementioned Boyle's law. We looked at each other in bewildered disbelief. Some laughed, nervously. This was ridiculous! Molecules were reduced to spheres of zero volume and diameter, yet they had mass. They bounced randomly off one-dimensional walls. The ideal gas law did emerge, but the procedure looked fake, contrived somehow to reach a previously known conclusion.

What did we expect? At secondary school, we had accepted $PV = RT$ as inherited wisdom. We had been told that it agreed with empirical measurements—well, to a degree, as real gases lead to somewhat different outcomes. We were satisfied with these assurances and did not ask for a more reasoned foundation. But if, nonetheless, we were given what pretended to be a logical justification, we expected something more complex. It could not be so ridiculously simple, with simplicity bought at the expense of making patently unrealistic assumptions, such as zero-volume spheres in a one-dimensional world!

How did we gradually come to accept it? Right away, van der Waals adjustments were added to the ideal gas law, granting volume to molecules, etc. This went beyond secondary school physics. We came to see how relatively small adjustments could turn the law for ideal gases into something that looked more realistic as a model and fitted many actual gases in practice. This way, we slowly began to grasp the predictive power of a method that dared to start from a situation simplified to an unrealistic degree and then added further realistic features only gradually.

Two less commendable considerations helped us to accept the method. First, we knew that what we were taught was the authoritative method in physical sciences. If one did not accept it, one would have to drop out or become a closet dissident. Second, even the van der Waals adjustments made our calculations so much more laborious (this was precomputer age!) that we came to appreciate the practical advantages of keeping our models as simple as possible—the simplest we could get away with and still make some predictions. The context is quite different in today's social sciences. The logical model approach is as yet far from authoritative, and computer programs reduce the urge to keep things simple. If computers had existed in year 1600, the traditional Ptolemaic circles moving along circles may have competed with the new-fangled Keplerian ellipses indefinitely.

The model to be presented next has none of the importance of the ideal gas law. It was chosen as an example because of its simplicity. Still, it has the same ingredients I encountered as a freshman. Furthermore, the refined model presented thereafter faintly echoes the van der Waals adjustments, in the sense of making the coarse model slightly more realistic—and more involved mathematically.

4

Example of Model Building: Electoral Volatility

- The foremost mental roadblocks in predictive model building are refusal to simplify and reluctance to play with extreme cases and their means. These roadblocks have little to do with mathematical skills.
- "Ignorance-based" models focus on conceptual constraints and extract the most out of near-complete ignorance. They ask: What do we already know about the situation, even before collecting any data?
- Eliminate the "conceptually forbidden areas" where data points could not possibly occur.
- Locate the conceptual "anchor points" where the value of x imposes a unique value of y.
- Once this is done, few options may remain for how y can depend on x—unless you tell yourself "It can't be that simple."
- Dare to make outrageous simplifications for an initial coarse model, including as few variables as possible. Leave refinements for later second approximations.
- A low R^2 may still confirm a predictive model, and a high one may work to reject it.

This chapter develops a quantitatively predictive logical model for a specific issue—volatility of voters and its conceivable dependence on the number of parties that run. Why this particular topic? It so happens that here the model is mathematically very simple, at least in first approximation. Indeed, this is one of the relatively few cases where the model has the linear form so familiar to social scientists. Thus, the reader's attention can focus on model-building skills, without being distracted by a possibly unfamiliar mathematical format. This is important for countering the impression that model-building skills are largely mathematical. A good grasp of high school and college mathematics helps of course, but many skills and mental roadblocks in model building are elsewhere.

A coarse approximate model is constructed first, expanding on an earlier shorter version (Taagepera 2007*b*). A second approximation follows, leading to a more refined model. Some broad contrasts emerge between predictive and descriptive approaches.

Constructing a Coarse "Ignorance-Based" Model

Volatility (V) stands for the percentage of voters who switch parties from one election to the next. When more parties run, voters have more choices for switching. Hence, if the number of parties (N) has any effect on volatility of voters at all, it should be in the upward direction. In mathematical terms, we would expect $dV/dN > 0$. This is a directionally predictive logical model.

A technical side issue is how to measure the number of parties when some are large and some are small. Here, the effective number of components is used: $N = 1/\Sigma(v_i^2)$, where v_i is the fractional vote share of the ith party (see Taagepera 2007*c*: 47–64). Since we compare two elections, N should be taken as the average N at these two elections, assuming that these are not excessively different.

Another side issue concerns the occasional voter. Voters may switch parties, but they also may switch to not voting at all. For simplicity, we first omit the "party of nonvoters." We can make it more complex later on.

The first mental roadblock in model building may set in at this point: *refusal to simplify*. Ah, the reader may say, you are naive or cheating. You ignore the hard reality that there are always people who sometimes vote and sometimes do not. In the words of a critical journal referee regarding a different topic: "I am skeptical that there is much value of operating at such a high level of generality. Huge amounts of real-world variation are consigned to nowhere." Actually, model building consigns them to a much better place, namely the next-level analysis. Making things complex is easy; the challenge is to simplify, to ferret out the essential. This is what Occam's razor is about. Galileo's study of falling bodies would have gotten nowhere if he had worried about feathers right from the beginning. He did not ignore feathers but consciously put them aside for a while. Note that reluctance to simplify has nothing to do with mathematical skills.

So we have the directional model $dV/dN > 0$. What should we do next? This may look self-evident to many social scientists. Collect data, run a linear regression $V = a + bN$, and see whether the slope $dV/dN = b$ is positive. If it is, the directional model is confirmed. Report the numerical value of slope b, its level of significance, correlation coefficient R^2, and possibly also intercept (a). Case closed. But hold it.

Are the resulting numerical values of a and b in a reasonable range, or are they surprisingly high or low? Such questions are rarely asked in today's social sciences, where the attitude tends to be that what is, is. Is not science about finding out what the world *is* like, leaving what it *should* be to religion? Right? Wrong.

Recall that science is very much about what *should* occur when some inevitable or plausible assumptions are made. Science is about such logical consequences. Of course, the expected outcomes must face a reality check. This is when data collection and statistical analysis enter, at a later stage. Let us first ask: *What do we already know about volatility and parties, even before collecting any formal data?*

The first response might be that, without data, we know nothing. But this is not so. We often take some of our knowledge so much for granted that we do not even realize how much we know. Teasing the most out of what we know can lead to a quantitative model that is based on near-complete ignorance, yet is of considerable predictive value. For short, I have called such models "*ignorance-based models*" (Taagepera 1999*b*).

The first step in constructing quantitatively predictive models often echoes the aforementioned advice by Sherlock Holmes: Eliminate the impossible, and a single possibility may remain—or at least the field is narrowed down appreciably. As a starter, *delineate the field in which data points could not possibly lie*.

Volatility cannot be less than 0 or more than 100%. The number of parties (N) cannot be less than 1. These *conceptually forbidden areas* are shown in Figure 4.1, where volatility is graphed against the number of parties. All this may look so obvious as not be worth three sentences, but it has consequences that are not so obvious. At this point, we assume that at least one party obtains some votes in both elections. This restriction excludes from consideration the unlikely situation where a single party

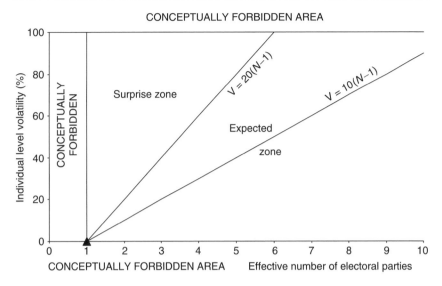

CONCEPTUALLY FORBIDDEN AREA

Figure 4.1. Individual-level volatility of votes vs. effective number of electoral parties—conceptually forbidden areas, anchor point, and expected zone

has all the votes in one election but loses them all to a brand new party in the next election.

Next, observe that there is a *conceptual extreme case*. Suppose only one party runs at the first election, and only the same party runs at the next one. This means that $N = 1$, and switching to another party is impossible. Hence, volatility must be 0. This point ($N = 1$, $V = 0$) is marked in Figure 4.1 with a black triangle. It is a conceptual *anchor point*. At $N = 1$, even a slight deviation of V away from 0 would violate logic.

A second mental roadblock may enter here: *reluctance to play with extreme cases* that rarely or never arise in practice. One may argue that talking about one-party elections is beside the point, because democratic countries always have more than one party running. Logical models, however, must not predict absurdities even under extreme conditions. Again, this mental roadblock has nothing to do with mathematical skills.

If V increases with N, our simplest tentative assumption could be linear increase: $V = a + bN$. But the anchor point adds a constraint. All acceptable lines must pass through the anchor point. For $N = 1$, we must have $V = 0$. Plugging these values into $V = a + bN$ yields $0 = a + b$, so that $a = -b$. This means that, among the infinite number of upward sloping straight lines, only those will do where the intercept equals the negative of slope:

$$V = -b + bN = b(N - 1).$$

Without any input of data, the conceptual anchor point approach has already narrowed down the range of possibilities. Instead of two unknowns (a and b), we have only one. This is a tremendous advance in parsimony.

Now we move to shakier grounds. Consider a high effective number of parties, say $N = 6$, which is rarely reached. The reader may share a gut feeling that even with such a high number of parties to choose from, not all voters will switch parties. If so, then $V = 100\%$ at $N = 6$ would be a *highly surprising* outcome, although it is not conceptually impossible. The line $V = b(N - 1)$ that passes through this point is shown in Figure 4.1. It requires that $100 = b(6 - 1)$; hence $b = 100/(6 - 1) = 20$. Thus, the equation of this line is $V = 20(N - 1)$. Any data point located above this line would be highly surprising, although we cannot completely exclude the possibility, in contrast to the conceptually forbidden areas. Hence, this zone is marked as a *surprise zone* in Figure 4.1.

So $V = 20(N - 1)$ is about the highest value of V that would not utterly surprise us, at given N. Do we also have a lowest value? We do not. Even with a very high number of parties, it is still conceivable that party loyalty of voters could be complete. Thus, no limit higher than $V = 0$ can be proposed, meaning a horizontal line in Figure 4.1.

Without any real data input, we have now narrowed the reasonably *expected zone* of occurrence of data points to the cone between the lines $V = 20(N - 1)$ and $V = 0$. *In the absence of any other knowledge*, we have no reason to expect the actual line to be closer to either of these two extremes. Therefore, our best guess would be *the average of the likely extremes*, meaning $V = 10(N - 1)$. This line is also shown in Figure 4.1.

A third mental roadblock may enter here: *reluctance to take the mean of the extremes*. Suppose $N = 4$. Then $V = 20(N - 1)$ yields $V = 60$ while $V = 0$ yields 0. This is an awfully wide range. How could we assert that $V = 10(N - 1) = 30$ is more likely than any other number between 0 and 60? Is it not time to acknowledge that "We just do not know"? This would be a mistake. We still do know something. Our best "minimax bet" would be the mean of the extremes. The central values within the range would surprise us less than the extremes. True, the mean slope $b = 10$ actually stands for $b = 10 \pm 10$, which implies a huge range of possible error. Still, this entire range of b, from 0 to 20, means a considerable reduction in possibilities, compared to the directional model "I'll accept any positive slopes." Once more, reluctance to use the mean of the extremes has little to do with the mathematical skills needed for calculating the mean.

Testing the Coarse Model

Before resorting to any data, we have reached a predictive model based on near-complete ignorance:

$$V \approx 10(N - 1).$$

Compared to the directional model $dV/dN > 0$, this one predicts volatility much more specifically. If we ask "What volatility would you predict when $N = 4$?" the directional model $dV/dN > 0$ would answer: "Any positive V will do." Such a model is bound to be right, but its predictive value is nil because it covers too much ground. It is a qualitative model—or a semi-quantitative, if you really stretch it. In contrast, the model $V = 10(N - 1)$ would answer: "V will be *roughly around* 30." This prediction may be off by ±30, upon testing with data, but it does offer a specific value. In this sense, this is a *quantitatively predictive model*. It is not "deterministic" in the sense of claiming that all data points will fall on the specific line. It rather expresses the expectation that about one-half the points will fall above and about one-half of the points will fall below the line $V = 10(N - 1)$.

In sum, this model makes two distinct predictions, one very precise and the other quite fuzzy:

1. If any straight line fits at all, the prediction $a = -b$ is absolute, due to respect for the conceptual anchor point. When regression with $V = a + bN$ is carried out, this model predicts that the two adjustable constants/coefficients will have exactly the same numerical value, with changed sign. If the values of b and $-a$ differed appreciably, it would sink the model, the more so if R^2 is high. On the other hand, if they pretty much agree, then we really should repeat the regression with $V = b(N - 1)$, which respects the anchor point and has only one adjustable coefficient, rather than with $V = a + bN$, where a and b can vary separately, ignoring the anchor point.

2. The prediction that slope b would be around 10, in contrast, is extremely fluid. It means: "If you force me to guess at a specific number, I would say 10." Even values appreciably different from 10

would not impair the basic model. They would just help to specify the numerical value of b, to be plugged into the model $V = b(N - 1)$.

Only at this stage would we need some data, so as to test the predictions $a = -b$ (exactly) and $b \approx 10$ (approximately). But we do not yet need to run a regression. All we need is the mean N and mean V for a set with many data points. Plug these means into $V = b(N - 1)$, and b is determined as $b = $ mean $V/($mean $N - 1)$. We will see how close b is to 10. For the first and crucial prediction, we will have to regress with $V = a + bN$ and see whether $a/b = -1$, say within ± 0.1.

A uniform data-set is available from Oliver Heath (2005), for state-level elections in India (1998–99). Many parties competed in some of these states, while few did in some others. Mean $N = 3.65$ and mean $V = 31.6$ lead to $b = 11.9$, a result within 20% of our very coarse expectation of 10. This input of still limited information (mean N and V only) enables us to predict more precisely that

$$V = -11.9 + 11.9N.$$

The actual best fit reported by Heath (2005) is

$$V = -9.07 + 11.14N \quad [R^2 = 0.50].$$

At $N = 1$, it would yield $V = 2.07$. On a 0–100 scale, this is rather close to the conceptually required $V = 0$. The ratio $a/b = -9.07/11.4 = -0.80$ is within 20% of the conceptually required value, -1.00. The scatter of data around the best-fit line is appreciable, and the R^2 for $V = -11.9 + 11.9N$ is almost as high as it is for the best-fit line. Therefore, the difference may well be due to random fluctuation in data. The quantitatively predictive model $V = b(N - 1)$ is confirmed within $\pm 20\%$, with b specified as 11.9 rather than the initial estimate of 10. For most practical purposes, this would be close enough.

Refined Ignorance-Based Model

It may look quite impressive how close our predictive model came to the descriptive best-fit line. This model, however, involves a conceptual flaw, right from the beginning. For simplicity's sake, we assumed a linear increase, which led to $V = b(N - 1)$. The attentive reader may have noticed that any such upward line would project to a volatility of more than 100% for a sufficiently high number of parties. When $V = -11.9 + 11.9N$, it would surpass 100% whenever $N > 9.34$. True, hardly any party systems have such a high effective number of parties, but remember: *"Predictive models must not violate logic even under extreme conditions."*

So we will have to refine the model. We must avoid predictions that extend into the forbidden area $V > 100$. This refinement requires some facility with exponential equations. A quick overview of the latter is given in the Appendix to Chapter 8. Some readers may wish to bypass the next section and simply accept its results.

This is the point where elementary school mathematics no longer suffices. The wonder is how far we have proceeded with little beyond arithmetic. Possible mental reservations against this approach have little to do with mathematical skills.

As an output variable approaches a conceptual ceiling, further increase in the input variable that drives it finds it ever harder, so to say, to achieve any further increase. The simplest way to express this extremely general phenomenon mathematically is $dy/dx = k(C - y)$, where C is the ceiling value for y, and k is an adjustable "rate constant" (see Chapter 8 for more details). This "differential equation" says that further increase in y is proportional to the remaining distance between y and the ceiling. Integration leads to a nonlinear equation: $y = C[1 - A e^{-kx}]$. It is an exponential equation where A is a constant that depends on the initial conditions. This equation applies, among others, to the amount of a new element produced by radioactive fission, over time x. The ceiling is imposed by the initial amount of fissionable material.

Now consider volatility. At a large number of parties, a further increase in the number of parties can be expected to become ever less efficient in inducing further volatility. The general exponential equation becomes $V = 100[1 - A e^{-kN}]$, where the anchor point $V = 0$ at $N = 1$ requires that $1 - A e^{-k} = 0$ and hence $A = e^k$. The result is

$$V = 100[1 - e^k e^{-kN}] = 100[1 - e^{-k(N-1)}].$$

How could such a predictive model be tested? It would be inappropriate to use straight linear regression, which would return us to the coarse linear model. However, the nonlinear equation above can be transformed into linear by transposing and taking natural logarithms:

$$\ln\left(1 - \frac{V}{100}\right) = -k(N - 1).$$

This means that linear regression against N must be carried out on $\ln(1 - (V/100))$, not on V itself.

In the case of Heath's data (2005) for state-level elections in India, the rate constant k can be calculated by plugging in the mean N (3.65) and the mean $\ln(1 - (V/100))$. The latter is around -0.384, by my rough calculations. For these means, $k = 0.384/(3.65 - 1) = 0.145$, so that the model predicts

$$V = 100[1 - e^{-0.145(N-1)}].$$

How Precisely Can the Number of Parties Predict Volatility?

Figure 4.2 shows the data points (from Heath 2005) and the curves for the exponential model, the coarse linear model, and the empirical linear fit. The latter two models pass by definition through the point of mean N and V. The exponential curve does not but comes close, because the mean $\ln((V/100) - 1)$ corresponds to $V = 31.9$, close to the mean $V = 31.6$ Above this point, the empirical linear fit lies between the two models. At lower values, the three curves can hardly be distinguished. With this degree of data scatter, all three approaches yield about the same R^2.

It can be seen from Figure 4.2 that the coarse model works about as well as the refined one throughout the usual range of volatility. Hence, we can

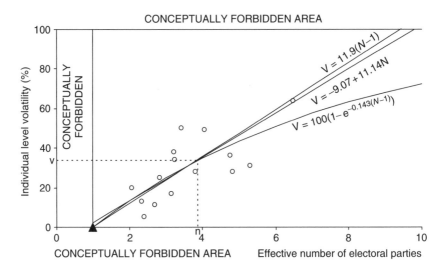

Figure 4.2. Individual-level volatility of votes vs. effective number of electoral parties—data and best linear fit from Heath (2005), plus coarse and refined predictive models

use the simpler model, as long as we keep in mind its limitations. This is a general observation: One must be aware of the refined model, so as to know when a simplification can be used. In physics, classical mechanics is more convenient to handle than the relativistic, and it does well, as long as speeds fall much short of the speed of light. For volatility, the coarse model is more convenient and does well, as long as there are effectively less than five parties.

It would be simplistic to expect that the effective number of parties alone fully determines volatility. Numerous other factors obviously enter. Therefore, the precision of the model should not be exaggerated. While 11.9 is the slope in the coarse model that happens to fit the Indian data, we should round it off to 12 for the purpose of broader worldwide prediction, and introduce a likely error range (ε):

$$V = (12 \pm \varepsilon)(N - 1).$$

How large a range of fluctuation could we expect? If we estimated the slope b on the basis of a single individual state in India, the results could range from 1.4 to 21.4, meaning 12 ± 10. For many elections *under roughly the same conditions*, a coarse rule of thumb would suggest an error equal to the square root of 10, which is about 3. Thus, my prediction for the range of average slopes in other countries is

$$V = (12 \pm 3)(N - 1),$$

provided that India's political culture corresponds to an average tendency of voters to switch parties. The Indian voter is reputed to be unusually prone to change parties, but this impression may arise from the rather large number of parties available.

How does this outcome differ from the descriptive linear regression equation, $V = -9.07 + 11.14N$? The quantitatively predictive model could in principle have been devised prior to any input of data. This means that it is not specific to India—it is expected to apply to all countries, albeit with a wide range of error. The Indian data just helped specify the slope b and verify that $a/b = -1.00$. The equation $V = (12 \pm 3)(N - 1)$ makes a universal quantitative prediction, with a specified range of likely variation.

In contrast, the regression equation deals solely with a particular set of Indian data. It offers the best fit to these data, with several decimals. It is the best way to *postdict* for these data—but for these data alone. Of course, it is a useful starting point for pondering the broader implications of the parameter values obtained. One could have done

Table 4.1. How does the number of parties (*N*) affect volatility (*V*)?—predictive and descriptive approaches (modified from Taagepera 2007*b*)

Predictive	Descriptive
Incipient model: $V = f(N)$, $dV/dN > 0$	Incipient model: $V = f(N)$, $dV/dN > 0$
How might things connect?	Do not prejudge, beyond asking "Is $dV/dN > 0$?"
1. Limits, and anchor point $V(1) = 0$.	Get data!
2. $(N-1)$ switching options $\rightarrow$ try V	Run regression
proportional to $(N-1)$	
3. High slope unlikely $\rightarrow$ $b < 20$	Report regression equation: $V = 11.14N - 9.07$
Quantitatively predictive model:	Hypothesis $dV/dN > 0$ proven
$V = bN - b$; $0 < b < 20 \rightarrow b \approx 10$	
Gather and transform data in the light of	No further prediction to test
the model: mean N and	
$V \rightarrow V = 11.9N \rightarrow 11.9$	
Test the predictive model with data: $\rightarrow$	Any coefficient values are accepted
close agreement. Could have been	
appreciably off, but did not	

the regression first, observe that $|a| = 9.07$ and $b = 11.14$ are remarkably close, and wonder whether there might be some logical reason for it. This is how I reacted upon seeing the analysis by Heath (2005), and the coarse model immediately took shape. Unfortunately, social scientists who deal with regressions all too often neglect such follow-up. Hence, they stop short of extracting the quantitative maximum out of their results.

Why would social scientists limit themselves to confirming merely the direction of impact ($dV/dN > 0$, in this case) when they also measure and publish its quantitative extent? One of the reasons may be that automatic fitting with $V = a + bN$ introduces two distinct parameters, *a* and *b*, which makes comparison of data-sets hard. Seemingly, one would have to compare both slopes and intercepts. Here, the quantitatively predictive model simplifies comparisons by indicating that one parameter alone should suffice to characterize the relationship in various party systems.

The Main Contrasts Between Predictive and Descriptive Approaches

Table 4.1 reviews the main contrasts between the predictive and descriptive handling of the sample problem, volatility. Beyond the incipient directional model ($dV/dN > 0$), the descriptive researcher would proceed immediately to data analysis. The predictive model builder would ask: Can we make the model more specific? How might things connect logically?

Following the Sherlock Holmes principle of eliminating the impossible, the predictive model starts by specifying the *boundary conditions*. It then considers further *logical constraints*, which leads to a conceptual *anchor point*. A number of simplifying assumptions may have to be introduced at this point. Next, one may look for the *simplest equation* that satisfies all logical constraints. Predictive models rarely can be linear without violating some boundary conditions, but linear approximations can be used, as long as one specifies their range of applicability.

The next step often concerns the *plausible range of values of coefficients and constants* in the model. Not just any positive values of slope b are acceptable in this case. So a range is established, such that values outside this range would surprise us. Given nothing but such a range and asked to guess at b, our best minimax bet would be the mean of the extremes.

Now, and only now, do we have to enter limited data into the predictive model, although we can enter data earlier, too, to inspire and guide model construction. Merely inserting the mean values of N and V leads to a full predictive model. Here, the numerical value of the single coefficient derives from this minimal data input, while the format is based on reasoning alone. Only past this stage would detailed data enter, for testing the predictive model through regression. In general, models must first be transformed into a linear form, before linear regression makes sense, but here the coarse model already is linear.

Heath (2005) exemplifies well the descriptive approach to the same issue, asking merely: "Do multiparty systems have higher levels of volatility than two-party systems?" The conceptual model is limited to this cautious question about the *direction* of impact. Linear regression immediately follows. The format used, $V = a + bN$, is not based on the specifics of the issue on hand. Linear regression is just what many social scientists tend to apply automatically to any relationship—it is a Pavlovian reflex. No expectations are voiced about how steep or shallow the slope might be, or what value the intercept might have. The numerical values in the regression equation derive fully from the data and from nothing else. Coming *after* data analysis, this equation represents a *postdictive* model.

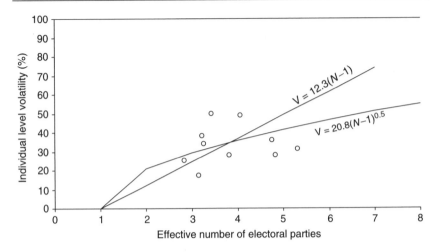

Figure 4.3. Individual-level volatility of votes vs. effective number of electoral parties—truncated data (from Heath 2005) and two models that fit the data and the anchor point

Can Data with Low R^2 Confirm a Model?

For descriptive (or directionally predictive) models, the answer is "no," because data are all there is. Any slope b in the regression equation $y = a + bx$ is accepted, as long as the sign of b is right. The only concern is how closely the data points crowd along the regression line. If R^2 is low, one has nothing.

Such a situation is illustrated in Figure 4.3. The data shown in Figure 4.2 has been truncated by omitting the one point with the highest and the four points with the lowest number of parties. Visibly, the best fit line now is almost horizontal. The slope might be slightly negative or positive, and R^2 is below 0.1. As far as descriptive analysis is concerned, all one could do is to report no correlation between V and N, and that is the end of it.

The outcome is quite different when we use the same data to test the predictive model $V = b(N - 1)$, where we expect a slope around 10. The new mean values of N and V are 3.87 and 35.3, respectively (as compared to 3.65 and 31.6 with the full data-set). The new estimate of slope is $b = 35.3/2.87 = 12.3$, hardly different from the previous 11.9. The expectation that slope is around 10 is confirmed, regardless of the low value of R^2. It would be nice to obtain a high correlation coefficient, but this is hardly essential.

It does not mean that the model $V = b(N - 1)$ is equally well confirmed by the truncated data-set as by the full one. The difference between $R^2 \approx .1$ and $R^2 = .50$ still matters. Suppose someone makes a logical argument for a square root model, $V = a(N - 1)^{0.5}$. Such a model is shown in Figure 4.3, along with the linear. It is fitted to go through the mean point, and it respects the anchor point (1;0). The truncated data could not discriminate between the two models, while the full data-set fits the linear model better. While not able to give preference to the linear model, the truncated data-set would still confirm that this simple model is plausible, until proven otherwise. It would take a much higher R^2 to discriminate between the linear and exponential models in Figure 4.2.

What distinguishes the predictive approach from the descriptive, in the context of Figure 4.3, is that the descriptive approach has nothing but the 10 actual data points at its disposal. When these points show no pattern, we effectively have a single point with some scatter around it. This is the data configuration in Figure 4.3. In contrast, the predictive approach adds the virtual data point at $N = 1$, $V = 0$. This addition of the anchor point may look weak, in the absence of real data at this location. Actually, it is extremely strong and precise, given our certitude that if we should ever get data points where $N = 1.00$, then every single one of them would have $V = 0.00$, with no margin of error.

Thus, even when $R^2 = 0$ for the actual data points, the predictive approach has not one but two very distinct points at its disposal, and two points determine a line. In the absence of any further knowledge, we can use this line as a first approximation for a predictive model. It would be less than optimal to refuse to do so and say "We cannot predict anything" when we actually can—within a margin of error. The extent of the scatter of points in Figure 4.2 (or 4.3) gives us an idea about the extent of possible error.

Actually, there is a situation where one might be happier with a lower R^2 (cf. discussion of Figure 3.2). This is when the best fit curve deviates from the predicted. In such a case, more scatter would leave more hope that further data might bring the observed pattern closer to the expected. This would be so only from the viewpoint of trying to preserve the existing model. There may be no need to preserve it. A high R^2 around an unexpected curve offers valuable guidance for adjusting the model.

In sum, there are more important considerations than high R^2, if one wants to make sense of nature. R^2 indicates by how much a regression equation *accounts* for some variance in y for given x, in a statistical sense. However, a high R^2 alone does not *explain* anything in a substantive sense that would allow prediction for other data-sets. It is nice to have a high R^2 (provided the best fit curve agrees with the model), but even a scattered data cloud does not sink a predictive model predicated on anchor points far away from the data cloud. A low R^2 may just indicate that the observed range of the input variable is too narrow to bring the trend into evidence, against a noisy background. One should then try to find ways to extend the range over which the model is tested.

On a broader note, data are not sacrosanct. They may be systematically distorted by some pervasive factors not included in the model, like the effect of gravity is by air friction. Or the data may not refer to the concept in the model but to a related, yet distinct concept. If one has a logically well-founded model, the first reaction to contradictory data might well be "Damn the data, full speed ahead!" One can sometimes outrun torpedoes and data. Later, of course, more suitable data must be located. Chapter 13 elaborates on this issue.

Some General Features of Constraint-Based Models

Quantitatively predictive logical models can at times be constructed prior to any input of data. Most often, however, some initial data inspire or guide model building, although these data might be much more limited than what would be eventually needed for serious testing. Oftentimes, even a cursory graphing brings out a pattern that makes one ask "Why?" This is the way the graph of volatility versus number of parties in Heath (2005) made me look for the reasons behind the regularity observed.

In building models, our choices are constrained in a highly constructive way by conceptually forbidden areas, where no data points can exist, and anchor points, through which the expected average curve must pass. The scientific quest for relationships need not establish that nature or God has chosen one particular form; it often suffices to show that any other choice would run into contradictions. Entering a forbidden zone or missing an anchor point would be among such contradictions. Let us review how such considerations entered the model for volatility.

1. Use boundary conditions, ceilings, and other logical constraints; establish anchor points.
2. Look for the simplest set of equations that does not violate the logical constraints.

3. Wonder about the possible range of values of coefficients and constants. Some limits are firm, while some are fluid. It may look unscientific to use such vague limits, but the reverse is true: It is not good science to ignore obvious limitations just because we cannot pin them down with two-digit precision. They still exist.

4. Use the means of data to estimate some coefficients in the predictive model. This step goes beyond dataless prediction but still precedes regression.

Continuity

The notion of continuity has been implicitly linked here to that of anchor points. In macroscopic natural or social phenomena, a small change in x mostly brings a small change in y. This means that the path from one anchor point to another (or to a conceptual ceiling) must form a continuous curve. Discontinuities do occur, for example, in aerodynamic theory (at speed of sound) and in utility theory. However, they are rather rare in *macroscopic* phenomena. At the microscopic level, the seemingly continuous electric current consists of discrete electrons and water flow has discrete molecules, but for large quantities of such particles, the micro-level granularity can be overlooked. Similarly, an electorate consisting of discrete voters can be treated as a continuous quantity, as long as there are thousands of them. One has to be cautious, of course, of not inadvertently stepping into territory where "granularity" can make a difference.

Note that the presumption of continuity applies to much of statistics as well. We presume quasi-continuity whenever we try to fit a distribution of discrete entities by a smooth normal curve (or other continuous curve), rather than as a discontinuous histogram.

Changes in slope (dy/dx) also tend to be continuous, and the same goes for the "slope of the slope" (d^2y/dx^2) and the higher derivatives (d^ny/dx^n). Moreover, the curves are expected to go monotonically up or down ($dy/dx > 0$ everywhere or $dy/dx < 0$ everywhere), *unless there is a reason* for reversal. If the data should present an unexpected kink in the pattern, the data should be checked. If the kink remains, the underlying reason must be discovered and worked into the model.

Conclusions

This specific example has introduced terms like forbidden areas, anchor points, and ceilings. It has illustrated the differing significance of the degree of correlation (R^2, in particular) when data is all we have (descriptive models) and when we also have a predictive model that goes beyond predicting directionality. Chapter 8 presents such notions in a more systematic form. Of course, a constraint-based approach is not the only one to building logical models. Chapter 11 expands into various model-building methods that were not needed in the specific case of volatility.

Appendix to Chapter 4

Further Refinements and Aggregate Volatility

Further improvement in predicting volatility may go in several directions. Data may be improved, addressing the "party of nonvoters" and the sticky problems that arise from party splits and fusions. Further input variables may be introduced. If further factors appreciably reduce the remaining variation in volatility, it may turn out that volatility's relationship to the number of parties deviates significantly even from the exponential model. In this case, one would have to review both the way the number of parties is measured and the way it could interact with volatility.

The term "interact" is used here on purpose. Up to now, we have proceeded as if causality were one-directional, the number of parties affecting volatility. This need not be so. Those who consider forming a new party may be encouraged if they know that voters are highly volatile and may easily switch to a new party. Thus, volatility may indirectly affect the number of parties.

Could further work show that some other factor is actually more important than the number of parties? Heath (2005) found that the number of parties accounts for one-half of the variation in volatility ($R^2 = .50$). This suggests that we have pinned down the major determinant of volatility, or at least one of two major ones, as no other single factor can account for more, unless it is a factor that affects the number of parties and also affects volatility directly.

All previous models refer to *individual level volatility* (V_I). This can be determined only by exit polls where voters are asked their present and previous party preference—and hope that the answers fit the facts. It is much easier to determine the *aggregate volatility* (V_A), based on how the vote shares of parties change from one election to the next. This is a lower number than V_I, because voters switching from party B to party C and vice versa may cancel out. It may also be of more interest. How could we estimate V_A?

In principle, aggregate volatility could range from 0 (full cancelling out of individual shifts) to V_I (no cancellation at all). Hence, it can be expected to be around one-half of the individual volatility, *on the average*. On the strength of the model for V_I and the value of slope constant $b = 12$ specified by the Indian individual volatility data, we can presume that the slope would be around 6 in a coarse model for aggregate volatility, as long as N remains moderate:

$$V_A \approx (6 \pm 1.5)(N - 1).$$

When initially constructing this model for aggregate volatility, I desisted from collecting any data. This way, it would truly represent a purely theoretical quantitative prediction regarding aggregate volatility, derived from data on individual volatility. Since then, Mainwaring and Torcal (2006) have reported aggregate volatility figures that lead to slopes ranging from 2 to 7 in the case of stable democracies. The slope can reach 15 in early elections in new democracies. Full testing remains to be done. Then we will now how close the prediction above was.

5

Physicists Multiply, Social Scientists Add—Even When It Does Not Add Up

- Most physics equations include few variables, which multiply or divide. In contrast, regression equations favored in social sciences often have many variables in additive–subtractive strings, with division almost unknown.

- Most physics equations include at most one freely adjustable constant, which has a substantive interpretation. Regression equations have more freely adjustable constants/coefficients than variables, and these coefficients lack substantive interpretation.

- Physics rarely offers alternate equations for the same phenomenon, with a different set of input variables and constants. This is frequent in regression analysis as practiced in social sciences.

- Physics expressions avoid inconsistencies and absurdities even for extreme cases. Social scientists often accept them.

- Physics equations are presented with prediction in mind. Tables of regression coefficients in social sciences reflect postdiction and often preclude even that.

- Physicists specify likely error ranges on predictions and present only meaningful decimals. Social scientists report correlation coefficients and often print meaningless decimals.

- Physics equations are reversible and transitive. Standard regression equations are unidirectional—different equations lead from y to x and from x to y. They are also nontransitive—regressing y on x and then z on y differs from regressing z on x directly.

- Hence, physics equations can form interlocking networks to join variables in a unique way, while standard regression equations cannot.

Physics and social sciences differ appreciably in typical mathematical format used for describing regularities. It has implications for what is considered a publishable result. This chapter describes the differences in format. The next two chapters point out how it affects falsifiability and even the very meaning of "results."

Table 5.1 shows the 20 "greatest equations ever" in physics (Crease 2004), based on an inquiry to which 120 readers of *Physics World* responded. They considered simplicity, practicality, and historical relevance for advancement of science. These top equations range from as simple as $1 + 1 = 2$ to Fourier transforms. Josep Colomer (2007) observes that physics has traditionally been "the model" for economics, which in turn has been a widely applauded model for other social sciences. Hence, "This list of physics equations can be taken as a benchmark to identify crucial properties of mathematical formulae that should also be found in other disciplines with similar scientific ambition" (Colomer 2007). The

Table 5.1. The 20 equations voted the most important for physics (Crease 2004), by rank

Euler's equation	$e^{j\pi} = -1$
Maxwell's equations	$\nabla.\mathbf{D} = \rho,\ \nabla.\mathbf{B} = 0,\ \nabla \times \mathbf{E} = \partial\mathbf{B}/\partial t,$ $\nabla \times \mathbf{H} = \partial\mathbf{D}/\partial t + \mathbf{J}$
*Newton's Second Law	$\mathbf{F} = m\mathbf{a}$
Pythagorean theorem	$a^2 + b^2 = c^2$
Schrödinger's equation	$H\Psi = E\Psi$
*Einstein's equation	$E = mc^2$
Boltzmann equation	$S = k \ln W$
One plus one	$1 + 1 = 2$
Principle of least action	$\delta S = 0$
*DeBroglie's equation	$P = h/\lambda$
Fourier transform	$F(x) = f(k)e^{2\pi kx}dk$
*Einstein's general theory of relativity	$G_{\mu\nu} = 8\pi G T_{\mu\nu}$
*Circumference of a circle	$C = 2\pi r$
Dirac equation	$i\gamma\partial\Psi = m\Psi$
Riemann zeta function	$\zeta(s) = \Pi[p^s/(p^s - 1)]$
*Hubble's Law	$v = H_0 d$
*Simplest ratio	$a/b = c/d$
*Ideal gas law	$PV = nRT$
Balmer series	$1/\lambda_n = R[1/2^2 - 1/n^2]$
*Planck's equation	$E = h\nu$

Asterisks mark the ones that follow the pattern $y = a\Pi x_i^b$.

following expands on his observations as well as a conference paper of mine (Taagepera 2005a).

Multiplication–Division Versus Addition–Subtraction

Nine of the 20 equations in Table 5.1 follow a common mathematical format: Any variable can be obtained by multiplication/division of one or more other variables, possibly multiplied by a constant. This general format is $y = a\Pi x_i^{b_i}$, where Π stands for "product," the exponents b_i are integers or simple fractions (mostly 1, 2, and 1/2), positive or negative, and a is a constant. When reduced to basic dimensions (length, time, etc.), only integer values ranging from -4 to $+4$ remain (Krantz et al. 1971: 455). The remaining 11 equations in Table 5.1 follow no common format. Thus, while $y = a\Pi x_i^{b_i}$ is by no means the only format, it is the most salient one.

This multiplicative format implies a linear format for the logarithms of the variables: $\log y = \log a + \Sigma b_i \log x_i$. While $\log a$ can have any value, the values of b_i are largely limited to ± 1, ± 2, $\pm 1/2$, and mathematical constants such as π. The implications of this major restriction are discussed in a later section.

In contrast, the most prevalent quantitative format in today's social sciences is linear regression of input variables, either directly as ordinary least squares (OLS) or after a standard transformation such as *probit* or *logit*. Factor analysis also maintains an essentially linear character. The general format is $y = a + \Sigma b_i x_i$, where a is usually called "the constant" or "intercept," while the b_i are called "slope," "coefficient," or simply "b." Any values of b_i can occur and are usually accepted, in contrast to the limited options for b_i in $\log y = \log a + \Sigma b_i \log x_i$ that follows from the multiplicative format.

To visualize the difference, compare the universal law of gravitation, $F = GMm/r^2$ (cf. Chapter 2) with a typical outcome in social sciences: $s = 12.906 - 0.477 V_0 + 1.172 E + 8.680 I$. The latter is the Baseline Model in a study of presidential accountability (Samuels 2004) that I will use later (Chapter 16) as an example of how existing descriptive research can be upgraded to predictive. Here s is vote swing for the incumbent's party, V_0 is its percent vote in previous election, E is percent change in GDP/capita, and I is a dummy variable that depends on whether the incumbent president runs for reelection. The gravitation equation assumes a broadly similar form when logarithms are taken: $\log F = \log G + \log M + \log m - 2 \log r$, but here all the slope coefficients are small integers.

Among the aforementioned 20 physics equations, addition occurs explicitly in $1 + 1 = 2$ and $a^2 + b^2 = c^2$, and implicitly at least in Maxwell's equations (compacted sums of partial derivatives) and Fourier series (limiting form of a sum). It is striking, however, that no addition of variables-cum-coefficients $(b_i x_i)$ occurs. (See Appendix to Chapter 5 for occurrence of addition in physics in a broader sense.) In contrast, such linear concatenation is a standard workhorse in social sciences. It is all too often treated as the only game in town.

Division: Widespread Versus Absent

It is quite unremarkable that the arithmetic operation of division occurs in physics equations. What *is* remarkable is its absence from regression analysis as practiced in social sciences. Nothing prevents inclusion of interactions that divide one input variable by another (x_i/x_j), but it just is not done. If x_i enhances y while x_j reduces it, linear regression automatically construes this relationship as subtraction $(a_i x_i - a_j x_j)$. The actual interaction might well be a division (x_i/x_j), but it cannot show up on its own. Is not it odd that we heavily depend on a format that never produces a division?

In contrast to division, social scientists do practice multiplication. They may on purpose add a product of two (or more) variables to the linear expression: $y = a + \Sigma b_i x_i . + c_1 x_1 x_2 + \ldots$. They then say they add an "interaction term" or simply that "I interact the [A] and [B] variables" (e.g., in Samuels 2004). Implicitly, the product of variables is proclaimed the only form of interaction that matters. This is the case in sophisticated elaborations on the "interaction term" by Brambor et al. (2006), and Braumoeller (2004), apart from end notes. Thus, the broad notion of interaction is narrowed down to only one out of innumerable ways variables can interact—and do interact in physics equations.

Minor transformations of variables prior to regression do occur in social sciences. Social scientists sometimes take the logarithm of some variable or include its square. Remarkably, they rarely include the inverse of a variable $(1/x_i)$. Yet the output variable may conceivably be linearly related to $1/x_i$ (cf. Figure 3.2). If so, then trying to fit it with x_i essentially replaces division by subtraction. It reduces the degree of correlation, but this should be our least concern. Much more important, it may miss the essential nature of the relationship. Remember the nondiscovery of the gravitation law (Chapter 2), despite preservation of satisfactory R^2!

A special multiplicative form occurs in multi-attribute utility theory (Keeney and Raiffa 1976: 234–8; Fishburn 1977): $(1 + cy) = (1 + cx_1)(1 + cx_2)$, which can be reduced to $y = x_1 + x_2 + cx_1x_2$. The latter may look like addition plus standard "interaction term," but it has crucial restrictions. It is far from $y = a + b_1x_1 + b_2x_2 + cx_1x_2$ where any values of $a, b_1,$ and b_2 are acceptable. As in the usual multiplicative expression, there is only one adjustable coefficient, c. Duncan Luce points out (personal communication, July 2007) that this is the only polynomial that can be transformed into a multiplicative form.

In sum, social scientists do not always approximate potentially multiplicative relationships by sums, but they all too frequently approximate potential divisions by subtractions. Many of us behave as if the arithmetic operation called division had not yet been invented.

Notation for Variables and Constants: One Letter Versus Several

It follows from frequency of multiplication in physics that the usual convention of algebra is respected: abc stands for multiplication $a \times b \times c$. If one runs out of letters and other symbols, subscripts or apostrophes might be used. In contrast, social scientists often prefer multi-letter designations for variables and constants.

Thus, many political scientists prefer to designate the "effective number of parties" (used in Chapter 4) as ENP even while Laakso and Taagepera (1979) used N_2 or simply N when they introduced this notion into political science. The multi-letter abbreviation presumably makes it easier to remember its meaning. It does not matter, as long as one limits oneself to addition. Physicists, however, would tend to interpret ENP as multiplication of three quantities: E times N times P—the same way they read GMm in $F = GMm/r^2$. As we later (Chapter 10) reach expressions like $(MS)^{1/4}$, in a definitely social science context, it becomes apparent how confusing the notation might become, if each of the quantities M and S were designated by a multi-letter abbreviation.

The Number of Variables per Equation: Occam's Razor Versus Garbage Can

Basic equations in physics rarely involve more than three input variables. This is so because physicists have found it advantageous to break

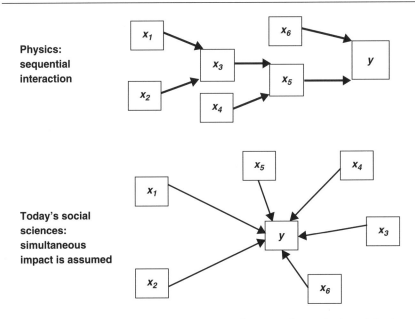

Figure 5.1. Typical ways variables interact in physics and in today's social science

up problems into smaller pieces. Most often it results in a sequence of equations of varied formats (though most often multiplicative) where each equation involves only a few variables (cf. Table 5.1). New variables gradually enter the sequence, as Figure 5.1 shows in a highly schematized way. (See the Appendix at the end of this chapter for an actual example.) Each step applies Occam's Razor.

In contrast, today's social scientists often throw numerous input variables into a single regression equation. While many regressions in social sciences have as few as a single input variable, more than 15 variables are included at times. As basic interaction pattern, it is assumed that all inputs affect the output simultaneously (see Figure 5.1). Occam's Razor is broken, thrown away and replaced by a garbage can that fits everything.

This does not mean that social phenomena involve inherently more numerous variables than the physical. Physicists just try to break up complex processes into a sequence of steps, each of which involves few variables. Quantitative social scientists tend to follow a contrary approach.

Imagine a cook assembling all the ingredients shown in a cookbook recipe, piling them together, passing them untreated through a blender, and calling the result a meal. It may work for gazpacho but for little else. Usually, ingredients must be processed separately, before they are successively introduced while cooking the meal. One must *think* how items relate to each other. This advice applies to science too. In particular, thinking about forms of relationships among various factors is at the core of quantitatively predictive logical models. In contrast, throwing all variables simultaneously into a grand regression is blender approach. All too often the output is inedible.

Are Dummies Dumb?

One special type of variables used in social science regressions is "dummy variables," for example, 0 for males and 1 for females, both preceded by a coefficient b_i, like any other variable. Sometimes it goes beyond dichotomy, for example, 0 for Muslims, 1 for Catholics, and 2 for Protestants. An extreme case I have seen replaced the variable "Age" (the effect of which may be nonlinear) by a string of dummies: 0 for ages 0–9, 1 for ages 10–19, etc.

There are no basic physics equations of comparable format (even when reduced to a linear form by taking logarithms). This is not the way positive and negative electric charges enter, or solids, liquids, and gases, or anything else. I cannot vouch for engineering applications, but once again, these are largely applications of more general laws over short ranges.

When going beyond dichotomies, the ordering of categories plays an arbitrary role. The dummies "0 for Muslims, 1 for Catholics, and 2 for Protestants" implicitly assume that Catholics are somehow intermediary between Muslims and Protestants. But even in the case of dichotomies, physicists would consider the effect of electric charge or biosocial gender in separate models rather than blithely assuming that one of the categories adds a fixed amount to the outcome. The use of dummies is questionable in many cases I have seen.

The Number of Freely Adjustable Constants/Coefficients: Too Many Notes

Maybe Mozart's music did not suffer from "too many notes," as the Emperor of Austria supposedly claimed, but standard data analysis in social sciences definitely suffers from "too many coefficients." Having many freely adjustable coefficients makes data fitting easier, compared to a single one, but the profusion of coefficients destroys their conceptual/ substantive significance. It is a direct result of replacing Occam's razor with a multivariable garbage can.

By a freely adjustable constant or coefficient, I mean one that can take any value, large or small, without raising objections. Basic physics has few of them. (More can arise in applications.) Recall that the exponents b_i in physics equations of format $y = a \Pi x_i^{b_i}$ tend to be small integers, simple fractions, or mathematical constants. Such nonadjustable constants tend to have a theoretical basis. The number of the remaining freely adjustable constants/coefficients is extremely limited. There is usually only one per equation, such as G in the gravitation law. Such a constant has a substantive interpretation—or at least a dimensional one (see Appendix to Chapter 13). Being scarce and substantive, these constants are not anonymous but tend to have names: universal constant of gravitation, Planck's constant, etc. Note that not a single one among the equations in Table 5.1 has more adjustable constants or coefficients than input variables.

The reverse is true for the linear regression format $y = a + \Sigma b_i x_i$, favored in social sciences. It has by definition more freely adjustable constants and coefficients than input variables—one b_i for each x_i, plus a. The number of variables themselves can be large, so that regression equations with more than 15 coefficients and constants can be observed. Even more coefficients per variable pile up when multiplicative "interaction terms" or other modified terms are added. These coefficients mostly lack direct substantive interpretation—they are statistical entities, not conceptual. In contrast to the sparse constants in physics equations, these prolific coefficients do not have names. Why bother naming them? Who would use these names?

It matters both for parsimony and potential substantive explana- tion whether the same degree of statistical fit is obtained with one adjustable coefficient (such as G in $F = GMm/r^2$) or with four (such as in $y = a + b_1 x_1 + b_2 x_2 + b_3 x_3$). If R^2 is equally high, then the former expres- sion accounts for the same variation using fewer coefficients. Thus, the efficiency per coefficient is higher. (This is most often so even with adjusted R^2.) Even more important, parsimony also makes it more likely that a logical path or process can be found to explain how the input should affect the output. Relationships are more diffuse in four-coefficient equations. The likelihood that all coefficients could be worked into a logical model is reduced, and the numerical values of coefficients are less likely to have permanence beyond the data set that generated them.

Even with the same initial number of freely adjustable coefficients, the multiplicative $y = kx_1^a x_2^b \ldots$ may have advantages over the additive $y = a + b_1 x_1 + b_2 x_2 + \ldots$ We may find that its exponents are close to small integers or simple fractions. Suppose linear regression of logarithms yields $y = 64 x_1^{1.76} x_2^{-1.17} x_3^{0.87} x_4^{0.07} x_5^{-0.15}$. Even if the last two exponents are statistically "significant," it makes sense to see how much fit is preserved when rounding the exponents to 2, -1, 1, 0, and 0, respectively, resulting in $y = kx_1^2 x_3 / x_2$. (Note that k is likely to shift away from 64.)

Here, parsimony is increased by eliminating two input variables. The remaining three may make some conceptual sense. Rounded-off values of the exponents might be tested with other data sets. In case of successful fit, the number of freely adjustable coefficients might be reduced conclusively, and their numerical values might acquire broader significance. At the early stage of research, x_4 and x_5 would just clutter up the main relationship. Only when this main relationship is logically explained would it be time to consider possible secondary effects. Instead of garbage can regression, there is sequential analysis.

This is not to say that linear regression of logarithms resulting from $y = kx_1^a x_2^b \ldots$ is an advisable way to proceed under most conditions. It is still overly mechanical. But it just may lead to conceptual ideas. In contrast, coefficient values close to integers have no special significance in a linear concatenation of variables themselves. Here, profusion of adjustable coefficients is irreducible when numerous variables are introduced together. One should always consider dropping the variables that improve the fit in only a minor way, even when they are "significant" in a statistical sense. Such variables often stop looking significant when a further, logically unrelated variable is added to the regression.

Such instability ("lack of robustness") suggests that not all statistically significant variables are meaningful in a logical sense—a feature all too often neglected in social sciences. Statistical significance expresses *at best* the probability that the correlations found are not due to random chance (see Chapter 6 for further reservations). Occasional correlation may well be random coincidence, unless a logical connective process can be established. This brings us to the next contrast with physics.

Alternate Equations for the Same Phenomenon: It is the Butler—Unless the Younger Uncle is Included

For a given phenomenon, physics may give complex sequences of equations and also simplified approximations for them, but it rarely gives competing alternatives with a different set of input variables and constants. Competing models for the same phenomenon do arise at times, but then the issue is not considered resolved until a single model emerges, either by discarding all but one or by integrating competing approaches, such as the wave-particle nature of light. Either way, a single way to calculate the output variable emerges.

Published social research follows this pattern only part of the time. One encounters many articles that offer several alternative regression equations for the same output variable (or closely related ones), adding or omitting some input variables or "interaction terms." These are *parallel* expressions for the same output. The output may be shown impacted by only one input ($x_1 \to y$) or by three in various combinations ($x_1 \to y \leftarrow x_2$ or $x_3 \to y \leftarrow x_2$) or simultaneously: $y \leftarrow x(x_1, x_2, x_3)$, as in Figure 5.1. Among such alternatives, the numerical value and statistical significance of the coefficient for the same input variable can differ appreciably. Such competing results are presented as different "empirical models" for the same phenomenon. All too often, the authors take no stand on which one should be preferred for the purposes of prediction or how their priority ranking could be tested.

To offer several "empirical models" often means that none is offered. Imagine concluding a detective novel as follows: The probability of the butler having done it is significant if one leaves out the younger uncle, but becomes nonsignificant if uncle is included, with R^2 being around .60 for both "models." An analysis that happily stops at this stage would satisfy neither Sherlock Holmes nor physicists. Most important, such analysis offers little to social and political decision-makers looking for scholarly advice. "Why do we tolerate long tables of numerous equations instead of just the one (or few) that really address the central question? Hardly anything is more annoying than reading a paper that has ten or twelve different "models" with this or that variable dropped or added, but with no real reason given" (Matthew Shugart, personal communication, March 2007).

Exceptions to this broad statement occur. The same behavioral laws may give rise to several distinct representations. But most parallel "empirical models" have no justification.

A perennial concern in physics has been to determine what remains constant in the midst of change—hence the notion of constants of motion and laws of conservation (of energy, mass, momentum, electric charge, etc.) that apply universally or under specified conditions. When several regressions for the same phenomenon are considered, one should compare the numerical values of coefficients for the same input variable, so as to locate some points of stability and constancy. Social scientists rarely do so. As a variable is regressed in the company of various other variables, any fluctuation in the numerical values for its coefficient all too often is deemed acceptable. This issue is handled in constructive detail later on (Chapter 16).

Conceptual Consistency: Concern Versus Acceptance of Absurdity

If the expression for a relationship produces contradictory or otherwise absurd results for some values of input variables, physicists are concerned. This is so even when these input values are outside the usual range, because conceptual consistency is at stake. Any inconsistency calls for modifying the expression so as to encompass all extreme cases. Models must not predict absurdities.

In contrast, social scientists often disregard such concerns. Consider a pure two-party system and suppose the linear fit $S = 2V - 50$ expresses well the relationship between the *observed* percentages of seats (S) and votes (V) of parties. My observation is that most social scientists would accept such a model even while it predicts *minus* 50% seats for zero votes, and an equally absurd 150% seats for 100% of votes. Their reasoning is that in practice the votes for either party always remain in the range from 30 to 70%, so what would happen at $V = 0$ or $V = 100$ is supposedly irrelevant.

Not so. Faced with the same issue, physicists would ask "but what if?" and would insist on finding a modified expression that satisfies the conceptual boundary conditions "$V = 0 \rightarrow S = 0$" and "$V = 100 \rightarrow S = 100$," while being close to $S = 2V - 50$ when V is around 50%. These conditions are satisfied by $S/(100 - S) = [V/(100 - V)]^2$, which leads to $S = 100V^2/(2V^2 - 200V + 10,000)$. Note that this form is essentially multiplicative.

Prediction Versus Postdiction

Scientific knowledge means ability to predict (in deterministic or probabilistic terms). This is possible with physics equations at several levels. Consider again the gravitation law $F = GMm/r^2$. Whenever the variables M, m, and r and the constant G are given, F can be predicted (within the limits of experimental error).

But there is also prediction in a wider sense. The constants in several law-like expressions may be connected. Thus G, combined with the mass (M_E) and radius (r_E) of the Earth, leads to gravity acceleration (g) on the surface of the Earth: $g = GM_E/r_E^2$. Gravity acceleration, in turn, also occurs in $T = 2\pi(L/g)^{0.5}$, the formula for the period (T) of simple pendulum of length L. Thus, two laws that involve some of the same variables or constants can combine into a new testable relationship. Prediction can turn out wrong. The model may not fit, either because it is faulty or because factors extraneous to the model enter. Deviations from prediction beg for explanation, which may lead to further insights.

Empirical regression equations rarely offer such creative inconsistencies. Almost any values of regression coefficients are deemed acceptable in today's social sciences, unless a variable that is expected to have a plus sign turns out to have a minus sign. There is no deviation from prediction when there is no prediction.

The argument could be made that all studies do not aim at building predictive models (see the Appendix to Chapter 15). The objective may be a tentative estimation whether a linkage is causal or not, in which case only the slope coefficient and degree of significance would matter. If accepted, this argument would highlight another contrast with physics. A mere claim that two variables are linked, without giving the mathematical form of the relationship (and hence ability to calculate one from the other) would not go far in physics.

The problem goes deeper and would remain, even if social scientists got into the habit of always using a single regression equation to plug in new cases. There simply tend to be too many freely adjustable coefficients. Anonymous regression coefficients, having existence only for a particular data set, inherently have little explanatory ability. Their large number, as compared to the sparse adjustable constants in physics equations, may make data fitting more precise, but there is a price to pay: No constants of a more durable nature emerge that could join several disparate phenomena. Without such unifying features, deeper explanation and the resulting prediction remain illusory.

Reporting Dispersion: Range of Error Versus Correlation Coefficient

Measurements are reported in physics with absolute or relative error indicated—which usually means the range of standard error. The same is done when new numerical values are inserted into existing equations. Correlation coefficients are offered quite rarely.

In social sciences, in contrast, an indicator of degree of dispersion is almost a must—most often it is a variation of R^2. It is sometimes given even while the equation for the best fitting curve to which it refers is not fully reported (by omitting the intercept). What about the range of expected error when plugging in new data? The question does not arise when no such use of regression results is envisaged.

The different formats for reporting dispersion in physics and social sciences are directly tied in with attitudes toward prediction. If one predicts, one must indicate the precision of such prediction. If one does not predict, looser concerns take over, including convention. King et al. (2000) note that jargon like "the coefficient on education was statistically significant at the 0.05 level" is common in social sciences but yields little usable information. As an alternative that makes sense, they offer "Other things being equal, an additional year of education would increase your annual income by $1,500 on the average, plus or minus about $500." Note the numerically specific estimates, plus range of reasonable uncertainty.

The Number of Decimals Reported: Meaningful Versus Meaningless

The number of decimals reported matters in natural sciences. The rule is: Show no meaningless ciphers. Decimals within the range of likely random error do not add to knowledge—they merely clutter up the place. In contrast, "the more the merrier" seems to be the custom in social sciences. This contrast may need elaboration.

Instead of indicating the likely error range of a numerical value explicitly, such as $b = 0.37 \pm 0.01$, natural sciences make use of the very number of ciphers reported. Thus $b = 0.37$ roughly implies $b = 0.37 \pm 0.01$ while

$b = 0.370$ would imply a more precise $b = 0.370 \pm 0.001$. But what about $b = 370$? Is it meant to indicate $b = 370 \pm 1$ or $b = 370 \pm 10$? The solution is to use the "scientific notation" where $b = 370 \pm 1$ becomes $b = 3.70 \times 10^2$ while $b = 370 \pm 10$ becomes $b = 3.7 \times 10^2$. By the same token, $b = 0.370$ becomes $b = 3.70 \times 10^{-1}$. In sum, the integer part is reduced to a number from 1 and 9, and the number of decimals indicates likely error.

In today's social sciences, coefficients and indices are most often shown with a profusion of decimals, simply because the computer spits them out. In what does $R^2 = .5273$ differ from $R^2 = .53$? The extra decimals are pure ballast. Social scientists routinely sin against the norm that *meaningless ciphers must not be shown.*

In the other direction, they sometimes omit meaningful ciphers. Around 2002, Kazakhstan had 16.7 million people and the Netherlands had 16.0 million people. In social sciences, these figures may be reported as 16.7 million and 16 million, respectively, because many social scientists erroneously think that terminal zeros are not worth reporting. Indeed, some computer programs aimed at social scientists routinely erase such zeros, and one must fight the computers to restore them. To a scientist, in contrast, reporting 16.7 million and 16 million would convey that the number was less precisely known for the Netherlands—only as 16 ± 0.5. Of course, *The World Almanac and Book of Facts* 2002 goes the opposite way, reporting 16,731,303 people for Kazakhstan and 15,981,472 for The Netherlands—a ridiculous degree of fake precision.

Reversible and Transitive Versus Unidirectional and Nontransitive

Most physics equations are algebraic. This means they are reversible, using algebraic transformations. One usually applies the gravitation law to calculate the attraction force when masses and their distance are given: $F = GMm/r^2$. But for such a calculation the numerical value of gravitational constant G is needed. How does one find it in the first place? By applying the law in the reverse direction, to known masses, distance, and also known force: $G = Fr^2/Mm$. Later on, the mass (m) of a newly discovered planet can be found, if one knows the mass of the Sun (M), their distance and the Sun's force of attraction on the planet (which itself can be calculated from its observed trajectory): $m = Fr^2/Gm$.

In contrast, one cannot reverse a regression equation, because every graph of x and y actually has two distinct regression equations: y on x

and x on y. Unless $R^2 = 1.00$, they differ. This crucial feature, well known to statisticians, seems little known among social scientists. We must use regression equation $y = a + bx$ to calculate y for a given value of x, but we must use the regression equation $x = a' + b'y$ to calculate x from y. If we use the value of y resulting from the first calculation, we do not get back the original value of x!

It follows from this unidirectionality that ordinary regression lacks transitivity. This means that if we regress z on y and then y on x, the resulting values of z differ from those obtained from direct regression of z on x. In contrast, most physics laws come in the form of algebraic equations that are transitive. Here, we can calculate z from x either directly or passing through y—and we do get the same result. All this is explained in more detail in Chapter 12, and a way out is offered. It is extremely important for the following reason.

Interlocked Equations Versus Isolates

The overall format in physics is a network of interlocked equations—cf. Figure 5.1. Each equation has few variables, but the same variables recur in many equations. We have seen how $F = GMm/r^2$ leads to gravity acceleration $g = GM_E/r_E^2$ which, in turn, also enters the simple pendulum formula, $T = 2\pi(L/g)^{0.5}$. Electricity has charge, force, field intensity, and voltage connected through short equations—see Figure 5.2 as discussed in the Appendix to Chapter 5—and this network continues to current intensity, resistance, capacitance, induction, etc. Indeed, most variables in physics are interlocked, however distantly. The quest for a "theory of everything" aims at completing such interlocking. (See Chapter 14 for misunderstandings of "TOE" in social sciences.)

In contrast, interlocked relationships are few in social sciences. When today's social scientists pile a large number of input variables into a single equation, some of them (such as literacy or per capita GDP) may occur in a large number of regressions. Yet the output variables remain disconnected. It is hard to establish basic relationships on purely empirical grounds in the first place—they require logical grounding. But even if individual relationships were developed on the basis of regression equations, they could not possibly be interlocked because standard regression equations are nontransitive. A *cumulative* science where relationships interlock can develop only on the basis of transitive equations.

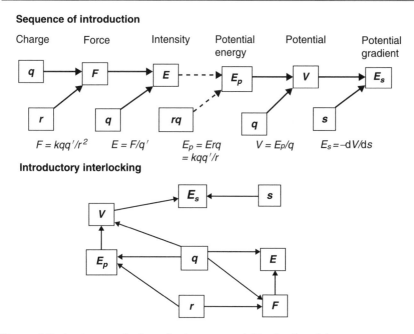

Figure 5.2. A sequence for introducing new variables in electricity

The patterns in physics and today's social sciences are akin to those of railroads in Europe and Africa. Europe has an interconnected network. From a given station on the continent, one can go to almost any other, just by changing trains. In Africa, most railroads start from a port city and end in hinterland, without connecting. Are networks of interlocking equations inherently impossible in social sciences, like railroads between separate islands in Indonesia? Or have the connections not been established because social scientists have not had the urge to look for them and the use of nontransitive equations makes connections unfeasible? At least one insipient interlocking network now exists—see Chapter 10.

Conclusions: Parsimony Versus Profusion

Table 5.2 reviews the contrasts presented. They are numerous and could have two reasons. Social and physical data may differ in their nature, calling for different treatment. Alternatively, today's social science, beguiled

Table 5.2. Typical mathematical formats in physics and in today's social sciences

	Physics	Social sciences
Basic operation	Multiplication/division: $y = a\Pi x_i^{b_i}$, leading to addition/subtraction of logarithms: $\log y = \log a + \Sigma b_i \log x_i$	Addition/subtraction: $y = a + \Sigma b_i x_i$.
Division of variables	Usual	rare
Variables per equation	Rarely more than 3	Often more than 3
Freely adjustable coefficients		
1. Per equation	Usually 1	Always more than 1
2. Per variable	At most 1	Always more than 1
Alternate equations for same phenomenon	Avoided	Presented often
Conceptual inconsistency	Cause for concern	Accepted
Prediction	Prime objective	Neglected
Measure of dispersion	Likely error, plus or minus	Correlation coefficient
Number of decimals	Indicates range of error	Meaningless
Nature of equations	Algebraic, reversible	Unidirectional, irreversible
Transitivity of equations	Transitive	Nontransitive
Networks of interlocking equations	Ubiquitous	Absent

by easy access to computerized statistics, may have neglected the aspects of scientific procedure that go beyond statistical analysis. Later chapters will sort it out.

Physics deals more in ratio variables and social sciences more in softer variables, but this is a difference in degree rather than in kind. Even when using ratio variables, today's social sciences restrict themselves largely to statistical approaches. The Appendix to Chapter 13 deals with the issue of different kinds of variables. For the moment, let us just observe that the mathematical formats are quite different, for whatever reason. The multiplicative format, so frequent in physics, is largely absent from the usual tool kit of social scientists. Physics uses sequential reasoning and applies parsimony in variables and coefficients at each step. In contrast, today's social science all too often shovels a profusion of variables and coefficients into a single regression equation. Some other contrasts follow directly, while some look separate.

Actually, social scientists do follow the principle of parsimony as long as they stick to qualitative methods. At this level, they tend to include few input variables. Multiple regression is the devil's favorite tool to induce social scientists to dump parsimony. Do not blame the tool. Blame those who misuse it.

Appendix to Chapter 5

Multiplication, Addition, and Ranking in Physics

Both addition and multiplication play of course roles in physics, and they are interlocked. The generalizations made in the section on "Multiplication–Division Versus Addition–Subtraction" need qualifications. Physics *measurements* are both additive and multiplicative (Krantz et al. 1971: 10; Luce et al. 1990: 19–20). Even the term "laws of physics" covers additive concatenations in at least two ways. One involves logarithmic transformation of multiplicative equations, as pointed out in the main text. The other concerns linear partial differential equations. Such expressions for laws of physics include sums of constants times differentials of different orders. Thus, multiplication and addition are incorporated in such expressions and, indeed, in the very definition of a derivative. The solutions of differential equations sometimes involve only multiplication of variables, but other types of solutions abound and at times explicit solutions do not exist. This becomes prevalent in quantum physics.

Besides using concatenation (including addition) and conjoint structure (including multiplication) physics even offers aspects where neither is possible, such as hardness (Luce 2005: 230). The operational definition for hardness of solids is which of two materials scratches the other. Thus, a ranking can be achieved, with no additive or multiplicative ability. This feature applies to many variables in social sciences. In sum, while rising to the level of multiplication, physics has not left behind addition or even sheer ranking. It just places more emphasis on multiplication—markedly more so.

An Actual Sequence in Physics—Basic Electricity

The sequential interaction pattern in Figure 5.1 is perforce schematized. Figure 5.2 shows the actual sequence in which a standard physics textbook, *Modern University Physics* (Richards et al. 1960: 381–437) introduces new variables relating to electric charges, fields, and potential (voltage).

Charges (q and q') and their distance (r) determine the force (F) of attraction/repulsion through $F = kqq'/r^2$. Force and charge define the electric field intensity (E) through $E = F/q'$. Electric potential energy (E_p) comes next. It could be defined on the basis of electric intensity, in conjunction with charge and distance, through $E_p = Erq$. This is shown as broken arrows in Figure 5.2. The textbook, however, finds it simpler to revert to charge and distance alone, through $E_p = kqq'/r$. Potential energy and charge define electric potential (V), through $V = E_p/q$. The potential gradient (E_s) is defined as change of V over distance s: $E_s = -dV/ds$. These variables are not just formal way stations in deducing potential from charge. The textbook offers examples of how each variable comes handy in various applications.

In contrast to the scheme in Figure 5.1, where new variables keep entering, Figure 5.2 has the same ones (q and r) re-entering in different roles. Hence, the chain can be replaced by a more parsimonious presentation of how new variables enter. The bottom of Figure 5.2 shows this interlocking. Only the links used in defining new variables are shown.

Actually, interlocking is complete in the sense that any of the variables (apart from E_s) could be expressed in terms of any other two or three variables, for example, $V = Er$ and $V = Fr/q$. This means that different textbooks may introduce variables in a different order. What they all have in common is sequential introduction of equations that involve only a few variables at a time. The result is an interlocked pattern, in contrast to the radial scheme for multiple regression approach, shown at the bottom of Figure 5.1.

Strikingly, the entire network makes do with a single constant (k). The latter is needed to connect mechanical units (force) to electrical units. The number of freely adjustable constants is much less than one per equation or per variable, in blatant contrast with regression equations.

Schemes like the ones in Figure 5.2 are not shown in physics texts. The format is taken for granted, and students internalize it early on. My scheme involves various simplifications, such as omitting vector notation and using k instead of its equivalent, $1/(4\pi\epsilon_0)$. They do not affect the argument.

6

All Hypotheses Are Not Created Equal

- Bones and hypotheses should remain hidden.
- The null hypothesis offers close to null prediction.
- Directional hypotheses are easy to satisfy and offer correspondingly vague predictions.
- Quantitative hypotheses (models) are hard to satisfy. They are the only hypotheses/models that offer quantitatively falsifiable predictions.
- Having "$p = .01$" does NOT mean confirmation in 99% of replications.
- The customary hypothesis-testing recipe in social sciences, "hypothesis $\rightarrow$ data collection $\rightarrow$ testing $\rightarrow$ acceptance/rejection," is only a single cycle in an ascending spiral:

  Initial hunch (qualitative hypothesis) $\rightarrow$ limited data collection $\rightarrow$
  $\rightarrow$ quick testing $\rightarrow$ quantitatively predictive model (quantitative hypothesis) $\rightarrow$ further data collection $\rightarrow$ testing $\rightarrow$ refined model $\rightarrow$ testing $\rightarrow$ further refining of model *or* data $\rightarrow$ testing...

The previous chapter pinned down a number of differences in mathematical format customary in physics and in social sciences. Would a shift to a multiplicative format go a long way to enable social scientists to detect patterns such as the one for gravitation law, if similar patterns existed in a social context? This could happen only in some lucky instances. Regressing logarithms of variables instead of variables themselves is still pretty mechanical and mindless. One has to think in terms of logical models. Chapter 4 pointed out some mental barriers to such thinking. There is another: fixation on "hypothesis" as the magical word. Hypothesis is a useful concept, but only when substance is built into it. Mere incantation of the term will not do.

Of Bones and Hypotheses

Social science students are told early on that "hypothesis testing" is the core of scientific procedure. Formulate a hypothesis, gather data, test the hypothesis, and either accept or reject it. This is indeed the basic framework of science—its skeleton, if you will. It is good for people to have bones, but it is bad if the bones show. So it is with the hypothesis testing cycle: it better remain hidden (Taagepera and Shugart 1989: 252). Compare the basic textbooks in physics and social sciences. The word "hypothesis" is more prominent in social sciences, while physics applies hypothesis testing in a subtler way, without parading the word itself.

In the early phase of research, the cycle often works on an informal level. The starting point might not even be more specific than a wild goose chase: "If I collect this kind of data and graph this versus that, something interesting may appear." The aficionados of the null hypothesis might reword it as " . . . nothing interesting will appear." One may also start with a more specific hunch based on qualitative observation, which may be quickly checked by further casual observations or thought experiments: "If I follow up on this hunch, to what result would it lead under this or that special or extreme condition?" One may call it a loose "testing" of the hunch, but the usual result is neither acceptance nor rejection but *modification* of the initial wording. Such an informal short cycle may be repeated many times over, with increasing collection of data and increasing specification of the hypothesis.

The trouble with explicit formulation of a formal hypothesis too early in the game is that it may destroy these "micro-cycles" of hunch-following, locking research into one long and hollow cycle of collecting extensive data for testing an insufficiently specific hypothesis. Moreover, in today's social sciences, the hypothesis is often couched in a sterile either/or format. But what if it is neither this nor that? What if it is an unexpected third way? Being open to the unexpected is essential for scientists; yet an excessively formal hypothesis formulation tends to fixate on the expected alternatives. In the case of null hypothesis, it fixates on a single expectation. Cycles and sub-cycles in scientific procedure are discussed in more detail in Chapter 14. For the moment, only the connection between hypothesis and falsifiability is addressed, covering some ground that has already been touched upon.

The Dance Around the Null Hypothesis

All hypotheses are not created equal. Some are qualitative, easy to satisfy, and offer only fuzzy predictions. Some others are quantitatively specific, hence immeasurably harder to satisfy, and offer specific predictions (Figure 6.1).

The least detailed is the famous *null hypothesis*—famous among social scientists, that is, but less so among physicists. Its focus is on disproving that some effect is due to chance. As early as 300 years ago, John Arbuthnot (1710) successfully proved that the excess of male over female births cannot be attributed to chance (Gigerenzer et al. 2004). Therefore, he considered proven that it was due to divine providence. And that is the catch: Rejecting the null hypothesis does not confront one's pet hypothesis with various alternatives. "The focus is on chance; to test substantive alternative hypotheses is not an issue" (Gigerenzer et al. 2004).

What I call the "null ritual" consists of three steps: (1) set up a statistical null hypothesis, but do not specify your own hypothesis nor any alternative hypothesis, (2) use the 5% significance level for rejecting the null and accept your hypothesis, and (3) always perform this procedure.   (Gigerenzer 2004)

One may well disprove the null hypothesis that Bob does not feel better when drinking milk, but it does not prove the positive hypothesis "Milk

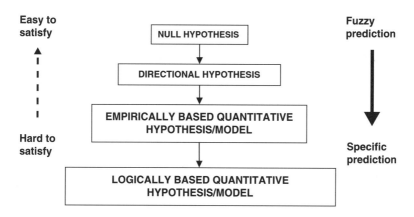

Figure 6.1. The hierarchy of hypotheses

73

is good for Bob" unless a causal process is established. Many alternative hypotheses must be considered. He may drink milk only at times when he feels good anyway—at breakfast or when it is warm. Drinking it at other times may have no effect or even a negative effect. Bob may feel good when not dehydrated, and milk just happens to contain water. Or drinking milk might make him drink less whiskey. Rejecting the null hypothesis says little about the validity of a given positive hypothesis, compared to various alternatives. "If there is one single severe problem with the null ritual, then it is the fact that *hypothesis* is in the singular. Hypothesis testing should always be competitive" (Gigerenzer et al. 2004).

Null hypothesis testing is just one statistical tool among many. Yet an editor of *Journal of Experimental Psychology*, Arthur Melton (1962), made it a necessary condition for acceptance of papers. Gigerenzer et al. (2004) call such rigidity "statistical ritual rather than statistical thinking" and document that the "null ritual" was "fabricated in the minds of statistical textbook writers in psychology and education" rather than emerging with any renowned statistician such as Sir Ronald A. Fisher (1935). In their use and misuse of statistics, much of social sciences remain at the level of Arbuthnot's divine providence: "What if there were no significance tests?" (Harlow et al. 1997). "Not much would be lost, except in situations in which we know very little," Gigerenzer et al. (2004) bluntly answer.

Directional Hypotheses

Even if a genuine connection is established by significance tests, we only get to know that x has *some* impact on y. In mathematical terms: $dy/dx \neq 0$. It says nothing about the direction of impact, much less about its intensity. It is nice to learn that drinking milk has an effect on my digestion, but as a guide for action it is worthless until I know at the very least whether it would make me better off or worse. Indeed, $dy/dx \neq 0$ allows for either direction or even both at once. Meeting a woman may never leave Jim cold: He always finds her either beautiful or ugly.

The next level of detail comes with *directional hypothesis*. It predicts that increasing x will increase y ($dy/dx > 0$) or decrease y ($dy/dx < 0$). Suppose the prediction is that drinking milk will improve my digestion. Now it becomes a guide for action. But how much do I have to drink? If a clear positive effect requires 100 L per day, forget it. This means we need to know not just the sign of the slope dy/dx but also its intensity: $dy/dx = b$.

It may also be that drinking two glasses has a positive effect but drinking 10 L no longer increases positive impact while producing negative side effects. Mathematically, $dy/dx > 0$ at small x but $dy/dx < 0$ at large x. We can presume that $dy/dx = 0$ occurs at some intermediary value x_0, an optimal stage still to be determined.

Quantitative Hypotheses and Models

To be of use as guide for action, we need a hypothesis more detailed than a directional one. Going beyond $dy/dx > 0$ or $dy/dx < 0$, we need the entire shape of the function $y = f(x)$—which is usually not a linear function over a wide range of x. Only then can we know how much milk to drink. Here we have the beginnings of a *quantitative hypothesis*. Of course, further factors may matter. Drinking milk may be good in the morning but less so in the evening. Mathematically, $y = f(x, t)$, within a 24-h interval. This functional form represents a more detailed quantitative hypothesis. It may be based on sheer empirical observation or on some logical reasons why milk acts as it does.

When advancing beyond null and directional hypotheses, our quantitative hypothesis may become quite complex in mathematical form plus various restrictions in its use. However, a "complex hypothesis" may sound odd to some of those social scientists who are conditioned to simple directional hypotheses. Therefore, it might be safer to talk about testing *quantitative models* rather than quantitative hypotheses. The term "model" carries its own risks in social sciences (see the Appendix to Chapter 6), but there is no way to avoid it.

Quite a few manuscript reviewers for social science journals are unable to distinguish between directional and quantitative hypotheses/models. Once the direction has been confirmed, such people see no point in finding the functional form of the relationship and the logical reasons behind it. For them, Galileo and the peasant of Tuscany are on par.

Degrees of Falsifiablility and Usefulness

The more detailed our hypothesis or model is, the more difficult it becomes to satisfy it—but also the more useful it becomes as a guide for action or further study (cf. Chapter 3). Rejecting a null hypothesis means confirming an utterly vague predictive model: "Something will happen." We may confirm that red sunsets do mean a change of weather tomorrow—for colder or for warmer. Verifying a directional hypothesis tells us a bit more. Suppose I predict "Red sunsets mean colder weather." Compared to the null hypothesis, the directional one reduces the possible outcomes by about one-half—but no more. Given that the chances of temperature remaining *exactly* the same are slim, I have an almost 50% probability of being right just by random chance. If, however, I offer a more specific model that predicts that a given degree of redness will result in a drop of more than 10 degrees, my chances of being right by random chance are severely reduced. If the model withstands such increased jeopardy, then it is so much more valuable as guide for choosing proper clothing.

A directional model can be valuable for preliminary studies but leaves the field much too open. A quantitatively predictive model predicts how much y corresponds to how much x. The more specific the model, the more valuable it is, if confirmed—and the harder it is to confirm. Recall the previous norm that "Hypothesis testing should always be competitive" (Gigerenzer et al. 2004). It becomes less stringent for more complex models. They sort of compete against themselves by making so specific predictions that it is unlikely that a different model would predict exactly the same specifics. However, data with wide scatter may leave room for many models—cf. Figure 4.3.

A regression equation based on sufficient data seems to qualify as quantitatively predictive, conditional on "all other factors remaining the same"—*ceteris paribus*. "But how do we know that all *ceteris* remain *paribus*?" as my colleague Bernie Grofman (2004) is fond of asking. This is when "How things *should* be?" enters. If we know *why* x affects y to the extent it does, then we also have a better idea of which conditions could alter this extent.

This is why the goal of social sciences should be to develop quantitatively predictive models which are logically grounded rather than merely empirical. All too many social science projects that go beyond the null hypothesis are satisfied with a directional hypothesis. They should proceed beyond it.

Can the given model be proven inadequate? Is it "falsifiable"? It is difficult to declare a regression-based "empirical model" false, when the underlying directional hypothesis involves only a loose prediction. The R^2 can be disappointingly low, but as long as the slopes b_i have the expected signs, the form $y = a + \Sigma b_i x_i$ as such cannot be declared false within the range of data used. Even when the data cloud y versus x shows a blatant curvature (such as data-set B in Figure 3.1), many political scientists unflinchingly put a straight line through the cloud. Curvature is even easier to ignore when no graphs are shown (see Chapter 15).

Science deals with falsifiable statements. Few statements are as unfalsifiable as "Everything happens as God wills it," but linear regression "models" offer fair competition. Whatever is, is. The coefficients in such a "model" are based on data and hence cannot be tested with the same data. When tested with different data, their numerical values are likely to change. Hence, a regression equation is untestable beyond directionality, meaning it is unfalsifiable.

In contrast, the logically based model can be tested. It can be proven false. This can in principle happen the more easily, the more narrowly the functional shape and the possible values of constants and coefficients are specified. To the extent it passes, such a model has predictive value and may reflect underlying processes.

False Positives: "p = .01" Does NOT Mean Confirmation in 99% of Replications

It was pointed out earlier (Chapter 1) that medical research is finding an alarming rate of "false positives." This means that statistically "significant" differences are not confirmed upon replication. In many subfields of social sciences, too, factors reported significant "at the 99% level" ($p < .01$) in one regression often are reported only as "$p < .05$" or even nonsignificant at the 5% level in some other. Such discrepancies should be extremely rare—literally 1 out of 100, if $p < .01$ really meant replication in 99% of the cases, as it often is interpreted. How come discrepancies are visibly more frequent than that?

False positives can arise from "delusions about the meaning of $p < .01$," as Gigerenzer et al. (2004) put it. They offered students and instructors of psychology six false statements about the null hypothesis and found that quite a few accepted them as true. All these misperceptions go in the direction of mistakenly increasing our confidence in the meaningfulness of results.

Only one of these statements is addressed here. Suppose a simple independent means t-test indicates that the result is significant ($t = 2.7$,

$df = 18$, $p = .01$). Is it true that "You have a reliable experimental finding in the sense that if, hypothetically, the experiment were repeated a great number of times, you would obtain a significant result on 99% of occasions?" Among German psychology instructors not teaching statistics, 49% incorrectly responded "yes," and 37% did so even among those teaching statistics (Gigerenzer et al. 2004). Incorrect answers rose to 60% in the UK (Oakes 1986).

Why does not the above statement hold? Because of "model uncertainty" (Coleman 2007). The statement would hold "only if one knew that the null hypothesis was true" (Gigerenzer et al. 2004), which itself cannot be asserted on the given basis. Recall Arbuthnot's divine providence. "The statistical method assumes that the model being tested is correct. When the model is in doubt, the whole business is off to a wrong start. This is the best argument for having a logical or theory-based model" (Coleman, private communication, July 2007).

Coleman (2007) observes that "False positives—findings statistically significant results that are not actually true—appear to be much more common than previously recognized," from medical research to social sciences. He points out that a recent editorial in the *Journal of the Royal Statistical Society* (Longford 2005) deems much of contemporary statistics-based research a "junkyard of unsubstantiated confidence," precisely because of false positives.

The Tennis Match Between Data and Models

We began with the time-honored recipe "hypothesis → data collection → testing → acceptance/rejection." It oversimplifies the interaction between model and data. The actual interaction looks like a tennis match. Superficial data inspire the first coarse logical model. The model may suggest looking for different data that better correspond to what the model is about. It may also suggest looking for data at very low or very high values of x, because random fluctuations may blur the logically expected trend when the range of x is short. On the other hand, discrepancies between model and data may also motivate search for a more refined model. Some hidden assumptions may have entered the first round of model building and must be explicitly stipulated. Thus, the coarse model for volatility in Chapter 4 implicitly assumed that any positive values of volatility are acceptable, even those surpassing 100%.

It may also happen that the model works, but some data points are erroneous and need weeding out. If one works with weights of peas and one of them is off by three standard deviations, then probably a bean has slipped in. It would be unreasonable not to discard it, out of excessive respect for data. "Newton Fudged" is the title of a short piece in *Scientific American* (1973)—he manipulated observations to fit his models. Such data manipulation is a no–no by modern research standards. But true, Newton's calculations proved better than the data. The moral is: Report all data, but do not consider all data sacrosanct. If the model and data do not fit, *either* can be at fault.

In sum, scientific research most often looks like an ascending spiral, within which the recipe "hypothesis → data collection → testing → acceptance/rejection" represents a single cycle:

Initial hunch (qualitative hypothesis) → limited data collection →
→ quick testing → quantitatively predictive model (quantitative hypothesis) → further data collection → testing → refined model → testing → further refining of model *or* data → testing…

Conclusions

Table 6.1 reviews some general contrasts between predictive and descriptive approaches, as typified in physics and today's social sciences, going back to some features presented already in Chapter 1. Where physicists ask "*How much* effect does x have on y?" social scientists tend to limit themselves to a much looser "*Does x* have any effect on y?" Some of this vagueness is inevitable under nonlaboratory conditions, but social scientists have become so acclimatized that they tend to forget the "*how much*" part even when it can be answered. The utmost they all too often venture to propose is "If x goes up, then y goes down/up," meaning that the slope $b = dy/dx$ is negative/positive.

While the predictive approach truly *tests* a specific model, the statistics-based approach tests at best the direction of the effect. The result is passively descriptive to the point of rarely even asking *how steep* this slope should or could reasonably be. Whatever slope pops up from regression is reported, without pondering whether it makes sense or what it may tell us. Given that a large proportion of random outcomes can satisfy the

Table 6.1. Predictive vs. descriptive models (modified from Taagepera 2007*b*)

	Predictive models	Descriptive models
Fields of major occurrence	Physics	Today's social sciences
Broad question	*How much* effect?	*Is there* an effect?
Hypothesis level	Quantitative How should *y* be related to *x*? What is the form of $y = f(x)$? The sign of dy/dx is not enough.	Directional Does *x* impact *y*? If *x* goes up, does *y* go down? The sign of dy/dx suffices.
Model building	Think about relationship → most often nonlinear combinations of variables, frequently multiplicative.	Do not think much, just assume a simple mathematical form, often linear concatenation.
Testing/analysis	Try to transform into linear format, or use conceptually suitable nonlinear testing.	Feed relatively raw data into linear regression, and analyze it statistically.
End point	Two-way functional equation, may fit into a transitive sequence.	One-way regression equation, cannot fit into transitive sequence.
"Falsifiability"	Strict. Even at high R^2, the presumed functional form can prove to be wrong.	Loose. Even at low R^2, format $y = a + \Sigma b_i x_i$ cannot be declared false, as long as dy/dx has the expected sign.
Value	High falsifiability → the presumed model may reflect underlying processes.	No falsifiability → no explanatory power. Whatever is, is.

directional model, its degree of falsifiability is loose. Correspondingly, it has little explanatory or predictive power.

Appendix to Chapter 6

Devaluation of the Term "Model" and of Model Testing

A prominent social scientist writes me: "When I read an abstract preceding an article which starts with 'I present a model...,' I usually read no further than that!" One reason for such skepticism is that all too many "models" in social sciences remain qualitative or directional and hence are nontestable or cheaply testable. Those quantitative models that do go beyond directionality often are not tested beyond directionality or using a few convenient illustrative examples. Indeed, some subfields seem to have a tacit agreement between model builders and empiricists not to tread on each others' territory.

This means that impressive theoretical models are not faced with data and hence are safe against refutation. It also makes such models useless, which may explain the reaction to the term "model" above. On the other side, empiricists are left free to call statistical best fits "empirical models"—another devaluation of the term. They, too, can hardly be refuted. Due lip service is given to model testing as the core of scientific procedure, but in practice it is all too often reduced to directional testing.

The social scientist who devises a theoretical model and also submits it to quantitative testing faces double jeopardy. First, agreement of nonlaboratory data with models is bound to be limited. Second, he may irk both pure modelers and pure empiricists. A journal with *Theoretical* in its title recently returned such a manuscript without even sending it out to reviewers, because it soiled the purity of theory with testing. This journal is proud to publish only untested theory.

The reviewers of empirically minded journals, on the other hand, at times mistake a theoretically predicted curve for a botched-up statistical best fit, as they seemingly recognize only "empirical models." When they do recognize the theoretical nature of the model tested, they are liable to say that it fits the test data worse than the best statistical fit to these particular data—which is of course the case by definition. How could a *predictive* model for *all* data of the given type fit better than a *postdictive* fit based of these *particular* data, if the statistics is handled competently?

The alliance of pure modelers and pure empiricists against testing of models may suit both in the short run. But it cannot lead to science with predictive ability.

7

Why Most Numbers Published in Social Sciences Are Dead on Arrival

---

- Physicists, like people in general, start with causal models. Social scientists stand apart by often starting with empirical models.
- Depending on statistical method used, a variable may look "significant" in opposite directions. Only a logical model can tell which way it actually acts.
- The numbers published in physics are steppingstones for further inquiry, because they are few and other researchers often make use of them. The numbers published in social sciences are endpoints, because they are profligate and, once printed, hardly anyone makes use of them.
- Astronomy could not develop without overcoming the Ptolemaic syndrome of reducing all motion to circular. Social sciences must overcome their syndrome of reducing all relationships to linear.
- Given the dearth of laboratory-quality data in social sciences, even more emphasis should go into predictive modeling, so as to make the most of scarce and messy data. Paradoxically, the reverse has become the fashion.

Imagine a mental activity where the norms of thinking differ both from everyday thinking and the scientific one. Imagine a scholarly discipline where lots of numbers are printed but hardly any are read. This chapter describes such an activity and discipline. It documents to which extent the practices described do occur in social sciences in general and in political science in particular. It says nothing about the durability of qualitative finding in social sciences. Numbers are the issue.

Table 7.1. Thinking patterns during the course of solving an intellectual problem

Everyday thinking	Physics thinking	Today's social science thinking
Preliminary observation	Preliminary observation	Preliminary observation
How might things connect?	How might things connect?	Do not prejudge: get data!
Qualitative causal model (*loose* predictive model)	Quantitative causal model (*precise* predictive model)	Run regression
Pick affirmative evidence, overlook the contrary	Gather and *transform* data in the light of the model, test predictive model	Report regression equation (descriptive model)
Loose predictive model not systematically tested → hard to prove wrong = low falsifiability	*Precise* predictive model systematically tested → can prove to be wrong = high falsifiability	*No* predictive model to test → little that could prove to be wrong = low falsifiability

Everyday and Scientific Thinking—and How Today's Social Sciences Fit In

Scientific thinking differs from everyday thinking. If today's social science thinking differs from that in physics, it might be thought to be so because it still harbors features from everyday thinking. Surprisingly, Coleman (2005, 2007) suggests the reverse. Thinking in natural sciences is in many ways closer to everyday thinking, compared to what passes for scientific in social sciences. Table 7.1 shows the three-way similarities and contrasts.

In contrast to descriptive models that predominate in today's social sciences, both everyday and natural science thinking tend to operate by predictive models. Psychological research by Ahn et al. (1995) indicates that most people do not first observe covariation and then construct empirical models, like today's social scientists tend to do. People rather construct causal models first, asking how things *might* be connected, and then start looking for supporting evidence (Coleman 2007). This is also how major advances in natural sciences have proceeded, but with some important differences.

First, people in general tend to act as defense lawyers for their pet models. They emphasize supporting evidence and overlook the contrary. In contrast, scientists try to act as impartial judges when gathering and weighing evidence. Second, they try to make their models specific—and hence those models take a mathematical form. The prediction soon comes so specific that it is hardly possible that data might confirm the model by random chance. The more specific the predictive model, the less statistical machinery is needed to test it. Note that the predictive model may also affect the way data are collected or transformed prior to testing.

All this is all too often missed in social science analysis. A directional hypothesis tends to be the limit of predictive precision, before one rushes on to data analysis. One could understand such hurry, if social sciences had a surplus of good-quality data, compared to natural sciences, but the reverse is the case. Physicists can generate extensive relatively clean data under laboratory conditions, yet they do not expect passive data crunching alone to lead them to the laws of nature. Experimental findings serve mainly to guide predictive modeling.

Given the dearth of laboratory-quality data in social sciences, even more emphasis should go into predictive modeling, so as to make the most of scarce and messy data. Paradoxically, the reverse has become the fashion.

A Crazy Methodology?

This is the title of a study by Bernard Kittel (2006) in *International Sociology*, reacting to Nancy Cartwright's claim (2002: 142) that the "methodology is crazy" in macro-quantitative social science research. Kittel observes that "Currently the use of quantitative data and pooled time-series cross-section regression methods seem to be more or less a precondition for publication in most reputed social science journals." He assumes that "An important reason for the popularity of this approach is related to social scientists' attempts to mimic the natural sciences *or, at least, economics* [my italics], in order to defend the relevance of their research to audiences outside the social science community."

This is a fitting description. Two features stand out. First, mimicking is poor science. Yes, one should be inspired by more developed scientific disciplines, but it must go beyond superficial mimicking of external forms. It must aim at understanding the deeper reasons behind the forms, so that one gets a feel for what can or cannot be adopted under which circumstances. Second, even this mimicking of outer forms has been carried out unbelievably poorly, as the comparison of mathematical formats in Chapter 5 shows.

The reason is the quick shift of focus, even for mimicking, from natural sciences to "at least" economics, itself reduced to econometrics. This shift overlooks the fundamental ways in which the econometric approach itself differs from that of physics, in mathematical format and in underlying thinking. By the various contrasts highlighted in Chapter 5,

Table 7.2. Total government expenditure in % of GDP: How can it be predicted?

	Model 1 Pooled OLS	Model 2 Two-way FE	Model 3 Two-way FE + PW	Model 4 Two-way FE + LDV	Model 5 FD + one-way FE(T)
Lagged output	—	—	—	0.91***	0.23***
Unemployment	0.93***	0.71***	0.61***	0.02	0.40***
GDP/cap. growth	−0.90***	−0.51***	−0.20***	−0.36***	−0.21***
Dependency ratio	**−0.445***	**1.33***	0.93***	0.08	0.44***
Left cab. portfolios	**5.80***	**−1.26***	−0.20	−0.22	0.04
Christ. Dem. portf.	2.88**	−0.78	0.30	−0.42	−0.07
Trade	0.13***	0.02	−0.02	−0.03**	−0.03
Low-wage imports	**−0.16***	**0.34***	0.11***	0.03*	0.02
Foreign direct investment	0.09	0.14	−0.10	−0.01	−0.12*
Intercept (constant)	??	??	??	??	??
R^2	.58	.94	—	.99	.46

Condensed from Kittel (2006). $^*a \leq .10$; $^{**}a \leq .05$; $^{***}a \leq .01$.

Shown in bold are those variables which are statistically highly significant in opposite directions, depending on method used.

much of economics qualifies as social science. Could economists pin down the gravitation law? Those few in my very unrepresentative sample (Chapter 2) could not. By seeking inspiration in economics, the blind may have been seeking insights from the half-blind.

When comparing different societies, one "assumes that law-like relationships between social phenomena not only exist, but do so at the aggregate level of nation-states independent of time and space" (Kittel 2006). One aims to "causally explain and predict societal phenomena by relying on statistical and econometric techniques." Yet, it runs into various difficulties that lead Kittel (2006) to wonder about a "crazy methodology." A main difficulty in dealing with complex macro-phenomena by means of statistical analysis is lack of robustness of the coefficient values when model specification is varied.

Earlier chapters have pointed out that coefficient values and their statistical significance vary enormously when further input variables are introduced. Kittel (2006) goes one better by keeping exactly the same input variables and changing only the statistical approach. The output variable is total government expenditure. Table 7.2 reproduces his results in an abbreviated form. Coefficient values are shown, but I have omitted their standard errors. (These errors range from one-tenth to triple of the coefficient values.) Also, I have rounded off the coefficients to two decimal places, correcting for the bad habit of social scientists to report meaningless decimals, those within the range of standard error.

Detailed explanation of variables and methods used is not given here—for these, see Kittel (2006) and Kittel and Winner (2005). Suffice to know that all these methods are reasonably well known and considered legitimate. The question that concerns us here is: How could we predict (or at least postdict) the output variable from such a table of presumed "results"? The immediate answer is "We just can't," simply because Kittel (2006) omits the intercept term (which I have inserted in Table 7.2 as "??"). But assume that this gap is filled. What could we then predict/postdict?

The answer still is: hardly anything. A high Dependency Ratio strongly and significantly reduces the output variable (Model 1)—or it strongly and significantly enhances it (Models 2, 3, and 5), or has no effect (Model 4). The same applies for the impact of Left Cabinet Portfolios and Low-wage Imports. Depending on the model, such an input variable can either increase or decrease the output—yet always "significantly"! Pick your choice. Or leave the picking to sociopolitical decision-makers who need advice to make hard decisions. See how impressed they are with such ambiguous achievements by social sciences!

Kittel (2006) concludes: "The most striking observation is that findings in macro-quantitative research lack robustness." This evaluation draws on various other concerns, too, but the one highlighted here should suffice. Note that this havoc takes place when the *same* input variables are used! It may be better masked when some variables are added or replaced, as all too often is the case in today's social science analyses, but the lack of meaning can only deepen. This applies to levels of significance, coefficient values, and even the direction of impact. Recall the discussion of false positives in Chapter 6.

Is it a crazy methodology? Do not blame methodology. Blame people who misapply it, trying to replace the logical model building phase of scientific research with statistics.

Do Social Sciences Face a Ptolemaic Syndrome?

The irony is that, at the level of statistical sophistication shown by Kittel (2006), the mathematical effort required may well exceed what it would take to build a logical model that could then be properly tested by statistical approaches. (Exceptions occur in psychology and economics.) There are precedents for scholars sticking with a simple format and rejecting a more complex one, even when the repeated application of the simple format eventually leads to more complex convolutions, and even so still fails to account for all the observations. Consider the following.

Ptolemaic astronomy considered circle the perfect closed curve and also took geocentricity as self-evident. An ellipse that did not center on the Earth failed in both respects. But attempts to fit the observed paths of planets forced astronomers to construct circles whose centers moved along circles whose centers moved along circles. This epicyclic approach eventually became vastly more complex than what it tried to avoid—the Keplerian ellipse with one focus at the Sun.

Do many social scientists act as if the straight line were the perfect shape, not to be questioned? Plenty of complex statistical methodology is superimposed on a tacit linear assumption. It is time to ask whether social sciences face a Ptolemaic syndrome.

The Meaning of Published Results: Steppingstones Versus Endpoints

The contrast between dearth of coefficients/constants in physics equations and their profusion in social science equations was established in Chapter 5. Its main features are worth repeating, because the consequences reach far. Basic physics equations rarely have more than two or three input variables. Longer logical sequences are broken up into several interlocking equations. In contrast, the regression equations used in social sciences pretty often include long concatenations of variables.

The number of numerical constants and coefficients in a regression always surpasses the number of variables, because each variable has its own slope coefficient, in addition to the intercept constant. The resulting profusion of numerical values is multiplied when several regression equations are published for the same output, with slightly different input variables. In contrast, the number of freely adjustable constants/coefficients in physics equations hardly ever exceeds the number of variables. Most often, there is only one adjustable constant. Also, physics strives to eliminate competing models for the same phenomenon.

The implications are momentous. Physicists tend to view the reported numerical results and equations as steppingstones for further inquiry. Numerical values of constants are published sparsely, with the idea of other people using them. When the findings are of sufficient interest, other researchers soon retest them, and the resulting numerical values of

Table 7.3. The number of constants/coefficients vs. their impact (modified from Taagepera 2007*b*)

	Physics	Social sciences
Number of input variables per equation	Rarely more than 3	Often more than 3
Number of completely freely adjustable constants/ coefficients	Few. At most as numerous as input variables	Many. Always more numerous than input variables
Alternate equations for same phenomenon	No competing alternatives	Often several regressions are given, with slightly different variables
Later use of numerical values of constants	Same constant values often used over and over	Once published, practically never used again for anything
Do they have names?	Some do	It is out of question
The meaning of published numerical results	Steppingstones	Endpoints
	→ Cumulation of quantitative knowledge	→ Only qualitative cumulation of knowledge

constants are compared. Knowledge cumulates on a quantitatively precise level, where even minor discrepancies can trigger new inquiries. Some constants are so frequently used that they are given names.

In contrast, the profligate numerical values of regression and correlation coefficients reported in social sciences are endpoints. None of them has a name, because those reams of computer-produced numbers are practically never used again for anything. Once printed in journals, not even their authors take another look at them. They are dead on arrival.

The more regression "models" are offered for the same output variable, the more fleeting the numerical values of coefficients become. The numbers are crunched but not digested. While physics has cumulation of quantitative knowledge, any such cumulation in today's social sciences remains largely qualitative—or semi-quantitative at best. Table 7.3 resumes the inverse relationship between the number of numerical values published and their impact.

Does this Description Fit the Present Practices in Social Sciences?

Are social sciences really so addicted to regression analysis and related descriptive methods? Do the features described here represent the main line? Even if they do, how frequent are the redeeming exceptions? An appreciable part of social science publications do not pretend to be quantitative, and they are subject to other quality norms. The question here is, what do social scientists presently do when they do apply quantitative approaches to numerical data?

The only field I have systematically investigated is political science. Its flagship journal, the *American Political Science Review*, is a highly selective journal that publishes less than 10% of the manuscripts submitted. The criteria used presumably select for what is presently considered the best in political science. Inspection of the "Articles" section, from 2002 to 2004, shows the following.

Out of a total of 116 articles, 62 involved some numerical data treatment, the rest being qualitative studies, proofs of theorems, constructions of indices, or numerical data tabulation without further analysis. Among these 62 articles, 47 (i.e., 76%) used OLS, *probit, logit,* and other essentially linear regression approaches to input variables. The remaining 15 used a variety of other methods.

Was this regression analysis really so linear? Out of the 47 articles that used regression, 30 stuck with purely linear format. The other 17 had at least one "interaction term" of form $x_i x_j$, or some other nonlinear feature. No squaring of a variable was observed. Were these articles oblivious of division? None included a division of one variable by another, or the inverse of a variable. Only a couple took the logarithm of one or several input variables. No article took the logarithms of all the variables (input and output) so as to correspond to the multiplicative format $y = a\Pi x_i^{b_i}$.

The number of input variables ranged from 1 up to at least 19. The number of freely adjustable constants/coefficients always exceeded the number of input variables in the given equation. Several alternative regressions for the same or fairly similar output variables were offered in quite a few articles, which enhanced the ratio of numerical values of coefficients per input variable. I did not notice any comparisons of the numerical values of regression coefficients for the same input variable (or related ones) in different regression. If any such comparisons occurred, they were rare.

The precise proportion of articles that used several regressions for the same output variable was hard to pin down. The prize may go to Helmke (2002), who offers *logit* models for judicial antigovernment votes in Argentina under military rule and under two presidents. There seem to be only three output variables, but I may have missed subtle differences.

A total of 33 *logit* models are tabulated, with a total of 101 different numerical values of constants and coefficients, 44 of them statistically significant at $p \leq .01$. The number of input variables in a single regression is mostly 1, but it reaches 19 in one regression.

Is regression really used so little for quantitative prediction or even postdiction? Regression coefficients invariably were reported in tabular form rather than in an equation, suitable for plugging in numerical inputs. I did not notice a single occasion where an article applied the numerical coefficient values to calculate the expected value for a case outside the initial set. Indeed, 10 studies (21% of all studies that used regression!) failed to report the numerical value of the constant ("intercept," a), thus making prediction for specific cases impossible. The frequent occurrence of such omissions suggests that not only authors but also reviewers and editors do not pay attention to whether the results can be applied for prediction.

Correlation coefficients or other measures of dispersion were reported in all cases. No standard errors seemed to be reported, but I may have missed some. On the positive side, I did not locate any conceptual inconsistencies in these particular articles.

Do political scientists really make so little use of numerical values of regression coefficients, once published? I did not notice a single occasion where an article referred to the numerical coefficient values from a previously published regression. The numbers published in the *American Political Science Review* look indeed like endpoints rather than steppingstones toward further research.

As for quantitatively predictive logical models, I did not notice any. It could mean that none were submitted, or that they were blocked by regression-minded reviewers—recall the experience of Folk and Luce in psychology (see Chapter 1). It can be documented that some reviewers recommend rejection because they mistake logical models for poorly executed regressions. They are liable to say that the equation proposed "does not even yield the obvious best fit"—which means they mistakenly compare the degree of fit of an a priori model for any data of the given type to the a posteriori statistical fit of a particular data-set.

Other political science journals do not seem to offer a markedly different picture, except that some of them have tolerated the use of logical models. Is it different in some other disciplines in social sciences? My casual inspections do not suggest so, but I would welcome evidence to the contrary.

Conclusion: We Must Do Better than That

Three social scientists climbed up the mountain to consult with the Wise One. One had analyzed some data and found that Pearson correlation coefficient was $R = -.21$, and the relationship was significant at the .01 level (two-tailed). The Wise One plugged his computer to his solar-powered batteries, ran the SPPS program, and announced: "Your result is significant indeed." The other social scientist had also crunched similar data and found that the correlation was significant at the .01 level, but R had the opposite sign: $R = +.31$. Once more, the Wise One ran his program and announced: "Your result is significant."

The third social scientist, a mere novice, piped up: "But how can y significantly increase and decrease with x at the same time?" The Wise One spoke: "Your question is a set of $n = 1$ and therefore by definition devoid of statistical significance." The novice was happy and said: "Now I know that I can have my cake and eat it too in a statistically significant way." Some answers I have received in response to such concerns have been more elaborate in terms of statistical sophistication but no more convincing.

Nothing is wrong with statistical methods such as linear regression. Plenty is wrong with the way these methods have been overused and misused in social sciences. The limitations of complete dependence on descriptive methodology have been expounded in Chapters 5–7. Throwing all conceivable factors into a grand regression equation will not do. We must and can do better than that. The next six chapters pick up on Chapters 3 and 4, explaining various aspects of logical model building and offering examples. The mathematics involved is no more complex than what is needed to use statistics without misusing it—and there are overlaps. The payoff is in predictive results that are useful to society and, incidentally, can earn respect for social sciences.

Part II

**Quantitatively Predictive
Logical Models**

8

Forbidden Areas and Anchor Points

- How much air and food does one need to survive? Adding "Air plus Food" would falsely tell us that one could do without air, if food is plentiful! We must not add but multiply: Survival depends on Air *times* Food.
- The outcomes of sociopolitical processes often depend on the factor in *shortest* supply. This consideration makes multiplication of factors superior to their addition
- Naïve linear regression may not detect all relationships between physical or social factors, because most of them are curved.
- When x and y can conceptually take only positive values, linear regression should be carried out on their logarithms, not on the numbers themselves. This corresponds to fitting y with x raised to a power (an exponent).
- Various other constraints lead to exponential, simple logistic and more complex patterns. These functional forms most often leave parameters to be determined empirically.

Every specific problem requires different creative approaches to model building. No general recipe can be worded and converted into a canned computer program. One has to think. Still, some features occur frequently. This chapter presents some general guidelines for developing certain types of quantitatively predictive logical models. Conceptual constraints such as boundary conditions on input and output variables impose specific and usually nonlinear relationships among them. This is so, in particular, when variables can take only positive values (or zero)—which is frequently the case. The importance of boundary conditions has been stressed by Gary King (1997).

Here, I present a selection of relatively simple and widely occurring situations, where some areas are conceptually forbidden and some anchor points are conceptually mandatory. The norm of continuity (see Chapter 4) requires curves to join the various anchor points. Their slopes, too, must be continuous. Given the social scientists' excessive trust in linear relationships, I pay special attention to the extent straight lines can or cannot satisfy conceptual constraints.

Even simple situations quickly involve some high school and college mathematics, if one wants to follow their implications systematically. In particular, familiarity with exponent notation and logarithms is needed. The Appendix to Chapter 8 offers a simplistic introduction, kept to the bare minimum. If the mathematics becomes overly hard at the first reading, one may take the results on faith and move on to later sections. Once the usefulness of such models becomes apparent, it would supply motivation to internalize the mathematics needed.

For those proficient in mathematics, on the other hand, all this may be old hat. Indeed, the outcomes cover a fair part of the generic approaches used by statisticians. All too many social scientists are not aware of the simple constraints that underlie these generic forms, treating them as somehow mysteriously given. Many substantive situations involve such constraints, and being aware of them helps to determine when a given format can or cannot be used. It should become second nature to a model builder in social sciences to pin down such constraints and delimit the field of remaining options accordingly.

The following is limited to the situation where a single output variable (y) is suspected of being affected by a single input variable (x). The extension to several variables is discussed at the end of the chapter.

No Forbidden Areas: Linear Relationships

As a starting point, assume that both x and y are such that they can conceptually range from minus to plus infinity. This means a two-dimensional field open to functions $y = f(x)$, with no conceptually forbidden areas whatsoever. All sorts of functional forms are allowed, but we should favor the simplest, unless something precludes it. Here, the simple linear relationship $y = a + bx$ applies, unconstrained, because one can pass lines with any slopes $dy/dx = b$ through any point $(x_0; y_0)$. This is the simplest family of acceptable curves. It corresponds to the "interval group" in Stevens's (1946) classification of scale types (Luce et al. 1990: 113), except that it also allows for $b < 0$.

> **When x and y can conceptually range from minus to plus infinity, then linear regression should be carried out. This corresponds to fitting y to a linear function of x.**

By so doing, we do not assert that y is a linear function of x, but we test for this possibility. Oftentimes it works, but sometimes it does not, because other constraints and conditions enter. In the following, we introduce some usual constraints.

Only Positive Quadrant Allowed: Fixed Exponent Relationships

Many variables of direct or indirect interest to social scientists cannot take negative values: population, telephones per capita, usual inequality indices, the numbers of votes, parties, and social cleavages. These variables may reach 0 or, in the opposite direction, be so much larger than 1 that there is no limit short of infinity, at least in first approximation. These are "ratio scale variables." For them, only one quadrant of the previous field remains allowed: $x \geq 0$ and $y \geq 0$.

Most straight lines that pass through a given point $(x_0; y_0)$ in this allowed quadrant are conceptually disallowed. All downward sloping lines ($b < 0$) are forbidden, because at sufficiently high values of x, they would predict negative values of y. Even among the upward sloping lines, those with negative intercepts ($a < 0$) are also forbidden, because at sufficiently low positive values of x, they would predict negative values of y. Such lines are acceptable only for coarse models and as approximations over short ranges of x.

With most straight lines disallowed, we should look for the simplest family of curves that is fully acceptable. This means that all curves belonging this family and passing through any given point $(x_0; y_0)$ of the positive quadrant avoid absurdities, such as negative y for an allowed value of x. The fixed exponent function satisfies this condition:

$$y = Ax^k,$$

where k can take any real values and $A = y_0/x_0^k$ is positive. For any positive x, we get a positive y. This family of curves corresponds to the "log-interval (power) group" in Stevens's (1946) classification of scale types (Luce et al. 1990: 113) except that it also allows for $k < 0$.

97

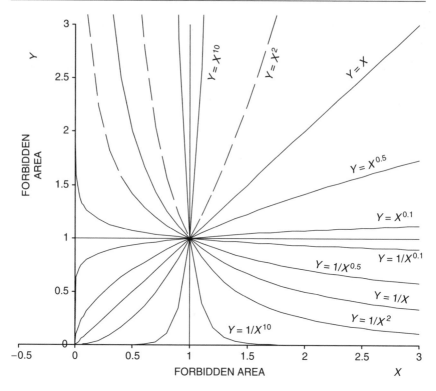

Figure 8.1. Fixed exponent functions—the simplest full family of curves allowed when x and y are conceptually restricted to positive values

Without loss of generality, we can take x_0 and y_0 as units of quantities x and y, respectively. This means shifting from x and y to $X = x/x_0$ and $Y = y/y_0$. Now the equation is simplified to

$$Y = X^k.$$

It can be shown that the slope dY/dX has a rather simple functional form:

$$\frac{dY}{dX} = k\left(\frac{Y}{X}\right)$$

slope is proportional to the ratio of variables. Figure 8.1 shows the corresponding pattern of curves. It fills the entire quadrant.

The curves in Figure 8.1 all pass through the point $(1;1)$, which divides the positive quadrant into four regions, depending on whether X and Y are larger or smaller than 1. The curves fall into two groups. For $k > 1$, these curves can be characterized as quasi-parabolic, as they include the positive halves of the parabolas $Y = X^2$ and $Y = X^{0.5}$. They all begin at $(0; 0)$, and they fill the lower left and upper right regions defined by $(1; 1)$. As a special case, they include the straight line, $Y = X$. For $k < 0$, on the other hand, the curves can be characterized as quasi-hyperbolic, as they include one branch of the hyperbola $Y = 1/X = X^{-1}$. These curves fill the upper left and lower right regions.

Variables of interest in social sciences often are nonnegative and have a conceptual anchor point at $(0; 0)$: When x is 0, y also must be 0. If so, then only the curves with positive k are possible. This is readily visible in Figure 8.1.

Which path is the likeliest for a continuous curve that must start at $(0; 0)$ and pass through $(1; 1)$—or any point $(x_0; y_0)$ in the general format? The paths $Y = X^k$ are the simplest paths mathematically. Using such paths in our models would certainly make it easier for students of social sciences. But do socially interesting *variables* know math, so as to follow these paths? They often behave as if they did. The reason is that any deviation from the fixed exponent equation would reflect the existence of some further constraint or condition that pulls the slope away from the simple value $k(Y/X)$. Later, we will consider such cases. But if we are not aware of any further constraints, our best bet is to assume a fixed exponent function, until proven otherwise.

In contrast, assuming a linear function would be among our worst bets. In particular, any downward sloping straight line is bound to run into the forbidden negative area. *Whenever data indicate a downward slope, a straight line fit will not do as a model for conceptually nonnegative quantities,* except as an empirical approximation over short ranges of x. In such cases, a division, $y = A/x^k$, with positive A and k, is the simplest conceptually acceptable format.

The simplest single function with such a format is the hyperbola, $y = A/x$. It implies that $x = 0$ leads to $y \to$ infinity. If such an outcome is not acceptable on conceptual grounds, then more complex curves must be used. For instance, suppose that y decreases with increasing x in the usual range of x but also must be 0 when $x = 0$. A curve of the form $y = Ax/(x + 1)^2$ might be considered. When $x = 0$, y is 0. But when x is large $(x \gg 1)$, then $y = Ax/(x + 1)^2 \approx A/x$.

How can testing by linear regression be used for nonnegative quantities? It requires first a transformation of both variables, so that their relationship becomes linear. Taking logarithms does the trick. Indeed, when $y = Ax^k$, then the logarithms of x and y are linearly related:

$$\log y = \log A + k \log x.$$

This means that any curve $y = Ax^k$ in the positive quadrant is related to a line in the open two-dimensional field. Given that $\log 1 = 0$ and $\log 0$ tends to minus infinity, we can "map" the entire positive quadrant into the entire two-dimensional field, by taking the logarithms of x and y. Such a "mapping" means that for every point in the positive quadrant, there is a corresponding point in the entire field. The resulting lines fill the entire two-dimensional field, unconstrained. This means that through any point ($\log x_0$; $\log y_0$) one can pass lines with any slopes k.

When x and y cannot conceptually take negative values, then linear regression should be carried out on their logarithms, rather than on x and y themselves. This corresponds to fitting y to a fixed exponent function of x.

By so doing, we do not assert that y is a fixed exponent function of x, but we test for this possibility. Oftentimes it works, but sometimes it does not, because other constraints and conditions enter. Simply regressing y on x would lead to conceptual absurdities whenever the slope is negative, because such regression line would extend into the prohibited negative values of y. So would those positive regression slopes that lead to negative values of y for any positive x.

Statistics and econometrics textbooks (e.g., Studenmund 2001: 203) recommend using the fixed exponent form instead of the linear when the statistical configuration of data calls for it. But even before any data are collected, we know that the linear approach should be rejected for conceptual reasons when x and y cannot take negative values.

Recall that a naïve introduction to exponents and logarithms is given in the Appendix to Chapter 8. For a given data-set, it enables the reader to determine the numerical values of constants in $y = Ax^k$.

Two Quadrants Allowed: Exponential Relationships

We now backtrack to the situation where the output variable y cannot take negative values, while the input variable x can take any real values. This is the case, in particular, when a nonnegative variable changes over time. Now two quadrants of the entire two-dimensional field remain allowed: $-\infty < x < +\infty$ and $0 \le y < +\infty$.

Under such conditions, *all* sloping straight lines are forbidden, because they would predict negative values of y either at sufficiently high or sufficiently low values of x. The only acceptable line through a given point $(x_0; y_0)$ in these two quadrants would be the one with zero slope ($y = y_0$ for any x). Straight lines are acceptable as approximations over short ranges, but they cannot be part of refined conceptually based models. In particular, $y = a + bt$, where t is time, is impossible over sufficient time spans when y cannot take negative values.

With straight lines disallowed, we should again look for the simplest alternative family of curves that is fully acceptable—even while recognizing that there is an infinite number of other possibilities. It is supplied by the exponential function

$$y = Ae^{kx} = A \exp(kx),$$

where k can take any real values and A must be positive. The expression "exp x" is an alternate way to write e^x, where $e = 2.718\ldots$ is the basis of natural logarithms. Like $\pi = 3.1416\ldots$, it is a universal constant in mathematics. If we want y to have a certain value $y = y_0$ when x has a given value x_0, then use $A = y_0 \exp(-kx_0)$.

One should watch the position of x in the equation. In the previous one-quadrant situation, x had a fixed exponent: x^k. In the present two-quadrant situation, in contrast, x itself is exponential to a fixed number: e^x. It matters.

Without loss of generality, one can shift from x and y to $X = x - x_0$ and $Y = y/y_0$, respectively. Now the equation is reduced to

$$Y = e^{kX} = \exp(kX).$$

The slope dY/dX of this curve has a truly simple functional form—the slope is proportional to the output variable:

$$\frac{dY}{dX} = kY.$$

As X increases, Y increases at an increasing rate. In the reverse direction, as X decreases, Y decreases at a decreasing rate. As Y approaches 0, its further decrease rate dY/dX also approaches 0; therefore Y can never reach zero level. In other words, restriction of Y to only positive values is implicit in the model $dY/dX = kY$.

Figure 8.2 shows the corresponding patterns. Given that $e^0 = 1$, the curves $Y = \exp(kX)$ all pass through the point (0; 1). This point divides the two positive-Y quadrants into four regions, depending on whether X is

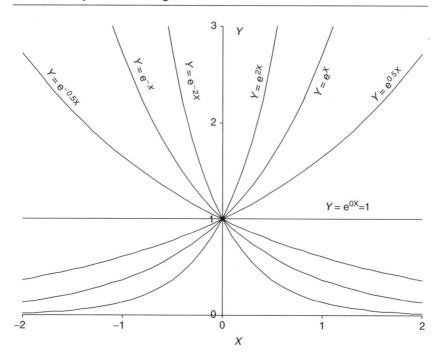

Figure 8.2. Exponential functions—the simplest full family of curves allowed when y is conceptually restricted to positive values while x is not

negative or positive and whether Y is smaller or larger than 1. The curves fall into two groups. For $k > 1$, the curves have positive slopes, and they fill the lower left and upper right regions defined by (0; 1). For $k < 0$, the curves fill the upper left and lower right regions.

Previously, restriction to the positive quadrant alone gave special status to the point (0; 0), which frequently functions as a conceptual anchor point. No such special points exist when two quadrants are allowed. Instead, there is a special exclusion point: no exponential curve with a finite k and passing through (0; 1) can pass through (0; 0).

What is the likeliest path of a continuous curve that must pass through (0; 1) in Figure 8.2—or any point $(x_0; y_0)$ in the general format? The paths $Y = \exp(kX)$ are the simplest mathematically. This is not to say that all relationships between unbounded x and bounded y must be exponential, but this is the simplest format they can follow. The linear format is impossible, except as a short-range approximation. If variables of interest in social sciences are conceptually restricted to two quadrants, yet do not follow the exponential pattern, it usually means that there are further constraints, and we better find out what they are.

How can testing by linear regression be used when x can take any real values, while y can conceptually take only positive values? All regression lines y versus x would lead to negative values of y for some values of x. This conceptual absurdity can be avoided by taking the logarithms of y (but not of x!), before regressing. When $y = A \exp(kx)$, then the natural logarithm of y is linearly related to x:

$$\ln y = \ln A + kx.$$

Hence, the exponential curves in the two positive-y quadrants can be mapped into straight lines in the entire two-dimensional field, by taking the logarithms of y. These lines cover the entire two-dimensional field, unconstrained. This means that through any point $(x_0; \ln y_0)$ one can pass lines with any slopes k.

When x can take any values, while y can conceptually take only nonnegative values, then linear regression against x should be carried out on the natural logarithm of y, rather than on y itself. This corresponds to fitting y to an exponential function of x.

By so doing, we do not assert that y is an exponential function of x, but we test for this possibility. Oftentimes it works, but sometimes it does not, because other constraints and conditions enter. One can actually use logarithms to any basis B, but then the equation above becomes $\log y = \log A + kx / \ln B$.

The converse situation, where the input variable x cannot take negative values, while the output variable y can take any real values, is not discussed here. It tends to occur relatively rarely. The format is $y = A + k \ln X$. For linear regression, y should be regressed against $\ln x$, not x itself.

Some confusion in terminology should be pointed out. The mathematics and physics texts I have checked call $y = A\, e^{kx}$ an "exponential function of x." Some statistics and econometric texts call $y = A + k \ln X$ a "semilog function of x" and $\ln y = A + kx$ an "alternative semilog form" (e.g., Studenmund 2001: 207–9). It is the latter that corresponds to the exponential function, $y = A\, e^{kx}$. The mathematics and physics texts designate x^a as "x to the power a," and a series $a_0 + a_1 x + a_2 x^2 + a_3 x^3 \ldots$ as a "power series." However, calling $y = Ax^k$ a "power function" or "power relationship" has met resistance by some social scientists who deal with political power. So

I have settled here for "fixed exponent relationship." Studenmund (2001: 203–6) refers to it as "double-log function," given that it corresponds to $\log y = \log A + k \log x$.

Two Quadrants Partly Allowed: Logistic Relationships

Sometimes the input variable x can take any real values, while the output variable y can take neither negative values nor positive values beyond some ceiling value $y = C$. This is the case, in particular, when x is time and y is a percentage. Now only parts of two quadrants of the entire two-dimensional field remain allowed: $-\infty < x < +\infty$ and $0 \le y \le C$. This is the constraint that underlies the *logit* and *probit* programs in statistics.

Once more, *all* sloped straight lines are conceptually disallowed. In particular, $y = a + bt$, where t is time, is impossible over sufficient time spans. The simplest family of acceptable curves that pass through a point $(x_0; y_0)$ in the allowed zone can be deduced from the simplest form for the slope dy/dx that expresses the two constraints:

$$\frac{dy}{dx} = k\left(1 - \frac{y}{C}\right)y.$$

Recall that restriction of y to only positive values is implicit in the exponential model $dy/dx = ky$. Multiplication of ky by $(1 - y/C)$ adds a further restriction of y to values less than C. Indeed, as x increases beyond the level $C/2$, y starts to increase at a decreasing rate, given that this rate is proportional to $1 - y/C$. As y approaches C, the difference $1 - y/C$ approaches 0 and hence the increase rate dy/dx approaches 0. Therefore, y can never reach C. This way, the restriction of y to values between 0 and C is implicit in the model $dy/dx = k(1 - y/C)y$.

Integration of $dy/dx = k(1 - y/C)y$ leads to the "simple logistic equation" (although it may not look very simple!):

$$y = \frac{C}{1 + A e^{-kx}},$$

where k can take any real values and A must be positive. If we want y to have a certain value $y = y_0$ when x has a given value x_0, then use $A = [(C - y_0)/y_0] \exp(+kx_0)$. The corresponding curve has been described as a "drawn-out S." For given ceiling C and basic rate constant k, a single starting point $(x_0; y_0)$ defines the entire curve.

How can testing by linear regression be used in such a case? The simple logistic equation is connected to the linear function in the following way.

Consider the ratio of the distances of y to its two limits: $(y - 0)/(C - y)$. The simple logistic function yields $(y - 0)/(C - y) = (1/A)e^{kx}$, which is an exponential function. Taking logarithms on both sides of the equation results in a linear equation in x:

$$\ln\left[\frac{y}{C - y}\right] = -\ln A + kx.$$

For $y = y_0$ when $x = x_0$,

$$\ln\left[\frac{y}{C - y}\right] = -\ln\left[\frac{y_0}{C - y_0}\right] - kx_0 + kx.$$

Before linear regression against x can be applied, y must be transformed in this way.

> **When x can conceptually take any values, while y can range from 0 up to a positive ceiling C, then linear regression against x should be carried out on the logarithm of $y/(C - y)$, rather than on y itself. This corresponds to fitting y to a simple logistic function of x.**

By so doing, we do not assert that y is a simple logistic function of x, but we test for this possibility. Oftentimes it works, but equally often it does not, because other constraints and conditions enter.

With $C = 1$, the transform is reduced to $\ln[y/(1 - y)]$. This is the transformation that the *logit* program in statistics carries out automatically. The *probit* program yields a fairly similar curve, but starting from quite different premises (normal error function), not discussed here.

The logistic model has substance when y actually can take values ranging between 0 to C, as is the case for growth curves of organisms and innovations. When something can take only values 0 or 1 and y represents probability of either outcome, then the *probit* approach makes more conceptual sense, but either way, such regression may become a model without meaning. Steve Coleman puts it as follows, based on Kennedy (1998: 239–40):

The idea that one can model binary choices with a continuous function makes regression possible but skirts the idea that one should actually have a reasonable theory or model of binary decision making. This is just a more complex case of social scientists skipping the messy business of theory to go straight to data analysis. As much as one can complain about mindless linear models, logistic models are this same problem multiplied. They also have serious statistical problems in estimating coefficients because models are very sensitive to errors in specification. Also there is no universally accepted measure for goodness of fit. (Steve Coleman, personal communication, July 2007)

Constraints on Three Sides

Constraints on three sides can occur in various ways. Consider the one where both x and y are constrained to the positive quadrant, and y also has a finite ceiling C: $0 \leq x < +\infty$, $0 \leq y \leq C$. This is the situation for volatility, in Figure 4.2. All sloping straight lines would stray into forbidden areas. As in the previous case, the simplest way to let y approach the ceiling, without ever reaching it, is to make the slope proportional to the remaining distance to the ceiling:

$$\frac{dy}{dx} = k(C - y),$$

where k is positive. This differential equation corresponds to an exponential approach to the ceiling:

$$y = C(1 - e^{-kx}) + y_0,$$

where y_0 is the value of y when $x = 0$. Alternatively, it can be written as

$$y = C - C \exp[k(x_0 - x)],$$

where x_0 is the value of x for which $y = 0$. In Figure 4.2, $x_0 = 1$. The resulting pattern can be deduced from Figure 8.2. Take the bottom right region alone, and reverse the direction of y. The shapes obtained are akin to the one for the refined model in Figure 4.2.

Testing by linear regression again requires first a transformation of the output variable. The equation above can be expressed as

$$\ln(C - y) = (\ln C + kx_0) - kx.$$

Hence, the logarithm of $(C - y)$ is a linear function of x.

When x can conceptually take any nonnegative values, while y can range from 0 up to a ceiling C, then linear regression against x should be carried out on the logarithm of $(C - y)$, rather than on y itself. This corresponds to fitting $C - y$ to an exponential function of x.

By so doing, we do not assert that $C - y$ is an exponential function of x, but we test for this possibility. It often works, but not always, because other constraints and conditions enter.

Constraints on All Four Sides

Finally, consider the case where both x and y are nonnegative and have finite ceilings: $0 \leq x \leq D$, $0 \leq y \leq C$. This is so, in particular, whenever both x and y are in percentages—or fractional shares that cannot surpass 1. By taking D and C as units, this case can always be reduced to $0 \leq X \leq 1$, $0 \leq Y \leq 1$, without loss of generality. Here, the share of acceptable straight lines is limited. It can be shown that the only lines $y = a + bx$ that have an allowed value of Y for every allowed value of X are those that satisfy both $0 \leq a \leq 1$ and $0 \leq a + b \leq 1$. The simplest family of curves that is acceptable depends on the nature of the conceptual anchor points. Two cases occur rather frequently.

Two anchor points. It may be that minimal and maximal Y must correspond to minimal and maximal X, respectively. Consider, for instance, female literacy (F), which is usually lower than male literacy (M): $F \leq M$. (We will overlook exceptions that occur at very high literacy.) Also $0 \leq F \leq 1$ and $0 \leq M \leq 1$. If so, then a country with zero male literacy ($M = 0$) must also have zero female literacy, because $F \leq 0$. Also, a country with full female literacy ($F = 1$) must also have full male literacy, because $1 \leq M$. This would mean two anchor points, (0; 0) and (1; 1). Then the simplest fully allowed family of curves is $F = M^k$, or more generally,

$$Y = X^k, \quad [2 \text{ anchor points}]$$

with $k \geq 0$. It includes the line $Y = X$ as a special case that corresponds to $k = 1$—and this is the only acceptable straight line. We found the same equation when the entire top right quadrant is allowed. The ceilings just limit the pattern to the one in the bottom left region of Figure 8.1.

Three anchor points. There may also be a further constraint that adds a central anchor point. For instance, in any two-party system, zero votes (X) must lead to zero seats (Y), and 100% of the votes must lead to 100% of the seats. Furthermore, in an unbiased system, 50% votes must lead to 50% seats. These three anchor points appear in Figure 8.3 as (0; 0), (0.5; 0.5), and (1; 1). Even the simplest curve cannot be very simple when

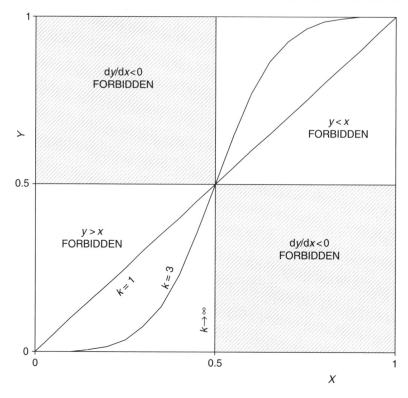

Figure 8.3. The simplest full family of curves allowed when x and y are conceptually restricted to the range from 0 to 1, with three anchor points—(0; 0), (0.5; 0.5), and (1; 1)

it must participate in a three-gate slalom. The simplest family that joins the three anchor points is

$$Y = \frac{X^k}{X^k + (1 - X)^k}, \quad \text{[3 anchor points, no bias]}$$

where k can take any positive values. It can also be expressed more symmetrically as

$$\frac{Y}{1 - Y} = \left[\frac{X}{1 - X}\right]^k.$$

When $k = 1$, $Y = X$—and this is the only straight line acceptable. As k ranges from zero to infinity, the curves fill in the lower left and upper right quadrants in Figure 8.3. (The other two quadrants correspond to

$k < 0$, which would impose $Y = 1$ for $X = 0$, and vice versa, contrary to our assumptions.)

The slope is also more complex than in the previous cases. It can be shown that

$$\frac{dY}{dX} = k\left(\frac{Y}{X}\right)\left[\frac{1-Y}{1-X}\right].$$

The slope is proportional to the ratio of the variables times the ratio of their complements. It is always positive or 0, for $k > 0$, When $X = Y = 0.5$, the slope equals k. When $X = 0$ or $X = 1$, the slope is 0 for $k > 1$; it tends toward infinity for $k < 1$. (For $k < 0$, $dY/dX \leq 0$ and the opposite anchor points (0;1) and (1;0) would be imposed.)

In the context of votes and seats, $dY/dX > 0$ means that more votes lead to more seats, as we would expect. Further restriction may be imposed. Nearly all electoral systems avoid favoring smaller parties at the expense of larger ones. It means that for the smaller party we expect $Y \leq X$ and for the larger one, $Y \geq X$. This constraint restricts k even further, to $k \geq 1$. It eliminates the top left half of the remaining lower quarter, and also the bottom right half of the remaining higher quarter, as shown in Figure 8.3. Any acceptable curve must be squeezed into the two remaining triangular areas.

By now, the allowed area is so tight that there is preciously little squiggle room away from the simplest family of curves, once the best fitting value of k is determined. As an example, the curve for $k = 3$ is shown in Figure 8.3. The actual patterns need not follow the simplest curves, but usually they do. Any deviation would need explanation in terms of further constraints or factors.

The lowest allowed value of k, $k = 1$, leads to $Y = X$, meaning perfectly proportional representation in the case of elections. When k tends to infinity, the curve in Figure 8.3 tends to the vertical line at $X = 0.5$, meaning that the larger party gets all the seats—or the only seat at stake, in the case of presidential elections.

This relationship applies in various contexts, whenever two and only two components split the total. Nor does it have to be an unbiased system. If $X = 0.5$ leads to $Y = 0.5 + b'$, then b' represents a bias away from 0.5. It can be positive or negative. The allowed triangles in Figure 8.3 would shift and bend accordingly, and the simplest family of curves is

$$Y = \frac{X^{bk}}{X^{bk} + (1 - X^b)^k}, \qquad \text{[3 anchor points, bias exponent } b]$$

which can also be expressed as

$$\frac{Y}{1-Y} = \left[\frac{X^b}{(1-X^b)^k}\right].$$

Here, the exponent b is connected to bias b' as $b = -\log 2/\log(0.5 + b')$. For unbiased system, $b = 1$. The expression for slope dY/dX is fairly complex.

Overview: Logically Predicted Forms, Empirically Determined Parameters

Table 8.1 offers a summary, depending on how the input (x) and output (y) variables are constrained from covering the entire range from minus infinity to plus infinity. In the case of patterns that cannot be linear on conceptual grounds, extracting most out of the data requires prior transformation of y and/or x, before linear regression makes sense. Even so, caution is advisable. These transformations may distort the distribution of random error, leading to extra problems.

Various other types of constraints and anchor points can of course occur, depending on the specific issue. Still, it is remarkable how many sociopolitical relationships fit the above description, at least as a first approximation.

As more constraints enter, a linear approach becomes ever more hopeless, and even the simplest curved solutions become more complex. Sometimes constraints impose a single equation, with no wiggle room

Table 8.1. Simplest formats resulting from conceptual constraints on ranges of occurrence of input and output variables

Number of constraints	Simplest format expected	Test by linear regression
None	Linear	y on x
One: x unconstrained, y positive (or zero)	Exponential	$\log y$ on x
Two: both x and y positive (or zero)	Fixed exponent	$\log y$ on $\log x$
Two: y ranging from 0 to a ceiling, C	Simple logistic	$\log[y/(C-y)]$ on $\log x$
Three: x positive, y ranging from 0 to a ceiling, C. Anchor point $(0; 0)$	Reversed exponential	$\log(C-y)$ on x
Four: both x and y ranging from 0 to a ceiling. Two anchor points: $(0; 0)$ and $(C; C')$	Fixed exponent	$\log y$ on $\log x$
Four: both x and y ranging from 0 to a ceiling. Three anchor points: $(0; 0)$, $(C; C')$, and an intervening one	Elongated S-shaped	More involved transformation of x and y

whatsoever, true to Sherlock Holmes's ideal. In most cases, however, only the mathematical format is prescribed or strongly suggested by the nature of the problem, including conceptual restraints, while one or more parameters are to be determined empirically.

It would be a mistake to think that such lack of full specification is peculiar to social sciences and represents a weakness for a theoretical model. Physics is full of empirically determined constants. In the aforementioned law of gravitation, the universal constant of gravitation (G) is determined empirically. Indeed, it could not be otherwise, whenever quantities lack a natural unit value (see the Appendix to Chapter 13). As for social sciences, in Coleman's (1981: 5) and Sørensen's (1998) view, models with a free parameter represent the general case for what they call substantive models.

Empirically determined parameters offer strength as much as weakness. Parameter k in the aforementioned equation $Y = X^k/[X^k + (1 - X)^k]$ enables us to express various situations for party seats and votes. When $k = 1$, it means perfect proportional representation. When $k = 3$, it expresses a moderate attrition of the minority in some parliamentary elections with single-seat districts. Finally, $k \to$ infinity corresponds to the stark attrition in presidential elections, where any number of votes short of plurality is translated into zero seats. Thus, empirically determined values of exponent k represent a measure of how disproportional a system is.

The essential part of a predictive model is that it predicts a *functional form* for the relationship among the variables, such as the exponential form in the refined model for volatility, $V = 100[1 - e^{-k(N-1)}]$. In this functional framework, empirically determined constants may be embedded, such as the constant k in the model above, as well as parameters that express the impact of various external conditions. If a later study should enable us to explain these constants themselves in still more fundamental terms, so much the better—it expands our predictive power. But the main thing is prediction of the functional form of the interaction.

Several Input Variables

The preceding discussion dealt with the situation where an output variable (y) is affected by a single input variable (x). Often we have reason to believe that several input variables matter. Should we combine them by addition or multiplication? It depends.

Annihilating Factors

Consider how much air (A) and food (F) one needs for survival and well-being (S). An addition "Air plus Food" ($S = a + bA + cF$) would erroneously tell us that one could do without air, if food is plentiful! Models must not predict absurdities. To reflect reality, we must multiply rather than add when the inputs are "annihilating" in the sense of a single zero input reducing the output to zero. Simple multiplication "Air times Food" ($S = kAF$) still leaves quite a few loose ends, but it at least tells us that either zero air or zero food would be lethal.

The outcome often depends heavily on the factor in the shortest supply. This consideration makes multiplication of factors superior to their addition in much of sociopolitical decision-making and related scholarly analysis. An underlying theoretical reason is that survival, food, and air are all quantities that cannot take negative values. The next section, however, warns us that nonnegative quantities need not always lead to simple multiplication.

Note further that the misleading $S = a + bA + cF$ needs three adjustable constants/coefficients, while $S = kAF$ may need only one. The philosophy of adding everything often piles up numerical constants/coefficients of doubtful significance, muddling the analysis. Adding an "interaction term," cAF, would be of only limited help. Indeed, in the presence of random error, the best fit with $S = a + b_1 A + b_2 F + cAF$ may still leave a slim possibility of survival without air, if food is plentiful. One must have the good sense to make the coefficients a, b_1, and b_2 exactly zero even if it reduces R^2.

The simple approximation $S = kAF$ fails when both inputs are plentiful. A surplus of air and food would improve chances of survival at a decreasing rate. This could be expressed by $S = [1 - \exp(-A/A_0)][1 - \exp(-F/F_0)]$, which at low A and F reduces to $S = kAF$, where $k = 1/A_0 F_0$). Such a second-approximation elaboration evolves from the multiplicative format, not from the additive.

In more abstract terms, consider two input variables, x and z. In principle, they could affect y in an infinite variety of combinations $y = f(x, z)$, the simplest being addition/subtraction ($y = a + bx - cz$), multiplication ($y = axz$), and division ($y = ax/z$). The approach depends on the problem on hand. Some options are excluded or made awkward by the range of values the variables can conceivably take.

When all three variables can range from minus to plus infinity, the linear pattern $y = a + bx + cz$ may well be the most suitable, because various other forms run into difficulties with negative values. In particular, $y = axz$ would presume that a product of negative values of x and z produces the same value of y as a product of positive x and y—which may or may not make sense for the given phenomenon.

In contrast, when all three variables can range only from zero to plus infinity ($x \geq 0$, $z \geq 0$, and $y \geq 0$), the picture is reversed. The restrictions noted previously for the quadrant $x \geq 0$ and $y \geq 0$ apply again. Most of the straight lines $y = a + bx + cz$ that pass through a given point $(x_0; z_0; y_0)$ are disallowed. In particular, all downward sloping lines ($b < 0$ or $c < 0$) are forbidden, because at very high values of x or z, respectively, they would predict a negative value of y.

The simplest family of curves that remains entirely in the allowed region is the product of x and z to some fixed exponent: $y = Ax^b z^c$, where A is a positive constant and exponents b and c can take any positive or negative values. Note that a negative exponent means division. Once more, the logarithms of the variables are linearly related: $\ln y = a + b \ln x + c \ln z$, where $a = \ln A$.

The preceding observations can be extended to any number of variables that cannot take negative values. The linear equation $y = a + \Sigma b_i x_i$ leads to conceptual inconsistencies avoided by the multiplicative form $y = a\Pi x_i^{b_i}$, which can be linearized by taking logarithms: $\ln y = a + \Sigma b_i \ln x_i$. Few laws of physics, however, multiply/divide more than three input variables, and the same can be expected for social relationships.

Enhancing Factors

Now consider the following problem, inspired by Daniel Bochsler's (2006) research. The number of treaties (T) between Swiss cantons may be enhanced by commonalities of border (B), language (L), and religion (R). However, these quantities are measured, they have natural zeros (complete lack of commonalities and treaties), and they cannot take negative values. Nonetheless, a model $T = kBLR$ would be absurd, as it would suggest that no treaties would occur even among neighbors unless they have some commonality of language and religion. Here, in contrast to the air and food example, none of the input factors are annihilating. Their presence enhances an output that could be positive even when one of the factors is nil.

How could we model such a situation? One simple possibility involves four constants: $T = T_0(1 + B/b)(1 + L/l)(1 + R/r)$. Here, T_0 is the base value of T when all input variables are zero. Positive constants b, l, and r are the values of B, L, and R that double the out put. In the complete absence of common border, language, or religion, the corresponding term becomes 1 and does not affect the outcome. But if several inputs are positive, they magnify each other's impact.

Here, simple logarithmic reduction to linearity is not possible. The model could be decomposed into an addition of T_0 plus three linear terms, three pair-wise multiplicative terms and a jointly multiplicative term $T_0BLR/(blr)$. We may seem to be back to a linear regression plus "interaction" terms, with a total of eight constants/coefficients. The latter, however, cannot take just any odd values. They all are combinations of the basic four coefficients (T_0, b, l, and r) and thus are subject to constraints. The simple model above is confirmed only if the coefficient values found by multiple regression do satisfy these constraints.

Recall (from Chapter 5) the special multiplicative form that occurs in utility theory (Keeney and Raiffa 1976: 234–8; Fishburn 1977): $(1 + cy) = (1 + cx_1)(1 + cx_2)$. It can be reduced to $y = x_1 + x_2 + cx_1x_2$. This expression is akin to the one above, with only two input variables and with only one adjustable coefficient.

These examples should caution us. We cannot unthinkingly multiply all input variables together just because they are restricted to nonnegative values. We must consider whether they are "annihilating" in the sense of a single zero input reducing the output to zero. If this is not the case, such inputs must enter in a different way.

Conclusions: Why Would the Simplest Forms Prevail?

I have highlighted the models based on ignorance—or rather near-ignorance, teasing the most out of what we know about constraints. Conceptually forbidden zones, anchor points, and continuity are important parts of our knowledge—knowledge we often take so much for granted that we do not even notice it, and hence fail to draw conclusions. Asking what would happen under extreme conditions can lead to insights, even if we agree that such extremes will never materialize. When the impossible is eliminated, the possible emerges with more clarity.

When proposing for consideration simple nonlinear mathematical forms, I may seem merely to dilute blind adherence to linear models. So a couple of models are offered, instead of a single linear one. Why should we expect that, among the many mathematical formats that satisfy some obvious constraints, precisely the simplest ones would apply? Physicist Eugene Wigner (1960) addressed a similar issue regarding natural sciences, which he implicitly reduced to physics alone.

His answer is that the physicist is a somewhat irresponsible character. If he finds that the relationship between two variables is close to some well-known mathematical function, he jumps to the conclusion that this is it, simply because he does not know any better options. Yet, it is eerie how often this irresponsible approach works out, as if mathematics were indeed the language in which nature speaks to us. Wigner (1960) deals with natural sciences only. It may not work in social sciences, but how would we know without giving it a try?

The models are presented here as equations devoid of an "error term." It by no means implies that they are rigidly "deterministic." They are deterministic for the mean outcomes even while they may be probabilistic for individual cases—like the equations for mean positions in quantum mechanics. For given x, the resulting value of y indicates the expected median of actual values, with one-half above and one-half below this level. In the absence of any other knowledge, it is more productive to use such a model rather than say that we do not know. If actual data tell us otherwise, this additional knowledge will have to be worked into the model.

Measures of degree of scatter, such as R^2, are the only measures of goodness for descriptive models, but they are less important for predictive models, where the location of data points in relation to the *predicted* mean expectation is critical (cf. Chapter 4), not their location regarding the actual empirical mean. When actual data (A) are regressed on the values predicted by a model (P), we expect not just any line $A = a + bP$ but specifically $a = 0.00$ and $b = 1.00$ so that $A = P$. If this is the case, then the predictive model holds even if R^2 is low. The reverse is also true: If a and/or b deviate markedly from 0 and 1, respectively, then the model needs revision, *especially* so when R^2 is high for this best-fit line.

The essential part of a predictive model is the predicted *functional form* of relationship among the variables. The model may include a constant or parameter, to be determined empirically. Due to conceptual constraints, predictive models rarely are linear. Linear approximations are useful in preliminary work, along with graphical representations, to get a feel for the empirical pattern. They are also useful at the very end, as practical simplifications. In order to know when a simplification can be used, one must be aware of the refined model.

115

Appendix to Chapter 8

Getting a Feel for Exponents and Logarithms

Many graduate students and even professors in social sciences seem ill at ease with exponents and logarithms. They may recall that "When numbers are multiplied, their logarithms add," but they have not internalized it, and hence they hesitate using logarithms. A simplistic introduction may help.

Exponents of 10

We use 10^3 as shorthand for $10 \times 10 \times 10$. Thus, $10^3 = 1,000$. More generally, **the "exponent" a in 10^a is the number of zeros that come after "1."** It follows that $10^1 = 10$. Also $10^0 = 1$, given that here "1" is followed by no zeros. It may look counterintuitive, yet this is the only consistent way to interpret 10^0.

If we multiply 100 by 1,000, we get 100,000. Using exponents, we have $10^2 \times 10^3 = 10^5 = 10^{(2+3)}$. This is how multiplication turns into addition. **When multiples of 10 are multiplied, their exponents are added:**

$$10^a 10^b = 10^{a+b}.$$

When multiplying 100 by itself 3 times, we get $100 \times 100 \times 100 = 1,000,000$. In the exponent notation, $10^2 \times 10^2 \times 10^2 = (10^2)^3 = 10^6$. Thus

$$(10^a)^b = 10^{ab}.$$

If we divide 10,000 by 10, we get 1,000. Using exponents, $10^4/10^1 = 10^3 = 10^{(4-1)}$. Division of numbers leads to subtraction of exponents:

$$10^a/10^b = 10^{a-b}.$$

Now consider the reverse situation: Dividing 10 by 10,000 yields $1/1,000 = 0.001$. The previous rule makes it correspond to $10^1/10^4 = 10^{1-4} = 10^{-3}$. The -3 corresponds to the number of zeros that *precedes* "1." It also means that

$$10^{-a} = \frac{1}{10^a}.$$

If we divide 100 by 100, we get 1. It corresponds to $10^2/10^2 = 10^{2-2} = 10^0$. This confirms that

$$10^0 = 1.$$

Fractional exponents of 10

The next question may sound crazy: What could $10^{1/2}$ or $10^{0.5}$ stand for? By the previous rule, it would mean "1" followed by one-half of a zero! It seems to make no sense. But hold it! When multiplying $10^{0.5}$ by itself, the previous rule yields 10, given that we have $10^{0.5} \times 10^{0.5} = 10^{0.5+0.5} = 10^1$. But this is the very definition of square root of 10, which is 3.16: we have $3.16 \times 3.16 = 10$. Thus, **$10^{0.5} = 10^{1/2}$ stands for square root of 10**. Figuratively, it is as if 3.16 were "1" followed by one-half of a zero.

Similarly, the cube root of 10 is the number that leads to 10 when multiplied by itself 3 times. It is 2.154, because $2.154^3 = 10$. We could then argue that 2.154 is somehow like "1" followed by one-third of a zero, because $10^{1/3} \times 10^{1/3} \times 10^{1/3} = 10^{1/3+1/3+1/3} = 10^1$ leads to "1" followed by a full zero.

But if 3.16 is "1" followed by one-half of a zero, and 2.154 is "1" followed by one-third of a zero, then 3.00 should be "1" followed by somewhat less than one-half of a zero, if we want to be consistent.

Fact is, we can actually assign an exponent of 10, a sort of a "fractional number of zeros," to any number between 1 and 10. For instance, 2 is 10 with exponent 0.30. How can we prove it? Note that $2^{10} = 1,024$, which is quite close to $1,000 = 10^3$. Thus, $2^{10} \approx 10^3$. Put both sides of the equation to exponent 1/10: $(2^{10})^{1/10} \approx (10^3)^{1/10}$. Multiplying through leads to $2 \approx 10^{0.30}$.

This "fractional number of zeros" to follow "1"—this is what we call *decimal logarithm*, designated as "log." Thus, log 3.16 = 1/2 = 0.500, log 2.154 = 1/3 = 0.333, and log 2 = 0.30. By definition, $10^{\log 2} = 2$. More generally, for any number a,

$$10^{\log a} = a.$$

What could the logarithm of 5 be? We have $5 \times 2 = 10$. Hence, $10^{\log 5} \times 10^{\log 2} = 10^{\log 10}$. This means that log 5 + log 2 = log 10 = 1. If log 2 $\approx$ 0.30, then log 5 $\approx$ 1 − 0.30 = 0.70. We conclude that $5 \approx 10^{0.70}$.

What about the logarithm of a number larger than 10, such as 316? Given that $316 = 3.16 \times 100$, log 316 = log 3.16 + log 100 = 0.50 + 2 = 2.50. There are ways to calculate the logarithms of any numbers between 1 and 10 precisely. Once we know these, we know the logarithms of all numbers—just do what we did for 316. We divided by multipliers of 10, until the number fell between 1 and 10. Then we took the log of that number and added to it the number of zeros in the multiplier of 10.

What are logarithms good for?

They turn multiplications and divisions into additions and subtractions. $AB = C$ can be written as $10^{\log A} 10^{\log B} = 10^{\log C}$. By the rules for exponents, we also have $10^{\log A} 10^{\log B} = 10^{\log A + \log B}$. Hence, **$AB = C$ corresponds to log A + log B = log C**. Also, $\log(A^2) = \log(AA) = \log A + \log A = 2\log A$. More generally,

$$\log(A^m) = m\log A.$$

Note that m enters here, not log m.

But who needs going through logarithms, when one can do the multiplication directly? True, we can easily do the multiplication A^m, as long as m is an integer. But consider something like $y = 2.2(0.2)^{0.47}$. It will be shown soon that we do face such expressions in model building, yet we cannot compute them directly. However, we can take logarithms on both sides: $\log y = \log 2.2 + 0.47 \log 0.2$.

How do we find the logarithms of such numbers? On a usual pocket calculator, $\log 2.2$ is found by entering "2.2" and pushing the LOG/10^x key. (On some calculators, one must push LOG, "2.2" and "=.") This way, we get

$$\log y = \log 2.2 + 0.47 \log 0.2. = 0.342 + 0.47(-0.699) = 0.013.$$

Once we have $\log y = 0.013$, we take the "antilog" of 0.013, meaning $10^{0.013}$. On a usual pocket calculator, we find $10^{0.013}$ by entering 0.013 and pushing the "2nd function" and LOG/10^x keys. We obtain $y = 10^{0.013} = 1.03$.

This is a most important property of logarithms: They turn exponent expressions, which we cannot compute directly, into multiplications: **$y = x^m$ corresponds to $\log y = m \log x$.**

Most pocket calculators offer a shortcut for $2.2(0.2)^{0.47}$. Enter 2.2, push "×" (MULTIPLY), enter 0.2, push y^x, enter 0.47, push "=" so as to get $2.2(0.2)^{+0.47} = 1.03$ directly.

When do we need such calculations? When x and y can take only positive value, it was observed that the simplest model to satisfy these constraints is $y = Ax^k$. Given a data-set with such constraints, which numerical values of constants A and k would correspond to this data-set?

Calculations of constants in $y = Ax^k$

Consider a set such as set B in Figures 3.1 and 3.2, which may fit $y = Ax^k$. Suppose the following two points can be taken as typical: $y = 2.2$ for $x = 0.2$ and $y = 0.8$ for $x = 1.7$. How can we determine the constants A and k?

Plug these coordinates into $y = Ax^k$. The two points give us

$$2.2 = A(0.2)^k \quad \text{and}$$
$$0.8 = A(1.7)^k.$$

Divide member by member, so as to make A cancel out: $2.2/0.8 = (0.2)^k/(1.7)^k$. This means $2.75 = (0.2/1.7)^k = (0.118)^k$. Take logarithms on both sides: $\log 2.75 = k \log 0.118$. Insert numerical values of logarithms: $0.439 = k(-0.930)$. Hence $k = -0.47$.

Now the previous $2.2 = A(0.2)^k$ becomes $2.2 = A(0.2)^{-0.47}$. Multiply on both sides by $(0.2)^{+0.47}$. We get $2.2(0.2)^{+0.47} = A(0.2)^{-0.47}(0.2)^{+0.47}$, and the latter simplifies to A. Calculate $2.2(0.2)^{0.47}$ the way we did in the previous section. We obtain $A = 1.03$. We previously found $k = -0.47$. In sum, $y = Ax^k$ becomes $y = 1.028x^{-0.47}$. This is the equation for this data-set, assuming that the two points were typical.

We should check our result for calculation mistakes. We used (0.2; 2.2) to calculate A. Now plug the x value of the other point (1.7; 0.8) into $y = 1.028x^{-0.47}$. We get $y = 1.03(1.7)^{-0.47} = 0.80$, in agreement with original data. Therefore, most likely no mistakes have been made.

How do we decide which two points to choose for calculating the constants in the equation? The best way is to regress log y on log x, pick two points on this regression line, far away from each other, and plug them into $\log y = \log A + k \log x$. Visually choosing two actual points as "typical" is an approximation that sometimes suffices.

Exponents of numbers other than 10, and logarithms on other bases

The formulas established for exponents of 10 apply to any number n. In particular, $n^a n^b = n^{a+b}$ and $n^a/n^b = n^{a-b}$, leading to $n^0 = 1$ and $n^{-a} = 1/n^a$. Also $(n^a)^b = n^{a.b}$. It follows that the **bth root of n is $n^{1/b}$** Combining with $(n^a)^b = n^{a.b}$ leads to **bth root of n^a is $n^{a/b}$**.

These relationships frequently enter model building and testing.

Logarithms can be established on bases other than 10. The only one needed for models in this chapter is the "natural logarithm," designated as "ln," based on $e = 2.718 \ldots$ The previously established relationships apply: $AB = C$ corresponds to $\ln A + \ln B = \ln C$, and $y = x^m$ corresponds to $\ln y = m \ln x$. Note that $\ln 10 = 2.3026$ and $\log e = 0.4341$. When $\log x$ means logarithm to the base 10, then we always have

$$\ln x = 2.3026 \log x,$$

and conversely,

$$\log x = 0.434 \ln x.$$

Most pocket calculators have separate keys for LOG (and 10^x) and LN (and e^x).

9

Geometric Means and Lognormal Distributions

- Geometric means are often more meaningful than arithmetic means, because they are closer to the central figure (median). Take three incomes, 4, 10, and 100 units. The arithmetic mean (38) depends too much on the largest income. The geometric mean (16) is closer to the median.
- To calculate the arithmetic mean of n numbers, add them, then divide by n. For the three numbers above, $(100 + 10 + 4)/3 = 38$. For geometric mean, multiply them, then take the nth root. For the three numbers above, enter $100 \times 10 \times 4 = 4{,}000$ on a pocket calculator, push key "y^x", enter 3, push key "$1/x$," push key " $=$ " and get $4{,}000^{1/3} = 15.87 \approx 16$.
- When x and y can conceptually take only positive values, their distributions cannot be normal and may be lognormal.
- This discrepancy becomes serious when running a normal distribution yields a standard deviation larger than one-half of the mean. In such a case, one should dump the normal fit and try a lognormal fit instead.

The previous chapter showed that conceptual constraints impose specific and usually nonlinear relationships among the variables. It follows from such nonlinearity that the central tendency is often better expressed by geometric than by arithmetic means. By the same token, lognormal data fits often are called for, instead of desperate attempts to fit data into a Procrustean normal distribution.

The simple instructions above for calculating geometric means were included on the recommendation of a prominent social scientist, one with sufficient self-assurance to acknowledge that he or she did not know how to calculate the geometric mean of more than two numbers on a pocket calculator. For one person who dares to ask for such advice, there must be many more who dare not ask. Yet without ability to calculate geometric means without the help of computer programs one may not develop a feel for what they represent and when to use them.

Arithmetic Versus Geometric Means

What often most interests us is the median. The median means a size such that half the cases fall below and half above it. But we often calculate the arithmetic or geometric mean, instead, because they are simpler to calculate.

To calculate the arithmetic mean (A) of n numbers, add them, then divide by n. For geometric mean (G), multiply them, then take the nth root; this is possible only for all numbers positive. It can be shown that $G \leq A$ in all cases. Their relation to the median (M) varies. Most often $G < M < A$, but both A and G can be smaller than M—as for 9, 10, 10—or larger than M—as for 10, 10, 11. Which mean should we use? Consider the following two cases.

What is a meaningful average weight of mammals? Humans might be close to median, since one can think of many smaller and also many larger animals. Consider a small mammal such as a mouse (about 3 g), a human (some 100 kg), and a large mammal such as a blue whale (some 30 tons). Take the mean you are most used to, the arithmetic mean, and what do you get? We get 10 tons (plus a few negligible kilograms)—which corresponds to another pretty large whale. All other species would look less than average. The geometric mean, on the other hand, would be 21 kg, closer to 100 kg.

Now take the average population of members of the United Nations. The total population of these nearly 200 countries is about 6 billion. The arithmetic mean is 30 million. Yet less than 40 countries reach 30 million. The other 160 look less than average.

In both cases, the geometric means come closer to what we often really look for—the median. It may often seem unclear when to use the arithmetic and when the geometric mean. When negative values can occur, only the arithmetic mean can be used. When the variables can take only positive values, however, the geometric mean is preferable in principle. It is mandatory when the smallest and largest values differ by several orders of magnitude, unless one truly wishes to focus on whales and neglect mice and men. The reasons for this claim derive from previous chapter and will be explained further. But let us first consider another specific illustration.

As I was completing high school in Marrakech, the first Moroccan uprisings against the French "protectorate" took place in Casablanca. My friend Jacques Favreau, with family ties in high military circles, asked me to guess how many people actually were killed. My answer went roughly as follows. "The French official figure reported in the newspapers is 40. Our Moroccan servant says the native rumor mill talks of several thousand. Take this to mean 4,000. The geometric mean of 40 and 4,000 is 400." It turned out that I was off only by 100, compared to the confidential army estimate, which was about 300.

Jacques said I was the only person he knew who would use such an approach. But when in 2004 I asked 40 undergraduates at the University of California, Irvine to offer their best guess, the median guess was 600, much closer to the geometric mean, $x_G = 400$, than to the arithmetic mean, $x_A = 2,020$.

The model behind such everyday wisdom is *equal distortion*. When we do not know which side is more credible, our best guess is that both sides exaggerate in opposite directions, by the same *multiplicative* factor k (not by the same additive amount!). For the unknown number of deaths (x) in Casablanca, this means that $x = 40k$ and also $x = 4,000/k$, which leads to $k = 10$ and $x = 400$. It implies that both sides distort reality by the same factor 10. The median estimate of the UCI students, 600, suggests they were more suspicious of the government (deemed to understate the figure by a factor of $600/40 = 15$) than of the rumor mill (deemed to overstate it by a factor of only $4,000/600 = 6.7$). Maybe the students fed in some ideas about the ongoing war in Iraq.

I delve on this incident because the analogous choice between arithmetic and geometric means is essential for some predictive models, yet some of my colleagues seem suspicious of the geometric mean, as if the arithmetic mean were the only honest one in all circumstances. But apply arithmetic mean to Casablanca riots: $x_A = 2,020$. This would mean claiming that the rumor mill only doubles the number of the dead, while the government grossly understates it by a factor of 50. The UCI undergraduates have more common sense than that.

It matters which mean we choose. It can make an enormous difference in conclusions of many analyses—and the resulting policy decisions. Per capita GNP represents the arithmetic mean. Here, one millionaire outweighs a thousand paupers. If per capita GNP is reported as 10,000

Table 9.1. The relationships of arithmetic mean (x_A), median (x_M), and geometric mean (x_G) as the ratio of largest to smallest entry widens

Values of x	x_A	x_M	x_G
1	1	1	1
1, 2	1.5	1.5	1.4
1, 2, 5	2.7	2	2.2
1, 2, 5, 10	4.5	3.5	3.2
1, 2, 5, 10, 20	7.6	5	4.6
1, 2, 5, 10, 20, 50	14.7	7.5	5.2
1, 2, 5, 10, 20, 50, 100	26.9	10	10.0
0, 1, 2, 5, 10, 20, 50, 100	23.5	7.5	0
Adding the smallest nonzero reading:			
1, 2, 3, 6, 11, 21, 51, 101	24.5	8.5	9.0
Subtracting the smallest nonzero reading:	23.5	7.5	8.0

pounds it would be grossly mistaken to imagine that one-half the people earn more than 10,000 pounds and one-half earn less. Actually, only about one quarter surpass this level. The median income is much lower than the mean, and the geometric mean comes close to the median.

Table 9.1 illustrates the relationship between the means and the median. Many countries have coins or bills of 1, 2, 5, 10, 20, 50, and 100 units. These numbers have roughly uniform multiplicative spaces between them—2, 2.5, 2, 2, 2.5, and 2, respectively. As we combine such values over ever wider ranges, the geometric means remain close to the medians, while the arithmetic means exceed the medians ever more— they heavily reflect the size of the largest single component. It can be seen that one has to be on guard when the highest reading surpasses the lowest by more than a factor of 10. When this ratio reaches 100, the arithmetic mean most likely tells us little about the median. This simplistic example has its pitfalls, but it conveys the main story.

The sticky point comes when one of the readings is a perfect zero. Consider the median number of telephones per capita for member countries of the United Nations. The geometric mean is likely to reflect the median better than does the arithmetic mean. However, if a single country fails to have a single telephone, the geometric mean drops to zero. The effect is illustrated in the bottom part of Table 9.1. Here, the geometric mean becomes meaningless, while the arithmetic mean still exceeds the median heavily. What should we do?

One operational way is to add the smallest nonzero reading to every reading, as shown at the bottom of Table 9.1. Then take the geometric mean and subtract the added part. The resulting pseudo-geometric mean is close to the median in the given case. This coarse approach is awkward in a mathematical sense, but it tends to reflect the median.

Normal Versus Lognormal Distributions

The ability of the arithmetic mean to reflect the median is very much connected to whether a normal distribution is possible. When a variable x can in principle extend from minus to plus infinity, random values of x may be distributed according to the so-called normal distribution (although many other distributions are also possible). What is so normal about it? It is a prime example of an "ignorance-based model." When no finite values are excluded in principle, because there are no conceptual lower or upper limits, the very absence of any further knowledge leads to the equation for normal distribution:

$$f(x) = [1/2\pi)^{0.5}\sigma] \exp[-(x - x_A)^2/2\sigma^2].$$

The *functional form* is prescribed by our ignorance, but the values of arithmetic mean (x_A) and standard deviation (σ) are not specified in the normal model. These parameters are determined empirically.

When some social data are normally distributed, we do not ask about the specific social factors that cause such a form of distribution. We accept the idea that such a distribution tends to happen *precisely in the absence* of any causal factors. Obviously, we are interested in the numerical values of the parameters that specify the given normal distribution—arithmetic mean and standard distribution—because these are the parts that convey substantive meaning. They may need explanation, or they may be of help in explaining something else.

A nice feature of the normal distribution is that the arithmetic mean equals the median and the mode (the point with the highest frequency of occurrence). We do not have to keep separate track of them. In contrast, the geometric mean may not be defined. This is so because a normal distribution may include negative readings.

The picture changes drastically when x can conceptually take only positive values, however small or large. Now the distribution of x cannot be perfectly normal, because the normal curve includes negative values. Try fitting the number of telephones per capita in member countries of the United Nations with a normal distribution. You would find that the standard deviation exceeds the mean. This would imply that more than $1/(2e) = 18\%$ of the countries have a negative number of telephones!

Unfortunately, printing such absurdities has been acceptable in social sciences.

When x can take only positive values, the arithmetic mean, median, and mode may no longer be equal. The median still tells the same story as before: one-half of the cases are above the median. But the arithmetic mean is heavily affected by the largest values. One person with a yearly income of 10,000,000 pounds would weigh as much as 1,000 people with an income of 10,000 pounds.

The problem subsides when we shift from values of x, which cannot be negative, to the logarithms of these values. These logarithms range from minus infinity (for $x = 0$) to plus infinity and hence can be normally distributed. In terms of decimal logarithms, the person with 10,000,000 pounds would contribute 7 while a person with 10,000 contributes 4, which is not an overwhelming difference. In Table 9.1, the logarithms of 1, 2, 5, 10, 20, 50, and 100 are 0, 0.3, 0.7, 1, 1.3, 1.7, and 2, respectively, and their mean agrees with their median.

Now take the antilog of the arithmetic mean of the logarithms. The result is precisely what we call the geometric mean. And the normal distribution of log x corresponds to what is called the *lognormal* distribution of x itself. In principle, whenever x is quasi-continuous and can take only positive values, a lognormal (rather than normal) distribution of x may be expected (although other distributions are also possible). The geometric mean can be expected to correspond to the median, while the arithmetic mean exceeds the median.

Still, normal distribution fits practically as well as the lognormal in many cases where x can take only positive values. When does it happen? The ratio of standard deviation to the arithmetic mean serves as a warning signal. Suppose data are fitted to normal distribution, and the standard deviation found is comparable to or even larger than the arithmetic mean. Then a normal fit is unacceptable, because it implies that negative values do occur. A lognormal fit (or still something else) should be tried instead.

On the other hand, if the arithmetic mean is many times larger than the standard deviation, one does not have to worry—the zero point is so far away that it might as well be minus infinity, as far as this particular normal distribution is concerned. This is the case, for example, for the heights of adult women. When the ratio of standard deviation to the (arithmetic) mean is smaller than one-half, one is on reasonably safe grounds—normal distribution differs little from the lognormal and the arithmetic mean can be used as a proxy for the median (and for the geometric mean). One should dump the normal fit and try a lognormal fit instead when standard deviation exceeds one-half of the mean.

Even without formally fitting data with normal distribution, the following coarse test usually works. If the ratio of the largest to the smallest reading (both positive) is less than 10, then normal distribution differs little from the lognormal and the arithmetic mean can be used as a proxy for the median. If it is larger than 10, it becomes risky, unless the number of readings is very large.

Limpert et al.'s "Lognormal Distributions across the Sciences: Keys and Clues" (2001) shows more thoroughly why the lognormal distribution is often the better model, and why normal distribution has nonetheless been unduly popular. In particular, they introduce the notion of *multiplicative standard deviation* (s^*) and use it, in conjunction with median, to describe the basic properties of the lognormal distribution. Tabulating 61 examples, ranging from geology and medicine to linguistics and social sciences, they find s^* ranging from 1.03 to 33.15, with a median of 1.85.

Conclusions

Geometric means often express the central tendency better than arithmetic means. For the same reason, lognormal data fits often are called for, instead of desperate attempts to fit data into a Procrustean normal distribution. The following advice applies, with some reservations.

- In the absence of any other information, if a variable can range from minus to plus infinity, a normal distribution is our best bet, implying that the arithmetic mean is close to the median. (In the presence of further information, the bet may be off.)

- In the absence of any other information, if a variable can have only positive values, a lognormal distribution is among our best bets, implying that the geometric mean is close to the median. (In the presence of further information, the bet may be off—we may have a gamma distribution or something else.)

- However, if one tries a normal fit and standard deviation turns out less than one-half of the mean, then one might use this normal distribution. If standard deviation exceeds one-half of the mean, the normal fit should be abandoned in favor of lognormal.

- If negative values are conceptually excluded but zero values do occur, then neither distribution can fit. Neither mean adequately reflects the median, but a pseudo-geometric mean might approximate it.

- When there are grounds to hesitate between the arithmetic and geometric means, using the median might be the safest way, although it is awkward to calculate.

Appendix to Chapter 9

Dice and Distributions

The additive and multiplicative effects on distributions can be demonstrated with the help of ordinary dice. Limpert et al. (2001) suggest two dice, but three dice lead to more convincing results. Throw three dice and record both the sums and products of the three numbers. Repeat 25–100 times. The sums will approach a normal distribution, except at the extremes, where values of less than 3 and more than 18 cannot occur. The median can be expected to be 10 or 11, with arithmetic mean in that range. The products will have a visibly skewed distribution that approaches the lognormal, except at the extremes, where values of less than 1 and more than 216 cannot occur. The median can be expected to be 27 or 30 (as products of numbers 1–6 cannot be 28 or 29), with geometric mean in that range.

When only two dice are used, the expected distribution of sums is a symmetrical triangle with peak frequency at 7 points and the base ranging from 1 to 13. Hence, the product is distributed in a not quite lognormal way. Combining three or more random numbers, the normal and lognormal patterns establish themselves quickly. This is so even when there are only two outcomes (as in heads and tail) rather than six (as with dice).

"Log-Lognormal" Distributions

Are there variables for which one would have to take logarithms not once but twice, before their distributions are turned into normal ones? One could expect such "log-lognormal" distributions when the conceptual lower limit is not 0 but 1. Taking logarithms once would shift this limit to 0, and taking it once more would shift it to minus infinity, as required for normal distribution. Note that natural logarithms are mandatory when taking logarithms twice. For a given base, $\log x/\ln x$ is constant, but $\log(\log x)/\ln(\ln x)$ is not.

One such variable is precisely the multiplicative standard deviation s^* devised by Limpert et al. (2001): It must be at least 1 by definition. And indeed, I find that graphing the 61 values of $\ln(s^*)$ based on their table of s^* still leads to a skewed distribution that looks lognormal. Graphing $\ln[\ln(s^*)]$ leads to a fairy symmetrical distribution that approximates the normal. It centers roughly at the second logarithm of the actual median, $\ln\ln 1.85 = -0.49$, with standard deviation 0.40. The corresponding median of $\ln(s^*)$ is $\ln 1.85 = 0.61$, and its multiplicative standard deviation is $\exp(0.40) = 1.49$. Finally, what might be called the "exponential standard deviation" of s^* itself is $\text{expexp}(0.40) = 1.49$. This means that the range corresponding to standard deviation of the normal distribution of $\ln\ln s^*$ extends from $1.85^{1/1.49} = 1.51$ to $1.85^{1.49} = 2.49$.

Other continuous quantities that cannot fall below 1 include the effective number of parties (N), used in Chapter 4. Indeed, Rekha Diwakar (personal communication, November 2007) finds that the distribution of $\ln N$ still has a tail toward higher values of N, although less marked than it is for the distribution of $\ln N$. A fairly symmetric distribution, close to normal, is obtained with $\ln\ln N$. The data involves 7,005 district level observations in Indian elections 1952–2004, as analyzed by Diwakar (2007).

Mapping Any Limited Range on the Entire Range of Real Numbers

A normal distribution of x requires conceptually that all real values of x be possible, from minus to plus infinity. We have seen that $0 < x < \infty$ can be mapped into $-\infty < X < +\infty$ by taking $X = \ln x$, and $1 < x < \infty$ can be mapped into $-\infty < X < +\infty$ by taking $X = \ln\ln x$. A broader question is: How can such mapping be done for any constraint $B < x < A$, where B and A are real numbers? (The issue is more complex for $B \leq x \leq A$.) An ad hoc way to proceed is the following. There is no guarantee that these mappings would lead to a normal distribution—they merely make it conceptually possible.

The upper limit A can always be mapped into $+\infty$ in many ways; one of the simplest is $x' = 1/(A - x)$. Then $1/(A - B) < x' < \infty$. Mappings to the interval $(1; \infty)$ are also possible; one of the simplest, when $B < x$, is $x'' = (A - B)x' = (A - B)/(A - x)$.

Further mapping into $-\infty < X < +\infty$ can be achieved in several ways. The aforementioned $X = \ln\ln x'' = \ln\ln[(A - B)/(A - x)]$ is the simplest conceptually, as it keeps repeating the same transformation (taking logarithms). In terms of computational ease, it is simpler to use $X' = \ln[(A - B)/(A - x) - 1] = \ln[(x - B)/(A - x)]$.

In particular, if $0 < x < 100$, as is the case for many measures using percentages, then $A = 100$ and $B = 0$. Hence $X = \ln\ln[(100)/(100 - x)]$ and $X' = \ln[(x)/(100 - x)]$. Suppose that the median value of x is $x_{med} = 75$. Then its distribution *might* correspond to a normal distribution of $X = \ln\ln[(100)/(100 - x)$ around a mean and median of $X_m = \ln\ln[(100)/(100 - 75)] = \ln\ln 4 = 0.33$. Or it *might* correspond to a normal distribution of $X' = \ln[(x)/(100 - x)]$ around a mean and median of $X' = \ln[(75)/(100 - 75)] = \ln 3 = 1.10$. It remains to be tested whether either mapping leads to normal distribution, for a given distribution of x. But without prior mapping into the range $-\infty < X < +\infty$, an attempt to fit with normal distribution is conceptually flawed from the beginning.

"Less-than-Lognormal" Distributions

A puzzling case is the distribution of populations (P) of sovereign states (of which there were 190, as of 1993). This population should have a lower limit at 0. As expected, the arithmetic mean (32 million) exceeds the median (5.4 million), and the distribution has a long tail toward higher values. However, the geometric mean (4.1 million) falls below the median, and the distribution of ln P has a clear tail toward lower values. To obtain a symmetrical distribution, we should take logarithms, but not all the way, so to say.

A function $\ln^n x$ can be defined, where $\ln^0 x = x$, $\ln^1 x = \ln x$, and $\ln^2 x = \ln\ln x$. Fractional values of n correspond to going part-way toward taking logarithms (Taagepera 1973). By taking $\ln^{0.58} P$ for the sovereign states, a normal distribution can be obtained, with center corresponding to 5.6 million. However, it would correspond to a lower limit on P not at 0 but around –0.5 people!

10

Example of Interlocking Models: Party Sizes and Cabinet Duration

---

- Interlocking networks of equations, based on logical models, are possible in social sciences.
- Partial evidence for such a possibility is offered by a sequence of models that ties mean duration of governmental cabinets first to the number of parties and then to the number of seats in the electoral district and the entire representative assembly.

The overall format in physics is a network of interlocking equations (cf. Chapter 5). Each equation has few variables and constants, but the same ones may recur in many equations. (This is the underpinning of dimensional analysis, briefly discussed in the Appendix to Chapter 13.) Are such networks inherently impossible in social sciences? Or have none been found because social scientists have no urge to look for them and the nontransitive nature of regression equations makes it hard? The shortest proof that such networks are possible in social sciences is to present one, albeit with some reservations.

From Assembly Size and District Magnitude to Mean Duration of Cabinets

If a democratic political system had to be characterized by a single number, it would be the number of parties in the representative assembly, best expressed by the effective number of parties (N) as defined in Chapter 4. Among the many political and even socioeconomic features that it affects, the mean duration of government cabinets (C) clearly matters, because it influences the time span over which policies are implemented in a consistent way. The larger the number of parties, the shakier the cabinets tend to be.

The number of parties, in turn, depends on two institutional factors: assembly size and electoral district magnitude. The magnitude (M) of an electoral district is the number of seats allocated in it. It can range from 1 (single-seat districts) to the number of seats (S) in the entire representative assembly. A larger district magnitude enables more parties to win seats. At given magnitude, a larger assembly offers more parties a chance to be represented.

During the last quarter-century, a chain of logical models has been established to connect cabinet duration to the effective number of parties and the latter to assembly size and electoral district magnitude. Assembly size itself depends on population (P). The dominant causal pattern acts through two intervening variables. The first is the number of seat-winning parties (N_0), that is, the number of parties that have at least one seat in the assembly. It is the largest number by which the party system in the assembly could be characterized. The second intervening variable is the fractional seat share of the largest party (s_1). It can be shown that the inverse of s_1, designated as N_∞, is the smallest number by which the party system could be characterized. The effective number is always in between: $N_\infty \leq N \leq N_0$. The main causal chain is shown in Figure 10.1. Note similarities and differences with the typical sequences in physics (Figures 5.1 and 5.2).

The logical models and empirical evidence for each stage are presented in detail in *Predicting Party Sizes: The Logic of Simple Electoral Systems* (Taagepera 2007c). The present overview gives the equations without proof, indicating only the type of model used. Boundary conditions enter repeatedly.

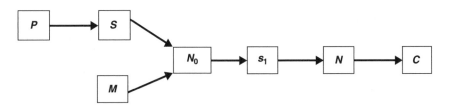

Figure 10.1. The main causal sequence leading from population, assembly size, and district magnitude to mean duration of cabinets

In a single district with M seats, at least one and at most M parties can win seats: $1 \leq p \leq M$. In line with the reasoning in Chapter 9, the geometric mean of these extremes is the most likely number of parties (subject to certain conditions): $p = M^{1/2}$. For the number of seat-winning parties in the entire assembly, assembly size imposes another set of limits: $1 \leq N_0 \leq S$. Combination with district level limitations leads to

$$N_0 = (MS)^{1/4}.$$

If so, then $N_0/(MS)^{1/4} = 1.00$ is expected, on the average, in the absence of any other information. The observed median is 1.15 for 16 single-seat systems and 1.12 for 14 simple multi-seat systems (Taagepera 2007c: 117).

The number of seat-winning parties restrains the largest party's fractional share to the range between the mean share and all the seats: $1/N_0 \leq s_1 < 1$. The likeliest share is the geometric mean of the limits: $s_1 = N_0^{-1/2}$. If so, then $s_1 N_0^{1/2} = 1.00$ is expected, on the average, in the absence of any other information. The actual median is 0.985, for 604 elections in 24 countries (Taagepera 2007c: 123). The $N_0 = (MS)^{1/4}$ above then leads to

$$s_1 = (MS)^{-1/8}.$$

If so, then $s_1(MS)^{1/8} = 1.00$ is expected, on the average, in the absence of any other information. The actual geometric mean is 0.985 for 30 single-seat systems and 1.068 for 16 multi-seat systems (Taagepera 2007c: 125, 128).

The effective number of parties, in turn, is constrained by the largest share. The logical limits are somewhat complex, but their geometric mean can be approximated as $N = s_1^{-4/3}$. It follows from previous $s_1 = (MS)^{-1/8}$ that

$$N = (MS)^{1/6}.$$

If so, then $N/(MS)^{1/6} = 1.00$ is expected, on the average, in the absence of any other information. The actual geometric mean is 1.036 for 14 single-seat systems and 0.953 for 11 multi-seat systems (Taagepera 2007c: 153).

Graphs showing these relationships are given in Taagepera (2007c: 118, 123, 126, and 129). Let us restate the overall pattern without using equations. The "seat product" MS imposes constraints on the largest conceivable number by which the party system could be characterized. The latter, in turn, imposes constraints on the smallest conceivable number by

Table 10.1. Logical connections (and R^2 of logarithms) between characteristics of party systems (Taagepera 2007c: 129, 153, 171)

	Seat product, MS	Seat-winning parties, N_0	Inverse of largest share, $N_\infty = 1/s_1$	Effective number (N)
Seat-winning parties	$N_0 = (MS)^{1/4}$	—		
Inverse of largest share ($1/s_1$)	$N_\infty = (MS)^{1/8}$ (0.51)	$N_\infty = N_0^{1/2}$	—	
Effective number	$N = (MS)^{1/6}$ (0.51)	$N = N_0^{2/3}$	$N = N_\infty^{4/3}$	—
Cabinet duration (years)	$C = 42/(MS)^{1/3}$ (0.24)	$C = 42/N_0^{4/3}$	$C = 42/N_\infty^{2/3}$ (0.35)	$C = 42/N^2$ (0.77)

which the party system could be characterized. Finally, the latter imposes constraints on the intermediary effective number. The chain ranging from MS to N involves no empirically determined constants. Hence, all later variables in the deductive chain can be directly connected to the seat product.

The logical models are quite different for connections to total population at the one end of the chain and to cabinet duration at the other. Both models consider the number of communication channels. As explained in next chapter, the outcomes are the *cube root law of assembly sizes*, $S = P^{1/3}$, and the *inverse square law of cabinet duration*, $C = k/N^2$, where the constant k is empirically determined as $k = 42$ years.

The way N is connected to seat product MS suggests an inverse cube root relationship between mean cabinet duration and the seat product (in years): $C = 42/(MS)^{1/3}$. While the number of parties cannot be prescribed by law, the seat product can. Thus, the latter equation makes institutional design possible, at least in principle.

The equations in the first column of Table 10.1 connect all output variables to MS. The top entries in each column show the connections between the successive variables in the deductive chain. Further down, the table shows the equations between ever more distant variables.

These relationships are multiplicative. Hence, linear correlation analysis must be carried out on the logarithms of the variables. In parentheses, Table 10.1 shows some resulting values of R^2. As the development of models proceeded, testing was carried out on somewhat different data collections, and not all links have been subjected to separate correlation analysis. Nonetheless, the main pattern is apparent: The values of R^2 tend to decrease as the logical distance between the variables increases, so that more random fluctuation enters.

Why the Role of Assembly Size Can Emerge
only from Logical Modeling

In this sequence of models, the role of assembly size highlights the limitations of regression in detecting truly significant factors. With the marked exception of Lijphart (1994), students of electoral systems have largely neglected assembly size. It may come as a surprise, therefore, that it features in the seat product at an equal level with district magnitude, the impact of which has long been recognized. The difference lies in their respective ranges. Because M ranges from 1 to several hundreds, its effect emerges with clarity from linear regression (especially when log M is used, as many political scientists do, because of its wide range). In contrast, S ranges only from 60 to 650 for countries above 1 million people. Therefore, its impact cannot emerge from raw regression over such a short range, as random fluctuation overshadows the systematic effect.

Only when logical model building suggests that assembly size *should* matter, is there motivation to look for special situations where the model could be tested. First, one is motivated to extend the range of S, by digging up data for oft-neglected tiny island countries, with parliaments as small as $S = 10$ for St. Kitts. Second, the study could be restricted to the relatively numerous single-seat systems, where the competing impact of M is eliminated and the model is simplified. I will focus on $s_1 = (MS)^{-1/8}$, which becomes $s_1 = S^{-1/8}$. We cannot run most sociopolitical relations under laboratory conditions. This makes it even more advisable to select data and try to extend their range in the light of logical thinking. This issue is revisited in Chapter 14.

Under such better controlled conditions, does the impact of assembly size on the largest seat share emerge? If it were merely a descriptive data fit, success would be considered modest, as the scatter around the best linear fit (log s_1 vs. log S) remains large: $R^2 = .26$ (Taagepera and Ensch 2006; Taagepera 2007c: 126). But it is not just a data fit. A prediction was made on logical grounds: $s_1 = 1.00S^{-0.125}$. How well is this prediction confirmed? The best linear fit of logarithms corresponds to $s_1 = 0.915S^{-0.108}$. On a log–log graph (Taagepera 2007c: 126), this line is almost indistinguishable from the predicted. The predicted line yields $R^2 = .245$—hardly less than the $R^2 = .256$ for the best statistical fit.

It comes as no surprise that many other factors and random fluctuation also affect the largest share, so that R^2 is low. The point is that the average impact of assembly size is predicted extremely closely. This is another example where the logical model is strongly confirmed even while R^2 is low (cf. Chapter 4, "Can Data with Low R^2 Confirm a Model?").

Causal Direction and Complex Systems

Under usual circumstances, institutional structure is a given (assembly size and district magnitude). It exerts pressure on party system and mean cabinet duration to conform to these constraints. During introduction of democracy, however, the existing party constellation largely determines which district magnitude is chosen, so as to preserve the party constellation. Even later, if factors external to the party system happen to produce undesirable outcomes, such as a sequence of unusually short-lived cabinets, then the electoral system may be altered. Hence, causality is two-directional in an asymmetric way vaguely reminiscent of punctuated equilibrium in biological evolution. Gradual adjustment of party system to electoral system over long periods may be interrupted by rather sudden adjustment of electoral system to party system.

The sequence of models presented applies directly only to simple electoral systems where all seats are allocated in separate districts, using standard proportional representation formulas or "first-past-the-post." Actually, some seats are often allocated outside the basic districts, or high legal thresholds are applied, so that district magnitude cannot be unambiguously specified. Exclusion of such more complex electoral systems is of little concern when establishing the basic pattern. Feathers in the wind are special cases where factors besides gravity enter. Similarly, complex electoral systems add further factors to the basic institutional variables, the effect of which must be established first.

Is It an Interlocking Network?

The rather unusual format of most steps in the sequence should give us concern. No empirically adjustable constants or lateral variables enter as we proceed from MS to N. Instead of a spreading network of equations, or a chain that introduces a new factor or constant at each link (cf. Figures 5.1 and 5.2), a single long chain extends from seat product to mean duration of cabinet. Such pattern is unusual in physics.

The typical equation in an interlocking network combines one or a few separate input variables with an empirically determined constant.

Recall Figures 5.1 and 5.2, and the constants R and G in laws of ideal gas $P = RT/V$ and gravity $F = GmM/r^2$. In the present chain, only $C = k/N^2$ follows this format. Elsewhere, the seat product is a single block that merely takes different exponents. The cube root law of assembly sizes ($S = P^{1/3}$) also lacks an empirically determined constant. It would seem that here we have, in a sociopolitical context, even more rigidly determined interactions than are usual in physics. How come?

Part of the answer is that here we deal with counting units that have no physical dimensions, such as length and time. Whenever physical dimensions enter, an empirically determined constant is needed to make the connection dimensionally sound (see elaboration in the Appendix to Chapter 13). Among our electoral variables, only cabinet duration has the physical dimension of time. Given that $1/N^2$ is a pure number, a constant k, with dimensions of time, is needed to make the equation $C = k/N^2$ dimensionally consistent. Its numerical value depends on units chosen: $k = 42$ when dealing in years but $k = 500$ when dealing in months.

Time or length intervals have no natural unit (unless some such unit develops at quantum level). In contrast, population and seats do have a natural counting unit: one person or one seat. In this sense, they belong to a special subclass of ratio quantities: In addition to a natural zero, they also have a natural "one." This feature explains why relationships devoid of a constant *can* exist among such quantities. It does not say, however, that all relationships between quantities with counting units *must* lack constants.

The dearth of constants in the chain described is related to its one-dimensional nature. The constant k in $C = k/N^2$ could conceivably recur in other contexts. If so, then lateral connections could be opened. Without such constants, lateral connections are less likely. Predictive models often predict only a mathematical format, a functional relationship, leaving parameters to be determined empirically (cf. end of Chapter 8). For establishing linkages, this feature is rather an advantage that we miss in the present case.

To show that interlocking networks of equations can occur in social sciences, it would be more convincing to present a multidimensional pattern of interactions rather than a single long chain of logical models. Still, such a chain is much better than nothing. Each individual link in the chain is logically grounded and can be separately tested empirically. Regardless of the one-dimensional configuration of the network, its linkages still reflect a basic feature of the usual pattern in physics.

All Predictive Models are not "Substantive"

When given a bag of green peas, I can predict with fair confidence that their weights are distributed lognormally—and roughly normally, when the largest peas are no larger than twice the smallest. This prediction is based on nothing "substantive" in a biological sense. It does not look into some biological process by which peas "coordinate" their weights so as to collectively oblige the lognormal equation. The prediction is soundly based nonetheless. Note that it deals only with the mathematical format. To predict the mean weight of peas and the standard deviation is another matter.

The exponential model of volatility in Chapter 4 is only faintly more substantive, in terms of social processes. The only arguably political substance enters when claiming that volatility is bound to be 0 when only one party runs. The upper limit of 100% is not substantive, for it applies to any values expressed as percentages of a maximum. The tendency of dV/dN to be proportional to the distance from a conceptual ceiling on V is not specifically social either. The model does not look into any process by which voters "coordinate" their shifts among parties so as to collectively oblige the model. This model still offers a theoretical basis for prediction.

This is why I prefer to talk of "quantitatively predictive logical models" rather than "substantive models" like Sørensen (1998) and Hedström (2004) do. Specifically social substance does enter some predictive models, but oftentimes these models depend on much broader conceptual notions—like anchor points, ceilings, and continuity. Such models certainly qualify as "theoretical," given that the predicted functional form is not empirically determined.

When features like anchor points suffice, insistence on substantive explanation in a narrowly social sense is as sterile as looking for a biological explanation for the size distribution of peas. It becomes especially sterile when coupled with the suggestion that, since the predictive model is not substantive anyway, one might just as well disregard it and throw all conceivable factors into a multiple regression. This would make it worse, because regression analysis is the least substantive approach conceivable. Using the example of factors that correlate with individual earnings, Sørensen (1998) has called it the "gas station" approach to theorizing:

This model, in fact, proposes a theory where each person receives x dollars from education, y dollars from family background, q dollars from gender, and z dollars from class. All of it adds up to the persons' yearly earnings. We can imagine people walking around pumps in a large gas station, getting something from each of the pumps. (Sørensen 1998: 248, via Hedström 2004)

I do not know whether Sørensen would be satisfied with the causal substance in the models presented in this book. But these models certainly make predictions on general, nonempirical grounds, in quantitative detail that can be contradicted by data.

Conclusions

Can interlocking networks of equations occur in social sciences? The example given here indicates that they may, on the basis of logical models. (Chapter 12 will show that such networks are impossible on the basis of usual regression approaches.) An important implication is that informed social intervention is possible. We know more than just the direction of the effect. We can estimate how much change in M is likely to induce a desired degree of change in C, on the average.

The sequence of models presented has the shortcoming of being a one-dimensional chain. Following up on the previous analogy with European and African railroads (Chapter 5), this sequence still looks like a single track. It penetrates much deeper into hinterland but still does not establish any side connections. Nonetheless, this sequence of models exhibits many other features of an interlocking network. At the level of descriptive analysis, variables like population and number of parties have been found to be statistically significant for numerous other outputs. To the extent that quantitatively predictive logical models can be constructed for these relationships, a multi-dimensional network of connections may develop.

At the present stage, it may be seen as wishful thinking. But let us also consider wishful thinking in the opposite direction—asserting that interlocking networks of logical models, as found in physics, cannot possibly develop in social sciences. The sequence presented here should make it pretty hard to hold on to such an article of faith.

11

Beyond Constraint-Based Models: Communication Channels and Growth Rates

---

- The number of communication channels may well turn out to be a major building block in constructing quantitatively predictive logical models in social sciences. It does determine representative assembly sizes and mean durations of cabinets.
- Some physical and social processes involve minimization or maximization of some quantities.
- Models for various processes can be formulated as differential equations, especially those that express rates of change in time, space, etc.
- The related notions of entropy and information have applications in social sciences.
- Some quantities are conserved during changes. We should try to determine them.
- Avoidance of logical inconsistencies may impose a unique expression for some social processes.

Among the multiplicity of ways to build quantitatively predictive logical models, this book has up to now focused on boundary constraints and anchor points as starting points for "ignorance-based models." This was prominent in the Sherlock Holmes principle (Chapter 3) and the introductory example of electoral volatility (Chapter 4). The approach was systematized later on (Chapter 8) and had implications for the use of geometric means (Chapter 9). Most models in the sequence presented in Chapter 10 use this approach.

This approach to model building is relatively simple mathematically and enters frequently, at least as a reality check. So it was worth introducing it in some detail. However, by now I run the risk of being pigeon-holed as another one-method person. Am I as much addicted to constraint-based solutions as some others are addicted to linear regression? It is time to point out briefly some other approaches I have used. The topics range from economics (trade/GNP ratios) to history (number of separate polities). This smorgasbord by no means covers the entire range of what is possible, but it extends the menu. Each social phenomenon has to be approached on its own.

The Number of Communication Channels

Society consists of individuals that interact. Hence the number of communication channels could be expected to be one of the most important factors in social sciences. On the micro level, individuals who dispose of more communication channels toward others tend to have more influence and power. Whom one knows matters. On the macro level, the number of communication channels is central to the aforementioned inverse square law of cabinet duration and cube root law of assembly sizes (Chapter 10), as will be shown shortly.

When a family has two children, the parents may have to adjudicate 1 potential conflict channel between them. With the advent of a third child, this number explodes to 3. I bear witness that this is so, indeed! Thus the number of communication channels (c) among n actors matters. The general formula is

$$c = \frac{n(n-1)}{2}.$$

Indeed, each of the n actors connects to each of the remaining $n-1$. This makes for $n(n-1)$ channels. But each channel has been double counted, approaching it from both ends. Hence we must divide by 2. It is easy to check that the formula agrees with the inter-child channels.

This formula may well turn out to be a major building block in constructing quantitatively predictive logical models in social sciences. For large n, it simplifies into $c \approx n^2/2$. Under some circumstances, we may have to distinguish between one-way and two-way channels, etc., introducing slight but important modifications.

Inverse Square Law of Cabinet Duration

When a representative assembly has n roughly equal-sized parties, the number of potential conflict channels among them is $c = n(n-1)/2$. Cabinets break down because of conflicts. The simplest assumption is that doubling the number of conflict channels cuts the duration of cabinets into half. The simplification $c = n^2/2$ can be used even when the number of parties is small, because intra-party conflicts also enter. It leads to an inverse square relationship between the mean duration of cabinets (C) and the number of parties. When the total number of parties is replaced by their effective number (N), the outcome is

$$C = \frac{k}{N^2}.$$

The constant k is empirically determined, like constant G is in the law of gravitation. Indeed, the law itself looks somewhat akin to the law of gravitation in form, but the reasons are quite different and no analogy should be sought.

For 35 polities analyzed in Lijphart (1999), the best linear fit to $\log C = \log k - 2\log N$ is obtained with $k = 42$ years, which is in the ballpark of the maximum length of a political career (Taagepera and Sikk 2007; Taagepera 2007c: 165–75). The predictive model

$$C = \frac{42\,\text{years}}{N^2}$$

is theoretical regarding the functional shape and empirical regarding the constant. The OLS regression line of $\log C$ versus $\log N$ corresponds to $C = 31.3\,\text{yrs}/N^{1.757}$. While the empirical slope 1.757 may look appreciably shallower than the predicted 2.00, the predicted slope accounts for almost as much variation, with $R^2 = .77$ as compared to $R^2 = .79$ for the best fit. As social sciences go, this is a high correlation. The corresponding graphs are shown in Taagepera (2007c: 165–75).

One might expect an even better agreement when the total number of parties is replaced by the number of parties within the cabinet itself, but surprisingly, the fit worsens appreciably. An important implication is that the pull from outside the cabinet matters as much as internal conflicts. Two broader issues are discussed in later chapters. First, is the actual exponent really lower than 2.00? Chapter 12 shows it may be an artifact of standard OLS regression—and this has wider ramifications. Second, several ways have been proposed to measure the duration of cabinets and the number of parties (when some are large and some are small). Have we been cheating by picking a particular combination of indices? Chapter 13 addresses this issue, and again wider implications emerge.

Cube Root Law of Assembly Sizes

A major reason for having representative assemblies is to reduce to a manageable level the number of communication channels involved in decision-making. Even in a small country of 1 million people, the total number of communication channels among them approaches a trillion (10^{12}). The use of a representative assembly carves out two much smaller subsets of channels: those in the assembly and those from representative to constituents. For a given politically active population (P_a), which assembly size (S) would minimize the total work load *on one particular representative*? As a first approximation, we may assume that this work load is proportional to the number (n) of relevant communication channels. With a very small assembly, the representative would have a low number of assembly channels but a huge number of constituency channels. With a very large assembly, the reverse would be the case.

It is a matter of setting up the function $n = f(S)$ and applying differential calculus to determine the value of S that minimizes n, for a given population P_a. Each representative has $(P_a/S) - 1$ constituency channels making demands on her or him. She or he has also $S - 1$ channels to the other members. At first glance, this $S - 1$ may seem the total number of assembly channels making demands on her or him. The resulting assembly size that minimizes n would be approximately $S = P_a^{1/2}$, an unrealistic size. Even a country of 1 million people would have an assembly of 1,000 members! Something must be missing. On closer thought, representatives do not just talk and listen to other representatives. They also need to "listen in" when other representatives interact. There are $(S - 1)(S - 2)/2$ such interactions that a representative needs to monitor. With this addition, the work load is minimized when

$$S = (2P_a)^{1/3}.$$

The details of model and testing are given in Taagepera (2007c: 189–90, 198–200) and in more detail in Taagepera and Shugart (1989: 173–83).

What is a politically active population? One may consider voters or the entire adult population, but the degree of literacy is also found to affect assembly size. A fair fit is obtained when P_a is operationalized as literate working age population. For countries with reasonably high literacy, P_a is fairly close to one-half of total population (P). Hence the simple approximation

$$S = P^{1/3}.$$

Minimizing or Maximizing a Function

Minimizing a mathematical function is a widespread method in physics. We also practice it in everyday life. How do we behave when walking over a meadow and encountering a plowed stretch? If it is easy to walk on, we will continue in an almost straight line, but if it is awfully muddy and time-consuming, we would try to cross at almost right angle to the plowed zone. This is so because we subconsciously try to minimize the total time the trip takes.

This is how light travels through a window pane. When it hits at an angle, it passes through glass at a lesser angle, and then continues through air at the original angle. It does so because its speed is lower in glass than in air, and light behaves *as if* it chose the angle that minimizes the total travel time. It does not "choose," of course, but it effectively behaves as if it did. Physics has equations to calculate the precise shift.

This is an example of how unanimated nature tends to act to minimize or maximize certain features. (I will not go into the reasons.) The same is observed with humans in the case of assembly size. Populations that start with relatively small assemblies often increase them within a few decades to fit the cube root of their population. This was the case for the United States from 1790 on (Taagepera and Shugart 1989: 175) and for the European Parliament in 1964–2004 (Taagepera 2007c: 260). Countries have not been aware of the underlying minimizing principle, any more than light is while crossing a window pane. Yet by trial and error countries gravitate toward the cube root law.

Minimization or maximization of some quantity y as an input x varies means devising the function $y = f(x)$ and then looking for the value of x at which $y = f(x)$ neither decreases nor increases, that is, the slope is zero. This is done by calculating the derivative dy/dx and then finding the value of x for which $dy/dx = 0$. Note that the existence of a minimum or maximum implies that these functions are nonlinear—as most relationships are (cf. Chapter 8). Kochen and Deutsch (1969) used this approach for optimal decentralization, offering a model for the number of warehouses that minimizes the combination of storage and delivery costs. Unfortunately, it seems not to have been tested empirically. Many opportunities to use this approach in social sciences may have been missed by researchers being unfamiliar not only with differential calculus (where help can be sought) but also with the very notion of minimization/maximization.

Rate Equations

Rather than try to express how things are interrelated macroscopically, it is often easier to construct models of how the outputs change when inputs are altered to a tiny degree. They have exceedingly different forms, depending on the specific issue.

Lanchester (1956) considered battle losses over short time intervals. Richardson (1960) studied arms races by setting up rates in time (dx/dt and dy/dt) for the arms budgets x and y of two countries:

$$dx/dt = ky - ax + g$$
$$dy/dt = lx - by + h.$$

What it says is that the other side's arms budget is seen as a threat that induces the country to increase its own arm budget (hence positive signs of k and l), while the already existing budget is a burden that induces the country to reduce it (hence negative signs in front of a and b). The constants g and h express the steady impact (positive or negative) of all sorts of other factors. Making $dx/dt = 0$ defines a stability line where the country with budget x feels no urge to change its existing arms budget, and similarly for $dy/dt = 0$.

It is hard to find suitable data to determine the numerous constants in such equations, before they can be used to predict the future course of arms races. Arms races just do not maintain sufficiently stable conditions long enough. Even more serious, it is difficult to distinguish mutually induced arms races from arms build-ups through domestic self-stimulation. But the rate equation approach as such has been much too fruitful in physical sciences to be written off in social sciences. A few social science examples follow. Two involve change over time (number of polities and world population), while the third starts out with change over distance (trade/GNP ratio).

Effective Number of Polities over 5,000 Years

The effective number (N) of polities (separate political entities) has tended to decrease over millennia. The simplest model is constant relative rate (percent rate) of decrease over time (t):

$$\frac{(\mathrm{d}N/N)}{\mathrm{d}t} = -k,$$

where the rate constant k is to be determined empirically. This is another ignorance-based approach. When we have no idea of whether the relative rate $(\mathrm{d}N/N)/\mathrm{d}t$ increases or decreases as the number N changes, our best average guess is that it remains the same. In other words, rate of decrease in N is proportional to N itself: $\mathrm{d}N/\mathrm{d}t = -kN$. Integration leads to exponential decrease:

$$N = ae^{-kt},$$

where a is a constant that depends on initial conditions. The corresponding curve becomes a straight line when $\log N$ is graphed against t (cf. Chapter 8).

We could actually have obtained this result more quickly by using boundary conditions, as in Chapter 8. Given that $0 < N < +\infty$ and $-\infty < t < +\infty$, two quadrants are allowed, and the simplest allowed family of curves is $N = ae^{-kt}$. But it is worthwhile to point out the constant relative rate approach, when we do not know if this rate goes up or down.

The number of polities could be based on their areas (A) or populations (P), leading to different numbers and rate constants. These numbers (N_A and N_P, respectively) can be predicted to be interrelated as

$$N_P = N_A^{1/2},$$

for the following reason. Large polities that most affect the effective number tend to form in the most densely populated areas. Hence the population-based number of polities can be expected to be lower than the area-based number of polities: $N_P \leq N_A$. For any given N_A, the lowest limit on N_P is 1. This would be the case if almost the entire world population were concentrated on a single state in a single fertile valley. (Nile valley 4,000 years ago came close.) Therefore, $1 \leq N_P \leq N_A$. In the absence of any other information, our best guess for N_P is the geometric mean of the extremes. The resulting square root relationship satisfies a conceptual anchor point: if $N_A = 1$, then also $N_P = 1$. If $N_P = N_A^{1/2}$, then we must have $k_P = k_A/2$ and $a_P = a_A^{1/2}$ in the exponential decrease equations $N = ae^{-kt}$.

145

The actual best fit lines (logN vs. t in centuries BC/AD) correspond to (Taagepera 1997)

$$N_A = 1300e^{-0.19t}(R^2 = 0.90)$$
$$N_P = 31e^{-0.08t}(R^2 = 0.68).$$

Here $0.19/2 = 0.085$ is indeed close to 0.08, and $1300^{1/2} = 36$ is fairly close to 31. These equations indicate the following average trend, over the last 5,000 years. The effective number of polities has been reduced by one-half every 3.6 centuries on the basis of area and every 8.7 centuries on the basis of population.

The width of the random fluctuation zones around these averages suggest that a single world state has a nil probability prior to 2600 AD, while a bipolar world ($N_A = 2.0$) could briefly occur by 2200 AD. Compared to the average secular trend, our present world is slightly overconcentrated regarding areas, but not regarding populations. This bodes ill for some of the largest sparsely populated polities: They may split up. All extrapolation is speculative of course, until we can logically explain why the halving times are around four and nine centuries. Still, when guessing at when "history will end," the best we can do is look at all the history we have got and extrapolate, very skeptically.

World Population Growth

Up to 1970, world population growth was faster than would be predicted by the exponential model $dP/dt = kP$. It is as if the rate "constant" k itself increased over time, during the last 20 centuries, or even the last million years. This growth could be modeled in terms of interaction between population (P) and technology (T). Both grow basically exponentially, but the rate "constants" depend on the other factor:

$$dP/dt = (kT^m)P$$
$$dT/dt = (hP^n)T.$$

Integration yields a quasi-hyperbolic equation:

$$P = A/(D - t)^M.$$

Here A, M, and D are constants. A fair fit with the widely disparate estimates of world population from −4,000 to +1970 was obtained (Taagepera

1976a) with

$$P = \frac{50 \text{ billion}}{(2005 - t)^{0.74}}.$$

Adding saturation effects, one could postpone the "doomsday," D, where the population would approach infinity (Taagepera 1979). The corresponding empirical constants could not be estimated until the slowdown in growth actually set on, in the 1970s. By now, this can be done, to some extent. The shift away from quasi-hyperbolic growth has been quite sudden, reflecting a sharp onset of depletion of resources (including water and space). Recent growth fits the simple logistic model (cf. Chapter 8)

$$\frac{dP}{dt} = k(1 - P/C)P,$$

where the ceiling (C) is the maximum sustainable size. It is still difficult to estimate the numerical value of C. Progress is being made toward fitting the hyperbolic and logistic parts of growth into a single model.

Trade/GNP Ratio

How is a country's trade related to its size? Consider the extreme cases. If a country occupied the entire world, its foreign trade would be zero: Imports/GNP = Exports/GNP = 0. On the other hand, if a country consisted of a single family, all their monetary transactions would be foreign trade, so that Imports/GNP = Exports/GNP = 1. In the actual intermediary cases one would hence expect trade/GNP to decrease with increasing country size. The same conclusion can be reached in a different way. If two countries join, their reciprocal trade would stop being international, so that the combined trade/GNP decreases.

To build a model, one can start with the differential equation used in physics for absorption of any flux of particles emanating from a point source in homogenous surroundings. The change in flow intensity (I) with distance (r) from the source is proportional to I itself:

$$\frac{dI}{dr} = -kI,$$

where k is the absorption constant of the surrounding matter. Consider the goods produced by factories as such a flux, absorbed by customers. Whatever flow continues beyond a country's border is export. The larger the country, the more goods are absorbed before reaching the border. The

Export/GNP ratio results from integrating the absorption of production by sources spread all across the country. A number of simplifying assumptions enter and only an approximate solution is possible (Taagepera 1976*b*). As measure of country size, a shift from geographical area to population improves results, as one might expect, given that customers absorb goods, not square kilometers.

Within the population range of actual countries, the following rough approximations to the model were found to fit (Taagepera and Hayes 1977):

$$\text{Imports/GNP} = 40/P^{1/3}(R^2 = .69)$$
$$\text{Exports/GNP} = 30/P^{1/3}(R^2 > .5).$$

Imports exceed exports in most countries, with the difference paid for in services, export of labor, etc. The combined equation for trade applied within a factor of 2 in 92% of the cases:

$$\frac{\text{Trade}}{\text{GNP}} = \frac{70}{P^{1/3}}.$$

This is the fractional ratio when P is the number of people. When population is entered in millions of people, the result is in percent. These approximations would not apply to very small or very large populations.

What is this model good for? It helps us to evaluate whether a country's trade is out of line with its size. China's low trade/GNP ratio in the 1970s was often interpreted as isolation, while in reality it largely expressed its large population. Of course, countries with different production profiles have different trade profiles. With about the same population, Saudi Arabian oil travels further than Romania's more diversified products. In fact, the model allows us to estimate a "characteristic absorption number"—the number of people a country's flow of goods encounters before it is reduced to $1/e = 0.37$ of its original intensity.

Avoidance of Logical Inconsistencies: The Law of Minority Attrition

A social process may be such that only one mathematical form can express it without running into logical inconsistencies. Compared to constraints imposed by anchor points and forbidden areas, avoidance of various other inconsistencies is a somewhat different application of the Sherlock

Holmes principle (Chapter 3): Eliminate the impossible, and only one outcome may remain. The law of minority attrition is one example.

If women are in minority at some lower echelon where positions are numerous, they tend to be an even smaller minority at higher echelons where positions are fewer. This sequential attrition applies to various sorts of minorities (Taagepera 2007c: 201–23). Minor parties in first-past-the-post elections may get a fair percentage of votes but a much lower percentage of seats. It goes beyond social selection processes. In volleyball, the total share of points won by the loosing team tends to exceed its share of games won.

In all such cases, the expected average outcome is expressed by the *law of minority attrition*, which also implies boosting the share of the larger components. In terms of seat and vote shares of parties A and B in a first-past-the-post system, it is

$$\frac{s_A}{s_B} = \left(\frac{v_A}{v_B}\right)^n,$$

with

$$n = \frac{\log V}{\log S},$$

where V is the total number of votes cast and S is the total number of seats available. This exponent n increases as the number of seats decreases, which accentuates minority attrition. For a pure two-party constellation, exponent n is actually the same as constant k in Figure 8.3.

For calculations of seat shares, it is more practical to replace the first equation by the following equivalent, where the summation is over all parties that receive votes:

$$s_A = \frac{v_A^n}{\sum v_i^k},$$

For degree of agreement with women's shares, party shares, and volleyball scores, see Taagepera (2007c: 208–13, 221–3). The law predicts that if women's share in the US House ($S = 435$) is about 5%, it would drop to about 2% in the US Senate ($S = 100$). This was the case in the early 1980s.

The derivation of the attrition law is based on avoidance of logical inconsistencies (Taagepera 2007c: 216–19). When more than two components (e.g., parties) are involved, $s_A/s_B = (v_A/v_B)^n$ is the only relationship between s_A/s_B and v_A/v_B that avoids inconsistency. With more than two stages (e.g., voters, electoral college, and final assembly), $n = f(V)/f(S)$ is the only relationship between n, V, and S that avoids inconsistency. The proof that $\log V$ is the only acceptable form of $f(V)$ follows similar lines.

A special aspect of minority attrition law is allocation of seats to member states in organizations like the Parliament of the European Union. Here two principles clash: representation proportional to population and equal representation of all member states. The compromise depends on the assembly size (S) as compared to the number of members (N) and total population (P). Conceptual extreme cases $S = 1$, $S = N$, and $S = P$ lead to (Taagepera and Hosli 2006; Taagepera 2007c: 255–68)

$$S_A = \frac{P_A^n}{\sum_i P_i^k}$$

where

$$n = \frac{(1/\log S - 1/\log N)}{(\log 1/P - 1/\log N)}.$$

If $S = 1$, the single seat goes to the largest member; if $S = N$, each member gets one seat; and the more S approaches P, the more representation proportional to population is approached. From the very beginning up to the Treaty of Nice, this pattern was followed by seats in the European Parliament (with n ranging from 0.67 to 0.72) and by voting weights in the Council of the European Union (with n ranging from 0.41 to 0.52). Instead of minority attrition, here we have minority enhancement, because "a member is a member."

The City–Country Rule: The Number of Components and the Number of Items in the Top Component

If the reader has a fair number of publications in scholarly journals, she or he may wish to carry out the following test. Count all the scholarly journals in which you have published. Also count your articles in the journal in which you have published most. Are these two numbers fairly equal? Now multiply either of these numbers by its natural logarithm. How close do you get to your total number of publications?

For large numbers, it tends to come close. Chapter bibliographies in *Political Science: The State of the Discipline II* (Finifter 1993) cite 281 journals at least once, and the most-cited journal is cited 317 times. The total citations are 1,834, while $281(\ln 281) = 1,584$ and $317(\ln 317) = 1,826$.

The underlying reason is the well-known *rank-size rule*, first observed for city populations (P) and ranks (r) in a country. The size (P_r) of the

rth ranked component tends to be the size of the largest component (P_1) divided by the rank:

$$P_r = \frac{P_1}{r}.$$

This rule fits the rankings of many quantities, but far from all, and the underlying reasons remain unclear. For the last component by size (rank L) it means $P_L = P_1/L$. Suppose this last component consists of one natural unit (one person, one citation), so that $P_L = 1$. Then $1 = P_1/L$ implies that the rank of the last component equals the size of the largest component: $L = P_1$. This is why the number of journals in which you have published may equal the number published in the top journal.

Total population (P) results from summation $P = \Sigma P_r = \Sigma P_1/r$ over all components, from 1 to L. It can be approximated by integration, leading to

$$P = P_1 \ln P_1 = L \ln L.$$

This also means that total population can in principle be estimated from the population of any component of known rank:

$$P = rP_r \ln(rP_r),$$

but the error can be large in practice.

In the geographical context, this relationship was called the city–country rule (Taagepera and Kaskla 2001), as it connects the country's population to the population of its cities. An important consequence is that we can reverse the equation and use the population of the country to predict the populations of all cities (or the distribution of your articles among journals). We can thus quickly tell whether the actual city populations are large or small, compared to this comparison base. Empirically, the largest city in the country tends to exceed the expectations—the so-called primacy effect.

This relationship may be of use in other social contexts that involve ranking of components by their size. We would, however, stand on firmer ground if we could understand the reason for the occurrence of the rank-size rule. Only then can we predict under which conditions it can be expected to occur. A partial explanation in terms of an ignorance-based model exists (Taagepera 2002).

Conserved Quantities

The notion of conservation covers broad grounds. It expresses the notion that nothing vanishes or appears unexplainably. In accounting, the amount of cash in the box must agree with sums received and sums paid out. Physics has laws of conservation of energy, matter, momentum, electric charge, etc. These quantities remain constant during various processes. Now consider the law of minority attrition. It can be expressed as $(\log S) \log(s_A/s_B) = (\log V) \log(v_A/v_B)^n = c$. Here c is a quantity conserved during the attrition process.

In party sizes (Chapter 10), the expression $s_1 N_0^{1/2} = 1$ might be considered a sort of a conservation law: The value of this particular combination of the number of seat-winning parties and the share of the largest party tends to be conserved. The same applies to the product of rank and population of a city within a country: $rP_r = P_1$—this product is conserved as one goes to cities at different ranks. In accounting and physics, conservation may be considered absolute, while $s_1 N_0^{1/2} = 1$ and $rP_r = P_1$ express only the average tendency. This difference must be kept in mind, but it is no grounds for disregarding a useful notion.

Conclusions

No canned computer programs can exist for constructing quantitatively predictive logical models. Each social phenomenon has to be approached on its own. Still, some concepts and methods keep popping up in a variety of contexts. The broad principle of avoiding inconsistencies and impossibilities enters practically all the examples offered here, in obvious or hidden ways. It mostly remains unstated in natural sciences, because it is taken for granted. It is transmitted to students through oral interaction in laboratories and field work rather than textbooks and lectures. For social sciences, my experience indicates that it often has to be made explicit.

Some approaches represent simple logic cast in mathematical language, such as avoidance of logical inconsistencies. Some hark back to physics, such as the notion of conservation of certain quantities during transformations. Intensity of a flow is a concept common to movements of people, goods, water, and neutrons, and the same broad dispersal and absorption models apply to all of them. The interrelated notions of entropy and information can be powerful (Coleman 2004), even while no examples are presented in this book.

Minimizing or maximizing a quantity is widely used in physics. It is often also the goal of human activity. Optimal decentralization (Kochen and Deutsch 1969) and assembly size are examples. Mathematically, minimization involves differentiating a function, which brings us to the panoply of differential equations as bases or tools for model building.

Expressing the rates in time is a widespread approach. Here it has been applied to arms races, decrease in the number of polities, and world population growth. The equations differ, depending on the problem, but workhorses like exponential and simple logistic equations often enter as building blocks. Note that they emerged in Chapter 8 as the simplest responses to conceptually forbidden areas.

Rates need not be rates in time. For the trade/GNP ratio, the central issue is the rate of decrease of some flow intensity in an absorbing space. The distance from which a university draws its students has similarities. So have labor flows toward metropolises.

The number of communication channels is a more specifically social notion. It enters in expressing phenomena as diverse as sizes of representative assemblies and mean durations of cabinets. Many other social interactions must be affected by this number.

Regularities in ranking patterns pop up in quite different contexts. They seem to tell us something about the underlying processes. Yet we still have a poor handle on what they tell us.

12

Why We Should Shift to Symmetric Regression

- For scattered data, Ordinary Least-Squares (OLS) regression produces two quite distinct regression lines: one for y versus x and another for x versus y. Both may differ appreciably from what your eyes tell you. Together, they define a single value of R^2.
- The more data are scattered, the more the OLS regression line, y against x, takes on a shallower slope than what your eyes tell you. "The OLS regression line is not a trend line." It is a mixed measure of slope and scatter.
- If data are scattered, OLS regression of y against x will disconfirm a model that actually fits. Hence good statistics can be death of good science.
- The OLS lines cannot form a system of interlocking of models, because they are not unique, cannot be reversed, and lack transitivity.
- Scale-independent symmetric regression avoids these problems of OLS, by offering a single, reversible, and transitive equation. It is extended here to multivariable regression.
- Symmetric regression is still merely regression. When linear regression amounts to mechanical data crunching, it remains so even when symmetric regression is used.

Even when the variables are transformed so that a linear relationship can be expected, testing by linear regression is not as straightforward as it might seem. Several ways to regress exist, and the Ordinary Least Squares (OLS) falls short in a serious way.

An essential aspect of logical model building is that various models form an interlocking network, as was illustrated for electricity in Figure 5.2 and for electoral rules, parties, and cabinet duration in Figure 10.1. One could use the seat product MS to calculate the effective number of parties (N), and then use N to calculate the mean cabinet duration (C). Alternatively, one could calculate C directly from MS, and the result would be the same. This is so because the models are expressed in terms of algebraic equations that have the property of transitivity.

In contrast, *OLS regression equations lack transitivity.* The model proposes linear relationships between the logarithms of MS, N, and C. Yet, regressing $\log N$ on $\log(MS)$ and then regressing $\log C$ on $\log N$ would *not* give the same result as regressing $\log C$ directly on $\log(MS)$, whenever R^2 is not a perfect 1.00.

This property, known to statisticians but much less to social scientists, makes it impossible to build interlocking networks on the basis of OLS regression equations.

This chapter elaborates on this problem with OLS and some related ones. More important, it also offers a way out in the form of symmetric linear regression, which has transitivity. More specifically, it is scale-independent symmetric regression. It was called the "impartial line" by astrophysicist Gustaf Strömberg (1940) who may have been the first to use it, and is termed "reduced major axis" in von Eye and Schuster (1998: 219–25). I extend it to multivariable regression.

The Standard OLS Regression Line Is Not a Trend Line

Figure 12.1 illustrates the core of the problem with some survey data. It shows Estonian respondents' ratings of their country's legal system versus their ratings of the Parliament, on a 0 to 10 scale. One might expect that many who completely distrust one of these institutions might also completely distrust the other, and the same might go for complete trust. In other words, (0; 0) and (10; 10) could be proposed as conceptual anchor points. In the actual graph, (0; 0) is heavily populated indeed, and (10; 10) is more populated than the neighboring combinations. Visually, the best fitting curve is close to the diagonal, $y = x$, with slope 1. But when we proceed to test this hunch by standard OLS regression, we find that the OLS "best fit" line has a slope shallower than 1, misses the anchor points, and does not agree with our visual impression.

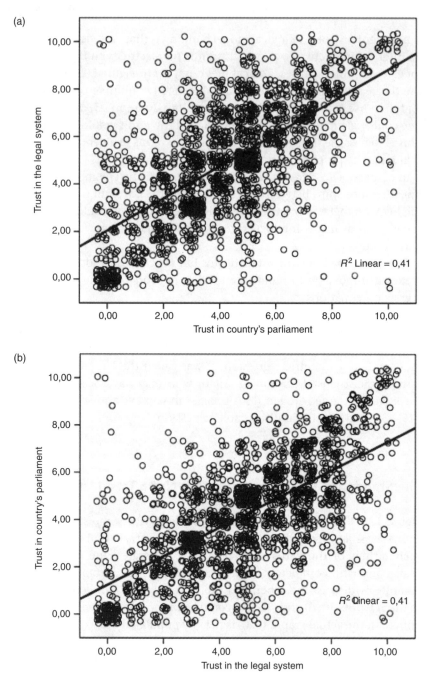

(a)

Trust in the legal system

R^2 Linear = 0,41

Trust in country's parliament

(b)

Trust in country's parliament

R^2 Linear = 0,41

Trust in the legal system

Figure 12.1. The OLS regression line underreports the expected slope, whichever way you graph the two variables (modified by Lühiste from Lühiste 2007)

The reader might recollect having noted such discrepancy when first introduced to regression and reluctantly becoming used to it when reassured that it is all right. Is it? "Don't trust your eyes" is risky advice. Claims of an optical illusion must be demonstrated, not just asserted. But even more is in store.

It would be as justified to graph the same data in the reverse direction, Parliament versus legal system, as shown in Figure 12.1b. Then one finds an OLS line that has a shallower slope than 1 on *that* graph—but that would mean a slope steeper than 1 when transposed on the previous graph! Whichever variable you take as y, the OLS slope is less steep than what your eyes tell you!

Why is it so? When $x = 0$, a few scattered points with positive y do occur, while no counterbalancing points with negative y can exist. This imbalance pushes the OLS line up at $x = 0$. The reverse happens at $x = 10$, so the regression slope becomes shallower than the visual best fit. Reverse the position of the variables, and OLS regression tilts in the opposite direction. Note that R^2 is the same for both graphs.

Standard OLS regressions of y on x and x on y yield different lines. This is so whenever correlation coefficient R^2 is less than a perfect 1.00. Neither line is what you might draw in as visual best fit line. As Peter Flanagan-Hyde (2006) puts it: "The least-squares regression line is not a trend line." This fact is well known to statisticians but much less so to social scientists, because most introductory statistics texts for social sciences do not highlight it, if they mention it at all. Welcome exceptions include Huck and Sandler (1984: 60–1), von Eye and Schuster (1998: 209–25), and Kennedy (1998: 141).

One of the few social science works where both regression lines are shown is *The Bell Curve* (Herrnstein and Murray 1994: 559–66). The example in their mathematical appendix deals with weight and height of people. It first shows weight regressed on height and presents it as "the best possible straight line passing through the cloud of points—the mathematically 'best' version of the line you just draw in by intuition" (1994: 562). Yet the very next page acknowledges that it is NOT the line you would draw in by intuition: *"Linear relationships don't always seem to fit very well* [their italics]. The best-fit line looks as if it is too shallow" (1994: 563).

To their credit, Herrnstein and Murray (1994: 565) later do show both regression lines. They argue that one line responds to "How much does weight increase with height?" while the other responds to "How much does height increase with weight?" This is not quite that simple when scatter is large, as will be shown later on, but it is good statistics for limited purposes. Yet, it presents momentous problems to science based on quantitatively predictive logical models, for the following reasons.

Why Good Statistics Can Be Death of Predictive Science

Suppose a logical model actually fits, but with appreciable random scatter. For given values of input variables, one can regress the actual output values (y_A) on those predicted by the model (y_M). The model is validated, if the best fit is $y_A = y_M$, meaning a line $y_A = a + by_M$ where the slope is $b = 1$ and the intercept is $a = 0$. Deviations from these values would indicate discrepancies between model and reality.

But should we regress y_A on y_M or, in the reverse direction, y_M on y_A? It should not matter, yet two different regression lines result. Regress the actual values y_A on model-predicted y_M, and you will find that the slope falls short of 1, meaning that y_A rises slower than y_M. The model seems disproved. Now regress y_M on y_A, and you will again find that the slope falls short of 1, but now it means that y_M rises slower than y_A! How can it be that y_A rises slower than y_M, which itself rises slower than y_A? (The intercepts also deviate from 0 in conflicting directions.) Either way, any logical model that actually fits is declared faulty by standard OLS regression, if scatter is large.

One does not have to regress expected values against the actual. The paradox arises whenever a linear relationship with a specified slope is expected. Consider two actual dilemmas from studies of party politics.

The first one comes from Chapter 11. Based on considerations of the number of communication channels, the predictive model $C = k/N^2$ connects the mean cabinet duration (C) with the effective number of parties (N). Taking the logarithms yields $\log C = \log 42 + 2 \log N$ when k is in years. This means a slope $s = 2.00$ is predicted. Empirically, the slope for regression of $\log C$ on $\log N$ is found to be only 1.76 (Taagepera and Sikk 2007), falling short of 2.00. The reverse regression $\log N$ on $\log C$ yields a slope corresponding to $1/s$. It is found to be 0.45; hence $s = 1/0.45 = 2.23$— which exceeds 2.00. Either way, $R^2 = .79$. Is the predicted slope 2.00 confirmed or disconfirmed? If disconfirmed, is it so because it is too low or too high?

Much earlier, Taagepera and Grofman (1985) proposed that "Parties minus issues equals one": $N - I = 1$, where N is again the effective number of legislative parties and I is the number of issue dimensions on which parties disagree. The logic behind this extremely simple model is the following. In the complete absence of issues ($I = 0$), there is no reason to expect more than a single catchall party. The model predicts that every new issue dimension tends to create one additional party of some significance. It works in the reverse direction too. When N parties exist for historical reasons, they tend to keep approximately $N - 1$ issue dimensions salient in inter-party debate so as to preserve minimal distinctions among themselves.

The corresponding data from Lijphart (1984) included 22 polities, with mean $I = 2.53$ and mean $N = 3.37$. Hence mean $(N - I) = 0.844$, just 16% short of the predicted 1.00. The prediction was

$$N = 1.00 + 1.00I. \quad \text{[logical model]}$$

Regressing N on I yielded

$$N = 1.264 + 0.834I. \quad [N \text{ on } I, \; R^2 = 0.56]$$

Here the slope 0.834 falls short of the predicted 1.00 (by 18%), while the constant 1.264 exceeds the predicted 1.00. However, Taagepera and Grofman (1985, note 4) also reported regressing I on N, with a result that would correspond, upon algebraic rearrangement, to

$$N = -0.370 + 1.481I. \quad [I \text{ on } N, \text{ and again } R^2 = 0.56]$$

In contrast to the previous equation, here the slope 1.481 exceeds the predicted 1.00 (by 48%), while the constant -0.370 falls short of the predicted +1.00.

So which way is it? Is the slope predicted by the logical model too low or too high, as compared to the data? It cannot be both! At the time, Taagepera and Grofman (1985) could only observe that the predicted line fell in between the two regression lines (except near the point where these lines cross). Given the two-way interaction between N and I, there is even more motivation than in the previous example to take some sort of a mean of the two regressions. How should such a mean be taken? The answer is symmetric regression, to be presented soon.

When researchers testing a quantitatively predictive logical model are unaware of the double regression line trap, they are likely to run a single regression and mistakenly conclude that the model is deficient even when this is not so. Moreover, the standard OLS equations cannot form an interlocking system of equations, because they are not unique. This is why good OLS statistics can be death of predictive science.

The Directionality of Standard OLS Equations

Recall that algebraic equations propose unique relationships between variables. They are reversible. Symbolically,

$$(x \to y) = (y \to x). \quad \text{[algebraic equations]}$$

They also have *transitivity*. One can calculate z from x directly, or z from y and y from x, and the result is the same. Symbolically,

$$(x \to y \to z) = (x \to z). \quad \text{[algebraic equations]}$$

This requirement is indispensable, if one wants to construct a knowledge system consisting of equations that interlock. When it comes to standard OLS, it has the following interrelated problems.

1. *OLS regressions of* y *on* x *and* x *on* y *yield different lines* whenever correlation coefficient R^2 is less than 1.00. Symbolically,

   $$(x \to y) \neq (y \to x). \quad \text{[OLS regression equations]}$$

   The difference is large when R^2 is low. Both regression lines are reported in conjunction with the same R^2, which itself does not depend on the direction of regression.

2. *OLS regression equations are not consistent in transfer* whenever correlation coefficient R^2 is less than 1.00. Combining the regression equations z on y and y on x does not yield the same result as regressing z on x directly. Symbolically,

   $$(x \to y \to z) \neq (x \to z). \quad \text{[OLS regression equations]}$$

   The difference can be large when some of the R^2 are low. Hence it is impossible to base an interlocking system of equations on standard OLS regression.

3. If one tests a theoretically supported law, and the data actually fit, *the slope of the OLS regression line y-on-x is always shallower than the actual slope*, relative to the x-axis, whichever variable one decides to designate as x. This is so whenever correlation coefficient R^2 is less than 1.00. The difference is appreciable at low R^2. If one tests the validity of such a law, such regression could hence lead to unfounded negative conclusion.

The Appendix to Chapter 12 offers illustrations that may help to get a feel for how these problems with standard OLS come about. The reason behind them is that standard *OLS regression equations are unidirectional.* This is so because regression *y*-on-*x* minimizes the sum of the squares of *vertical* distances from data points to the line, while *x*-on-*y* does the same for *horizontal* distances. Hence the least square formula used is asymmetric in *x* and *y* (see mathematics in the Appendix to Chapter 12). Using equality signs in OLS regression equations is misleading, as it falsely implies two-way equivalence. The regression equation of *y* on *x* should be shown as $y \leftarrow a + bx$, not as $y = a + bx$. This is different from regression equation of *x*-on-*y*, which should be shown as $x \leftarrow a' + b'x$.

Yet, both regressions yield the same R^2, because the formula for calculating R^2 is symmetric in *x* and *y*. The correlation coefficient is related to neither of the regression lines separately but combines the slopes of the two regression lines. Indeed, if *b* is the slope of *y*-on-*x* relative to the *x*-axis, and *b'* is the slope of the reverse *x*-on-*y* relative to the other axis (*y*-axis), then

$$bb' = R^2.$$

This striking relationship flows directly from the definitions of *b*, *b'*, and R^2, but I have not noticed it spelled out in any statistics book.

When both slopes are measured relative to the *x*-axis then the slope of *x*-on-*y* becomes $b'' = 1/b'$ so that

$$\frac{b}{b''} = R^2.$$

Thus R^2 *is the ratio of the slopes of regressions y-on-x and x-on-y,* when the latter are measured relative to the *same* axis. Since their ratio (R^2) is positive, *b* and *b''* have always the same sign—both lines go up, or both go down. As R^2 never exceeds 1, *b''* cannot be smaller than *b* : $b'' \geq b$. This means that *the slope of regression x-on-y is always steeper than the slope of regression y-on-x,* relative to the *x*-axis, for $R^2 < 1$.

At a perfect $R^2 = 1$, the two lines fuse. As R^2 decreases, the two regression lines move apart from each other and toward positions parallel to the two axes. At $R^2 = 0$, the *y*-on-*x* line is horizontal, while the *x*-on-*y* line is vertical, so that the two lines are orthogonal to each other.

The relationship $bb' = R^2$ offers a simple way to estimate R^2 from graphed data. Eyeballing on the graph often enables one to estimate the two best fit slopes, *y*-on-*x* and *x*–on-*y*, fairly accurately. (For *x*-on-*y*, the graph must be turned 90°.) Then, to obtain R^2, one multiplies the two slopes, keeping in mind that *b* and *b'* stand for the slopes relative to *different* axes.

Scale-Independent Symmetric Regression—A Single Line, with Transitivity

Several modification of standard OLS regression are available, so as to yield a single equation regardless of the direction of regression. In this sense they are symmetric. They all are reversible. However, most of them are not transitive, because they are not scale-independent. This means that when the scale for y is doubled (with the scale for x remaining the same), the visual slope is not doubled. In contrast, the slope is doubled in standard OLS, and thus the relationship to the scale is preserved.

Scale dependence affects *orthogonal regression*, devised early on by Pearson (1901), which minimizes the sum of squares of orthogonal distances from data points to the regression line. (Recall that regression y-on-x minimizes the sum of squares of *vertical* distances from points to the line.) It is also called major axis regression (von Eye and Schuster 1998: 210–33) and *principal components line* (Gelman and Hill 2007: 57–8). Scale dependence also affects the *bisector regression*, which halves the angle between the two standard regression lines, as described in von Eye and Schuster (1998: 220–5).

The only scale-independent symmetric regression seems to be what has been called *"impartial line"* (Strömberg 1940) and *"reduced major axis regression"* (Kermak and Haldane 1950; von Eye and Schuster 1998: 220–5). Thus it seems to be the only regression that could lead an interlocking system of equations, because it is both reversible and transitive. It minimizes the sum of the products of vertical and horizontal distances from data points to the regression line.

This *scale-independent symmetric regression,* reversible and transitive, seems to be "the mathematically 'best' version of the line you just draw in by intuition"—the description Herrnstein and Murray (1994: 562) mistakenly apply to standard OLS. Yet one hardly finds the term "symmetric regression" in indices of statistics textbooks, and an entire chapter on it can be found only in *Regression Analysis for Social Sciences* by von Eye and Schuster (1998: 209–36). They observe (1998: 230) that "In spite of its obvious benefits and its recently increased use in biology and astrophysics, symmetric regression is not part of standards statistical software packages," and offer the means for computing the "reduced major axis solution" (1998: 233–5). However, there is a quick way to calculate the symmetric slope whenever one already has R^2 and the standard OLS slope. It goes as follows.

If b is the slope of OLS regression y-on-x in relation to the x-axis, and b' is the slope of x-on-y in relation to the *same* axis, then the geometric mean (B) of these slopes can be calculated:

$$B = \pm(bb'')^{1/2}.$$

This is the slope of the scale-independent line symmetric with respect to the direction of regression, as presented in Strömberg (1940: 157). It must have the same sign as b and b''. It can also be calculated from OLS regression y-on-x plus R^2, without resorting to reverse regression. It results from previous $b/b'' = R^2$ that

$$B = \frac{b}{|R|}.$$

The slope of the symmetric regression line is the slope of OLS regression y-on-x, divided by the absolute value of correlation coefficient R. The absolute value of R must be used so as to give B the same sign as b and b'' have. Similarly,

$$B = b''|R|$$

Direct calculation of the symmetric slope from data is practically as simple as for the standard OLS, except for minding the $\pm$ sign:

$$B = \pm \left[\sum (y_i - Y)^2 / \sum (x_i - X)^2 \right]^{1/2},$$

where X and Y are the means of x_i and y_i, respectively. The sign of B is the same as for b and R, as it emerges from the summation $\Sigma(y_i - Y)(x_i - X)$. The full equation for the scale-independent symmetric regression line is

$$y = [Y - BX] + Bx.$$

It can be inferred from R^2 and the one-directional OLS regression equation, provided that the means X and Y also are given. This line satisfies the norm of transitivity:

$x \to y \to z$ is the same as $x \to z$ (see the Appendix to Chapter 12).

Recall the two examples from an earlier section. Regression of C on N yielded an exponent 1.76, while the reverse regression N on C gave 2.23. The geometric mean is 1.98, very close to the predicted 2.00 by the model $C = k/N^2$. This is too good to be true in most cases of logical model testing. The other example leads to a more realistic degree of fit.

For this other model, $N = 1 + I$, symmetric regression yields $N = 0.57 + 1.11I$. Let us compare the various equations, rounding all coefficients off to 2 decimals:

$$\text{OLS regression, } N \text{ on } I : N = 1.26 + 0.83I.$$
$$\text{Model} : N = 1.00 + 1.00I.$$
$$\text{Symmetric regression} : N = 0.57 + 1.11I.$$
$$\text{OLS regression, } I \text{ on } N : N = -0.37 + 1.48I.$$

The symmetric equation indicates that the theoretically expected slope is off by 11%, not 17 or 48%, as the separate OLS regressions would suggest. The model is confirmed within this appreciably lower level of error, which also affects the intercept.

For testing algebraically formulated predictive models, the following general advice emerges. Transform the model into a linear form. If no other way is possible, the line $y_{actual} = y_{expected}$ is available when no parameter values have to be determined. Run symmetric regression. The usual value of R^2 still applies. Problems may arise when the random error term is not normally distributed, but at least one avoids systematic underestimating of slope.

When scales are transformed so that the scale-independent symmetric regression line slope is ± 1 (i.e., $\pm 45°$ angle), then the orthogonal and bisector approaches lead to the same result. This outcome is obtained when the data are transformed in such a way that mean x and mean y are zero and the sum of squares of x_i equals the sum of squares of y_i (see the Appendix to Chapter 12).

Unemployment Versus Inflation Versus Unemployment: The Two Phillips Curves

The well-known Phillips (1958) curve connects inflation (I) and unemployment (U). Following up on Sargent (1999), Colomer (2007) points out that there are two ways to read it. The classical or monetarist view implies that decreasing unemployment increases inflation: U down $\rightarrow I$ up. The Keynesian view implies that when the government purposefully allows higher inflation, it will reduce unemployment: I up $\rightarrow U$ down. Both views agree that $dU/dI < 0$. However, the first approach leads to regression I-on-U, while the second leads to regression U-on-I. Different slopes result from OLS.

In Colomer's illustrative example (2007), a 5 percentage point decrease in U leads to a 5 percentage point increase in I (thus slope is -1 relative to U-axis), while a 10 percentage point increase in I leads to a 5 percentage point decrease in U—thus slope is $-1/2$ relative to I-axis, meaning a slope -2 relative to U-axis. The apparent conclusion is that the economic processes involved are unidirectional, presumably because the "monetarist" effect is direct, while the "Keynesian" effect is indirect.

This is possible in principle. It would be akin to hysteresis cycles in magnetism: It takes a stronger magnetic field to demagnetize a body than to magnetize it in the first place. But recall that "Whatever slope you predict is too high, if you believe OLS regression." The contrast in Phillips curves is precisely in that direction. The illustrative results correspond to $b = -1$ and $b'' = -1/2$, so that $b'' = -2.00$ and $R^2 = bb'' = 0.50$. Then the symmetric slope relative to U-axis is $B = b/|R| = -1/0.50^{1/2} = -1.41$.

Some hysteresis cannot be excluded for the unemployment–inflation cycle. One would have to determine the symmetric slope separately for periods where the government is deemed to intervene or to abstain. Different values of B may emerge. Until this is shown to be the case, it is more likely that the apparently unidirectional economic process is an artifact of using unidirectional regression. This observation may also apply to testing Okun's law regarding unemployment and Gross Domestic Product (Prachowny 1993).

It has been tacitly assumed here that the relationship of inflation and unemployment is linear. An exponential relationship $U = Ae^{-kI}$ is more likely, given that U cannot go negative while I can do so (cf. Chapter 8). However, a linear approximation might be sufficient over a limited range, as was the case for volatility in Chapter 4.

More than One Input Variable

Standard OLS is often applied to more than one input variable. How can the symmetrical approach be applied to regression with several variables? I have not found an explicit answer in published work. According to my calculations, shown in the Appendix to Chapter 12, multivariable symmetric regression of y on x, z, etc., corresponds to

$$y / \left[\sum (y_i - Y)^2\right]^{1/2} = A \pm x / \left[\sum (x_i - X)^2\right]^{1/2} \pm z / \left[\sum (z_i - Z)^2\right]^{1/2} \pm \ldots$$

and hence

$$y = a \pm \left[\sum(y_i - Y)^2 \Big/ \sum(x_i - X)^2\right]^{1/2} x \pm \left[\sum(y_i - Y)^2 \Big/ \sum(z_i - Z)^2\right]^{1/2} z \pm \ldots$$

Here A and a are constants, and $X, Y, Z, \ldots$ are the mean values of $x, y, z, \ldots$, respectively.

When taking the square roots, proper signs +/− must be inserted, as they emerge from the summations $\Sigma(y_i - Y)(x_i - X)$, $\Sigma(y_i - Y)(z_i - Z)$, etc. For instance, if $y = Kx/z$ is expected on logical grounds, we should run symmetric regression of actual $\log y$ against $\log x$ and $\log z$. The expectation is $\log y = k + 1.00 \log x - 1.00 \log z$, that is, one expects that, with proper sign, $[\Sigma(y_i - Y)^2/\Sigma(x_i - X)^2]^{1/2}$ is close to +1.00 and $[\Sigma(y_i - Y)^2/\Sigma(z_i - Z)^2]^{1/2}$ is close to −1.00.

With a single input, a simple relationship exists between the OLS slope, the slope of the symmetric regression line, and R^2: $B = b/|R|$. With more than one input, no such relationship can exist. One would again expect that the standard OLS coefficients fall short of the respective coefficients for symmetric regression, especially when R^2 is low, but I have not investigated the multi-input situation fully.

Connection to Scientific Practices

Physical scientists are accustomed to think in terms of interdependent variables, rather than dependent and independent ones. Some scientific relationships are indeed multidirectional. Take the law of ideal gases. It could be written $R = PV/T$, if one wants to determine the value of the universal constant (R) in the first place. It could also be written as $PV = RT$, if one wants to calculate the impact on pressure (P) and volume (V), when temperature (T) is changed from outside. It could also be written as $P/T = R/V$, if one wants to calculate the impact on pressure and temperature when volume is changed from the outside.

However, physical scientists think interdependence even when the law clearly follows a causal direction and could not be visualized in the reverse. Such is the case for the gravitation law, where force is a dependent quantity determined by masses and their distance. Should such laws be written with an arrow, like chemical reactions, rather than equality sign? Maybe we should be surprised that one gets away implying a two-directional causal path where only one causal direction makes sense. Yet, without transitivity, how could one construct a network of interlocking relationships?

This has implications for the future of social sciences. As long as social sciences depend heavily on standard OLS and related unidirectional regression methods, they are bound to face disconnected bits and pieces of relationships, because with OLS, $x \rightarrow y \rightarrow z$ is NOT the same as $x \rightarrow z$. If one wants to stick to regression equations as a major tool, symmetric regression offers a way out, at least to the extent of supplying nondirectional equations that satisfy the transitivity requirement.

Is Standard OLS Slope a Mixed Measure of Slope and Scatter?

When is scale-independent symmetric regression preferable to standard OLS? From the viewpoint of statistical concerns, Kennedy (1998: 26, 141) suggests the following approach. Regress y-on-x when measurement errors in y are relatively large, compared to those in x. When the opposite is the case, regress x-on-y. If the ratio of error variances is unity, use orthogonal regression. The trouble for the statistician is that these errors are usually not known well enough. The deeper trouble for the scientist is the unidirectional nature of equations.

The symmetric approach (in its scale-independent form) is definitely advisable when causality can act in either direction, at least under some circumstances. But suppose it is absolutely clear which is the independent variable. Could then standard OLS be preferable?

It may seem to depend on the purpose. If a logical model is tested and the value of its free parameter must be determined, then standard OLS would underestimate the actual slope. However, if the purpose is solely to postdict y empirically, for given x, then standard OLS may seem the way to go. But not so fast! Consider what happens when one omits a few data points with extreme values of x and y, as was done in Figure 4.3 as compared to Figure 4.2. Obviously, R^2 decreases. But what happens to the slopes of symmetric and standard OLS regression lines?

The slope of the symmetric regression line will change randomly, but it could not get systematically steeper or shallower, given that it is neutral toward reversal of y- and x-axes. The slope of the OLS line, y-on-x, however, will tend to decrease with decreasing R^2, because it has to approach 0 as R^2 approaches 0. The slope of the other OLS line, x-on-y, will of course get steeper, approaching the vertical slope of the y-axis.

Thus, Herrnstein and Murray (1994: 565) are right when saying that one of the OLS lines does "respond" to "How much does weight increase with height?" while the other "responds" to "How much does height increase with weight?" But it would be mistaken to conclude that when these lines respond, they respond with *unique answers* to these questions. It also depends on the degree of scatter.

Graph the precise areas of countries in South America in square kilometers versus their areas in square miles. The data points fall on a line $y = 2.590x$, or inversely, $x = 0.3861y$, with $R^2 = 1.00$. Now add random scatter to both area measures, and repeat this experiment several times. The symmetric regression line will wobble around $y = 2.590x$, but its average slope will approach 2.590, the more times the experiment is repeated. In contrast, the average slope of the OLS regression line y-on-x will be steadily lower than 2.590. The more one increases random scatter, the shallower the slope will tend to become.

If we did not know the relationship between square kilometers and square miles, such a determination would distort the relationship in one direction when we go from square miles to square kilometers and in the opposite direction when we go from square kilometers to square miles. Such distortion is less obvious in the case of social data where we do not know the slope ahead of time, but it is equally real. If we wanted to correct for this scatter dependence, we would have to divide the apparent OLS slope by R—which amounts to using symmetric regression.

With R^2 we have a pure measure of lack of scatter in the sense that it does not tell us anything about the slope of the data cloud. The slope of the scale-independent symmetric regression line is a unique measure of the slope. The slopes of the two standard OLS lines split away from this slope in a scatter-dependent way. It follows from previous $B = b/|R|$ and $B = b''|R|$ that $b = B|R|$ and $b'' = B/|R|$. Hence, as R^2 decreases from 1 to 0, b decreases from B to 0, while b'' increases from B toward infinity. Like R^2 is a pure measure of lack of scatter, the symmetric slope B is a pure measure of slope. In contrast, *the standard OLS slopes are mixed measures of slope and scatter.*

When we ask "How much does weight increase with height?", the standard OLS regression responds: "It depends on how scattered your data are." If you measure x and y with very rough rulers you get one slope. If you repeat the measurements with more refined rulers so that random measurement error is reduced, scatter also is reduced, and you get a steeper slope, even while the means of x and y remain about the same. My conclusion is that scale-independent symmetric regression may always be preferable to standard OLS. Of course, when scatter is small ($R^2 > .90$), symmetric and standard OLS regressions differ little.

Cautionary Note: Symmetric Regression Is Still Merely Regression

It might be wrongly concluded that shifting from OLS to scale-independent symmetric regression will do the trick and one can save oneself the effort of thinking in terms of how things *should* connect. No, one cannot escape that easily from thinking. Consider volatility (Chapter 4) in the light of symmetric regression.

The coarse linear model, based on the anchor point $V = 0$ for $N = 1$, predicts $V = b(N - 1)$. Knowing only the mean values of V and N leads to $V = -11.9 + 11.9N$. The best OLS fit V-on-N was reported by Heath (2005) as $V = -9.07 + 11.14N$ [$R^2 = .50$]. From this we can calculate the best OLS fit N-on-V as corresponding to $V = -49.7 + 22.3N$. Tilting the graph in Figure 4.2 by $45°$, one can see that this looks indeed like the best fit of N-on-V. It is grossly off the conceptual anchor point. But so is the symmetric regression line, though to a lesser degrees. Its calculation yields $V = -25.90 + 15.8N$. Here OLS, V-on-N, looks preferable to symmetric regression.

However, the line that one should take the most seriously is the one based on the anchor point and the means of V and N. This is the logically supported model (at low N), fitted to the data. It corresponds to the symmetric regression line one would obtain when adding to the actual data points an infinite number of virtual data points at the anchor point, thus forcing the regression line to go through the anchor point. The basic point is that any regression that does not respect conceptual anchor points is inadequate.

Appendix to Chapter 12

Three Interconnected Problems with Standard OLS

Same R^2, but Two Distinct OLS Regression Lines

We faced two distinct regression lines in Figure 12.1. Figure 12.2 illustrates it with the simplest possible example—only three points: A $(-4; -1.5)$, B $(2; -1.5)$, and C $(2; 3)$. The mean of x_i is $X = 0$ and the mean of y_i is $Y = 0$. No generality is lost by having the means at $(0; 0)$, because any data-set can be transformed to such an effect, by subtracting the means from all x_i and y_i.

The OLS regression line, y versus x, is the line that minimizes the sum of the squared *vertical* differences between these data points. This sum is visibly minimized when the line passes through A and halfway between B and C. This

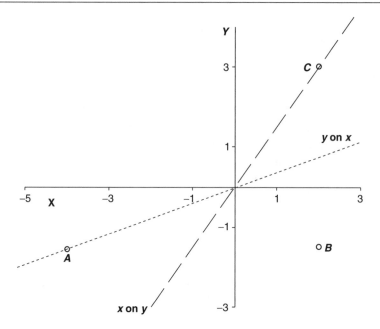

Figure 12.2. The same data-set yields two distinct regression lines—y vs. x and x vs. y

OLS regression line is the dotted line in Figure 12.2:

$$y = 0.375x.$$

When we regress in the reverse direction, x versus y, the axes should be reversed. On the existing graph, OLS minimizes the sum of the squares in the *horizontal x* dimension. This sum is minimized when the line passes through C and halfway between A and B. That OLS regression line is the dashed line in Figure 12.2:

$$x = 0.667y.$$

The correlation coefficient is the same, whichever way one approaches the problem:

$$R^2 = .25.$$

The two regression lines cross at the mean values $(X; Y)$ but diverge elsewhere. This is not an artifact of this simple data-set. The degree of divergence of the two regression lines would be the same for any data-set where $R^2 = .25$. Which

170

equation should we use? If we deduce y from x, we must use $y = 0.375x$, but if we deduce x from y, we must use $x = 0.667y$. Thus, $y = 0.375x$ really stands for $y \leftarrow 0.375x$, while $x = 0.667y$ stands for $x \leftarrow 0.677y$. Using equality signs in the OLS regression equations falsely implies two-way equivalence. Algebraically, with a genuine equality sign, the dotted line $x = 0.667y$ would be equivalent to $y = 1.5x$, not to $y = 0.375x$. But we cannot carry out such algebraic transformations on standard OLS regression equations.

We may check that R^2 is the ratio of the slopes of regressions y-on-x and x-on-y, when the latter are measured relative to the *same* axis. In Figure 12.2, $b = 0.375$ and $b'' = 1/0.667 = 1.5$, so that $b/b'' = 0.25 = R^2$.

All Roads Do Not Lead to the Same Rome

Take any data-sets for x, y, and z where some of the R^2 between them are rather low, and you can easily verify that $x \rightarrow y \rightarrow z$ is not the same as $x \rightarrow z$ for standard OLS. As a simple illustration, return to Figure 12.2 and add a data-set z_i identical to x_i. Then the means of z_i, x_i, and y_i are $Z = X = Y = 0$. As we go directly from x to z, the regression line is simply $z = x$ and $R^2 = 1$. But what happens as we go from x to y and then from y to z?

We go from x to y using $y = 0.375x$. We go from y to z using $z = 0.667y$, because regression z-on-y is the same as x-on-y. We end up with $z = 0.667(0.375x) = 0.25x$, rather than $z = x$. We have multiplied the previous value of x by R^2. If we accept this value of z as a new value of x (because of $z = x$) and continue to deduce z from x, we spiral in toward $X = Y = Z = 0$, the intersection point.

Suppose you take a walk out of Rome, and then return. Imagine your surprise when you find you do not get back to where you started! Also, when going to Naples directly, you end near a beach, but when you take a detour through Benevento, the Naples you reach may be far from the sea. It makes travel most uncertain. This is what standard OLS regression does to your data, because it is unidirectional.

Whatever Slope You Predict Is too High

Figure 12.1 showed that OLS regression y-on-x underestimates the slope relative to the x-axis, while reverse regression x-on-y overestimates the slope relative to the *same* axis. The nature of this artifact may become clearer from the example in Figure 12.3.

Suppose you compare the defense budgets of two competing countries, and the model predicts $y = x$, which also means $x = y$. You have no more reason to graph y versus x than x versus y. By the same token, regression in one direction cannot be preferred to the other. Suppose the actual points show some variation: (5; 10), (10; 5), (10; 15), (15; 10), (15; 20), (20; 15). The means of x_i and y_i are $X = Y = 12.5$.

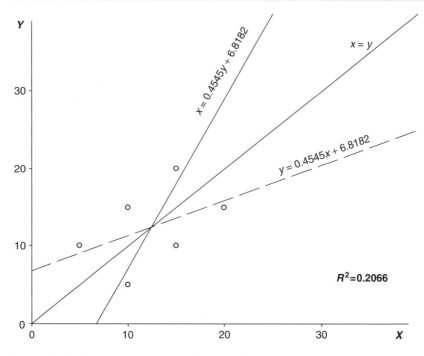

Figure 12.3. The two OLS regression lines under- and over-report, respectively, the expected slope

The pattern is visibly symmetrical regarding the predicted line, $y = x$, and a satisfactory statistical analysis should confirm it. However, when using standard OLS to regress y-on-x, the four central points relative to the x-axis balance themselves out and would lead to $y = x$, with slope 1.00; but the single point on the left pulls upwards, while the single point on the right pulls downwards. So the regression line (dashed line in Figure 12.3) has a shallower slope than 1.00, relative to the x-axis.

Now look at it from the viewpoint of regressing x on y. The four central points relative to the *vertical* y-axis balance themselves out and would lead to $x = y$, with slope 1.00; but the single point at the bottom pulls toward the right, while the single point at the top pulls toward the left. So the regression line (dotted line in Figure 12.3) has a steeper slope than 1.00, relative to the x-axis. All three lines cross at mean x and y (12.5; 12.5).

This is not an artifact peculiar to Figure 12.3. To bring out the underlying reasons in the most vivid way, only 6 points were shown, none of them on the line $y = x$. If one is uneasy about this peculiar configuration, one can add as many points as one would like on the line $y = x$. The R^2 would improve and the two regression lines would move closer to each other, but the qualitative discrepancy would remain.

The Mathematics of Symmetric Regression

Basic Equation

The OLS linear regression of y on x yields a line $y = a + bx$ such that

$$b = \frac{\sum (y_i - Y)(x_i - X)}{\sum (x_i - X)^2}$$

and $a = Y - bX$, where X and Y are the mean values of x_i and y_i, respectively. Conversely, the regression of x on y yields a line $x = a' + b'y$ such that

$$b' = \frac{\sum (y_i - Y)(x_i - X)}{\sum (y_i - Y)^2}$$

and $a' = X - b'Y$. Either way, the correlation coefficient is

$$R = \left[\sum (y_i - Y)(x_i - X) \right] / \left[\sum (x_i - X)^2 \sum (y_i - Y)^2 \right]^{1/2}$$

and

$$R^2 = \left[\sum (y_i - Y)(x_i - X) \right]^2 / \sum (x_i - X)^2 \sum (y_i - Y)^2.$$

In contrast to the expressions for b and b', the one for R^2 is symmetrical in x and y. An important implication of these definitions is that R^2 equals the product of the slopes of regression lines *relative to the axis on which the regression is carried out*:

$$b'b = R^2.$$

When both slopes are measured relative to the x-axis, then the slope of x-on-y is $b'' = 1/b'$, so that

$$\frac{b}{b''} = b'b = R^2.$$

Note that b, b', b'', and R are either all positive or all negative.

The equation for the reverse regression (x on y), $x = a' + b'y$, corresponds in the y versus x format to $y = (-a'/b') + (1/b')x$. Consider the line passing through $(X; Y)$ and having as slope (B) the geometric mean of the slopes $b'' = 1/b'$ of this line and b in $y = a + bx$:

$$B = \pm (bb'')^{1/2}.$$

Here B has the same sign as b and b''. In view of $b/b'' = R^2$, we have

$$B = \frac{b}{|R|}$$

and

$$B = b''|R|.$$

Direct calculation of B from data is straightforward, except for the $\pm$ sign:

$$B = \pm\{bb''\}^{1/2} = \pm\{b/b'\}^{1/2} =$$
$$= \pm\left\{\left[\sum(y_i - Y)(x_i - X)/\sum(x_i - X)^2\right]/\left[\sum(y_i - Y)(x_i - X)/\sum(y_i - Y)^2\right]\right\}^{1/2}$$
$$= \pm\left[\sum(y_i - Y)^2/\sum(x_i - X)^2\right]^{1/2}.$$

The line with slope B that passes through $(X; Y)$ is $y = A + Bx$, where $A = Y - BX$. Hence the equation of this line is

$$y = [Y - (b/|R|)X] + (b/|R|)x.$$

Symmetry Toward the Axes and Transitivity

The formal proof that the equation $y = [Y - (b/|R|)X] + (b/|R|)x$ is symmetric toward the axes, reversible and transitive, while the standard OLS is not, is available from rtaagepe@uci.edu

Orthogonal Regression Becomes Equivalent to Scale-Independent Symmetric Regression when Data Are Normalized

OLS regression of y on x aims at minimizing the sum of squares of vertical distances of data points to a line, $\Sigma(\Delta y_i)^2$. Instead, one could try to minimize the sum of squares of the shortest distance from data points to the line. This means orthogonal regression. Unfortunately, the resulting line is scale dependent. Indeed, as the relative scales of y and x are altered, the line that previously corresponded to the shortest distance from a data point to the line no longer does.

There is one privileged scale, though, the only one that makes the two usual OLS lines symmetric with respect to the axes. Here $b' = b$ and hence $B = \pm1$, so that the symmetric regression line is at 45° to the axes. The transformation consists of shifting to $x_j = (x_i - X)/[\Sigma(x_i - X)^2)^{1/2}]$ and $y_j = (y_i - Y)/[\Sigma(y_i - Y)^2]^{1/2}$. This way the OLS regression lines cross at $(0; 0)$. Moreover, $\Sigma y_j^2 = \Sigma x_j^2 = 1$.

Formal proof is available from rtaagepe@uci.edu that such a shift makes the two standard OLS lines symmetric with respect to the axes and that slope 1 minimizes the sum of squares of the shortest distance from data points to the line.

More than One Input Variable

With only one input variable (x), the symmetric regression is $y = a + Bx$, where $dy/dx = B = [\Sigma(y_i - Y)^2/\Sigma(x_i - X)^2]^{1/2}$. Transposing the latter yields

$$dy/\left[\sum(y_i - Y)^2\right]^{1/2} = dx/\left[\sum(x_i - X)^2\right]^{1/2}.$$

When more input variables are introduced, $y = a + Bx + Cz + \ldots$, and $dy = (\partial y/\partial x)dx + (\partial y/\partial z)dz + \ldots$, where $\partial y/\partial x$ is the partial derivative of y with respect to x. It follows from the above that

$\partial y/\partial x = [(y_i - Y)^2/\Sigma(x_i - X)^2]^{1/2}$, $\partial y/\partial z = [\Sigma(y_i - Y)^2/\Sigma(z_i - Z)^2]^{1/2}$, etc. In sum, multivariable symmetric regression is

$$y = a \pm \left[\sum(y_i - Y)^2 / \sum(x_i - X)^2\right]^{1/2} x \pm \left[\sum(y_i - Y)^2 / \sum(z_i - Z)^2\right]^{1/2} z \pm \ldots,$$

where $X, Y, Z, \ldots$ are the mean values of $x, y, z, \ldots$, respectively. When taking the square roots, we must insert the proper signs $+/-$, as they emerge from the summations $\Sigma(y_i - Y)(x_i - X)$, $\Sigma(y_i - Y)(z_i - Z)$, etc.

13

All Indices Are Not Created Equal

- Models are tested with data, but also data are tested by agreement with conceptual models.
- When competing indices exist to measure the same phenomena, one should use the ones that agree with logically supported prediction. These indices need not be philosophically "truer" measures of the underlying concepts. They are just more useful for prediction.
- The choice between two accepted ways to measure cabinet duration and three ways to measure the number of parties illustrates this advice.
- Clearest results emerge when symmetric regression is used for testing.

Whichever way predictive models may be set up, they are tested with data. In the light of the data, the model may have to be modified or even abandoned. It is a widely accepted norm that one can not argue with data. I disagree. Measurements are imperfect. Indices may not show what they are meant or thought to show. Testing models by agreement with data is only part of the game—data also are tested by agreement with models. More precisely, the way data are generated and processed is tested.

Give Preference to Indices That Best Fit a Logically Expected Relationship

Let us return to the relationship between mean cabinet duration and the number of parties, presented as $C = k/N^2$ in Chapters 10 and 11. The logical model does not refer to specific indices. It merely posits an inverse square relationship between conceptual quantities: (cabinet duration) = k/(number of parties)^2. It does not tell us how "cabinet duration" and "number of parties" are to be measured. Thus, it really means a relationship between a *suitable measure* of cabinet duration and a *suitable measure* of number of parties. A recurring problem in sciences is how to measure quantities that correspond to ideal concepts. We face it here.

We saw in Chapter 10 that there are several ways to measure the number of parties. Actually, one can base such a measure on $\sum p_i^m$, using any value of m, ranging from 0 (which leads to what was designated as N_0) to infinity (which leads to what was designated as N_∞). What was called the effective number of parties (N) corresponds in this notation to N_2. There may be still other ways to define a measure of the number of parties. There are also several ways to define and measure cabinet duration. Which indices should we choose, among the several alternatives?

My brief answer may at first glance look antithetic to the scientific method: Give preference to the indices that best fit a logically expected relationship. This may look like cooking the data—but it is not so. All ways to measure conceptual quantities are not created equal. Some are more useful than others. A major criterion for usefulness of an index is how it links up with something else, because only such linkages make prediction possible. Science is about establishing patterns, so that we can predict. Logically supported patterns are preferable to merely empirical, because knowing *why* a prediction works increases our confidence in it. It enables us to apply prediction in uncharted territories—and avoid applying it when the logical presumptions are absent.

Suppose that, on logical grounds, we expect a relationship $y = k/x^2$ between abstract concepts x and y. Suppose several indices ($X1, X2, \ldots Y1, Y2 \ldots$) compete to stand for x and y, respectively. Suppose that one and only one pair of indices, say $X2$ and $Y1$, comes close to confirming $y = k/x^2$. Then this pair stands out as the only one that offers logically supported predictability.

The likelihood that $Y1 = k/(X2)^2$ might fit by random coincidence is vanishingly small when data points are numerous and cover a fair range, because $y = k/x^2$ is only one among a multitude of downwards-sloping possibilities, ranging from $y = a - bx$ to $y = k/(x^4 - b)$, and so on. Chances are good that a logically expected and quantitatively specified relationship is for real, if one of the many combinations of alternative indices confirms it.

But even more is confirmed than the relationship itself. If the combination $X2$ with $Y1$ confirms the expected relationship and no other combination does, then $X1$ and $Y1$ themselves appear that much more useful. Hence their positions are reinforced as privileged measures of concepts x and y, respectively.

More often than not, indices that aim at measuring the same concept are somewhat correlated. Therefore, if one of the Y is connected to $X2$, so may be the others. Indeed, some other Y may conceivably correlate with $X2$ even slightly better than $Y1$, if one swears by R^2, but if the relationship found does not have the expected functional form, then this Y is not the preferred one.

The Need for Symmetric Regression

This is where symmetric regression becomes essential. Consider again the relationship between mean cabinet duration and the number of parties. Three measures of the number of parties have been used before: N_∞, N_2, and N_0. They all correlate with each other and hence with cabinet duration. The exponents n in $C = k/N^n$ correspond to the slopes on log–log graphs. Consider OLS regression of $\log C$ on $\log N_m$, where N_m stands successively for N_∞, N, and N_0. The exponent n is found to be 2.14 for N_∞, 1.76 for N_2, and about 0.93 for N_0.

On the face of it, the exponent for N_∞ looks closest to the logically expected 2.00. However, Chapter 12 has demonstrated that standard OLS regression systematically underestimates slopes, as compared to the theoretically predicted ones. The reverse regression of $\log N_m$ on $\log C$ must also be taken in account, and it yields different slopes. Taking the geometric mean of the two slopes (with respect to $\log N_m$ axis) corresponds to symmetric regression. With this adjustment, N_2 offers an almost perfect fit to the expected 2.00—the mean exponent is 1.98.

The three measures for the number of parties are logically connected by $N_2 = N_0^{2/3}$ and $N_2 = N_\infty^{4/3}$ (Table 10.1). If N_2 fits $C = k/N^2$, it leads to expectations $C = k/N_0^{4/3}$ and $C = k/N_\infty^{8/3}$. Table 13.1 shows the actual outcomes. For all three measures of the number of parties, OLS regression of $\log C$ on $\log N_x$ yields lower values of exponent n than predicted. Yet the reverse regression of $\log N_m$ on $\log C$ yields higher values of n than predicted. The geometric means of the two come relatively close to predictions. The slopes for N_0 are shown in parentheses, because they are not measured but approximately derived from known MS and the relationship $N_0 = (MS)^{1/4}$. The exponents for C versus MS, shown at the bottom of Table 13:l, are discussed in the Appendix to Chapter 13.

Table 13.1. Degree of agreement with predictive models of mean cabinet duration for standard OLS and symmetric regressions of logarithms

N_x	Predicted exponent	OLS regression		Symmetric regression	Deviation (%) from prediction	R^2
		C on N_x	N_x on C			
N_2	−2.00	−1.76	−2.23	−1.98	−1	.79
$N_\infty = 1/s_1$	−2.67	−2.14	−4.05	−2.94	+10	.53
N_0	−1.33	(−0.93)	(−3.10)	(−1.70)	(+28)	(.30)
MS	−0.33	−0.23	−0.77	−0.43	+28	.30

When N_2 is assumed to be the proper index for the number of parties in $C = k/N^2$, then it can be seen in Table 13.1 that the predicted exponent $8/3 = 2.67$ for N_∞ is also confirmed within 10%. The more uncertain result for N_0 deviates from the expected $4/3 = 1.33$ to a larger extent. The logical connection to cabinet duration is most direct for N_2, followed by N_∞ and then by N_0. Not surprisingly, R^2 decreases in the same order. In contrast, if one assumes N_∞ or N_0 to be the proper index for the N in $C = k/N^2$, nothing falls into place.

Now consider the measures of cabinet duration. Lijphart (1999: 132–3) uses two distinct ones. "Average cabinet life I," devised by Dodd (1976), is the more lenient one. A cabinet is considered to last when its partisan composition does not change. As long as the same parties or groupings participate, the same cabinet is considered to continue. Lijphart (1999) observes mean durations ranging from 1.3 to 31 years. This is the measure that confirms the model $C = k/N^2$, when used in conjunction with the effective number of parties, N_2.

A much more stringent measure ("Average cabinet life II") considers a cabinet terminated not only when its party composition changes but also upon an election, a change of prime minister, or a shift in cabinet type (minority, minimal winning, or oversized coalition). By these criteria, Lijphart (1999) observes mean durations ranging from 1.0 to 4.8 years. In particular, frequency of elections puts a severe upper limit on the range.

For data in Lijphart (1999: 132–3), the linear fit of logarithms corresponds approximately to Life II = 1.15(Life I)$^{0.45}$ when (and only when) both are measured in years. Scatter is so wide that Life II can be approximated with the square root of Life I. This purely empirical relationship depends on the time units used.

Correspondingly, the best fit of Life II with effective number of parties is quite close to Life II = 7 years/N. Here R^2 is not much lower than for Life I = 42 years/N^2, but there is a huge difference. The exponent "2" in Life I comes from a logical model, while the exponent "1" in Life II = 7 years/N lacks such an explanation. Combining Life II with the other measures of the number of parties leads to exponents of about 4/3 for N_∞ and 2/3 for N_0. Both fall much short of the expected 8/3 and 4/3, respectively. Thus Life II combined with the effective number of parties is the only combination of measures of cabinet duration and number of parties that fits the model $C = k/N^2$. These indices emerge as the best connected measures of mean cabinet duration and number of parties, respectively. They are the only ones that offer logically supported prediction, even while all other combinations of indices also offer empirical correlations.

Conclusions

When competing indices exist to measure the same phenomena, it is advisable to use the ones that agree with prediction based on logical models. No claim is made that these indices are "truer" measures of the underlying concepts in a philosophical sense. They are just more useful for prediction.

The mean duration of cabinets and the number of parties offer a handy illustration, because there are at least three ways to measure the number of parties and two accepted ways to measure duration. The results emerge the clearest when symmetric regression is used for testing. Thus, this illustration adds to the ones in Chapter 12 in pointing out the systematic shortcomings of one-directional OLS regression.

Appendix to Chapter 13

The Inverse Cube Root Relationship of Cabinet Duration and the Seat Product

An inverse cube root relationship between mean cabinet duration (C) and the seat product (MS) was suggested in Table 10.1: $C = 42/(MS)^{1/3}$. While the number of parties cannot be prescribed by law, the seat product can. Thus the latter equation makes institutional design possible, at least in principle. Is this relationship sufficiently firm to be called a law?

In Table 13.1, the exponent 0.23 resulting from OLS regression of log$C$ on log(MS) falls 30% short of the expected 1/3 = 0.33. This is what happens when R^2 is low and unidirectional OLS is used. Reverse regression of log(MS) on log$C$ produces a correspondingly high slope of 0.77 (relative to the MS-axis). The geometric mean is 0.43. This is still 28% higher than the expected 0.33. Here the shift to symmetric regression does not improve the fit.

The model $C = 42$ years/$(MS)^{1/3}$ still predicts mean cabinet duration within a factor of 2 for 19 cases out of 25. The six widely deviant cases are spread evenly: Botswana, Spain, and the Netherlands are above the predicted zone, while Mauritius, Papua-New Guinea, and India are below. Either we may tentatively accept the inverse cube root relationship as basis for uncertain prediction and institutional design or we would have to abstain from prediction altogether.

Dimensional Analysis

Chapter 10 hinted at a major difference between physics and social sciences. Physics has many dimensional quantities that emerge from measuring, while social sciences have many purely numerical quantities that emerge from counting. "Dimensional analysis is a method whereby physicists, engineers, and biologists often can arrive at the form of physical law simply by knowing exactly which variables are relevant—of course, that is a great deal to know" (Luce 1989: 262). The following tries to give a sense of what is involved, in simple terms. For full treatment, see Krantz et al. (1971: 454–544) and Luce et al. (1990: 307–26).

Counting and measuring differ fundamentally. Counting presumes existence of a natural unit, such as "one cow" or "one vote." Measuring involves comparison with a standard which most often is arbitrary, such as a month or a dollar. One can use different measuring units (such as years or euros), and it often makes no difference, as long as one specifies the units. In contrast, counting by half-cows or dozens of votes looks unjustified. (Sometimes both approaches could make sense— or both may have difficulties. One peasant may own five fat cows with total weight 2,500 kg, while another may own eight starved cows with total weight 2,000 kg. Which one can be considered wealthier depends on many factors.)

Most numerical values in physics emerge from measuring rather than counting. They are not pure numbers but products of a pure number and a unit of measurement. When units change, their number also changes, and the usual rules of multiplication apply. This means that the same time interval can appear as 120 times one second or 2 times one minute, given that 1 times one minute equals 60 times one second.

Different physical quantities have mutually incompatible dimensions. This means that seconds and meters cannot be added or subtracted, while seconds and minutes can, subject to a nondimensional multiplier of 60 s/min. However, even quantities with disparate dimensions can be multiplied and divided, and sometimes the outcomes have conceptual meanings. Thus, distance divided by time interval is what we call velocity. Such a division must involve both pure numbers and units. For instance, 10 km divided by 2 h equal $(10/2)$(km/h) = 5 km/h. We must divide units as well as the numbers—and the outcome must fit dimensionally.

Most physical quantities can be reduced to a multiplicative combination of 4 basic dimensions, often conventionally shown in square brackets: length $[L]$, time $[T]$, mass $[M]$, and electric charge $[Q]$. In dimensional terms, any volume is $[L^3]$, any velocity is $[L/T]$, and any acceleration is $[L/T^2]$. Equations must balance not only in numbers but also in dimensions (and hence units). Thus Newton's second law, force = mass × acceleration, implies that the dimension of force is $[\text{Force}] = [M][L/T^2] = [ML/T^2]$.

The universal law of gravitation, $f = GMm/r^2$, involves a universal constant, G. The latter cannot be a pure number, because the transposition $G = fr^2/Mm$ implies that $[G] = [ML/T^2][L^2]/[M^2] = [L^3/MT^2]$. At the end of complex calculations, a dimensional check is advisable. If dimensions do not fit, there is bound to be a mistake.

Dimensions always come in small integers (Krantz et al. 1971: 455). Even if a formula involves a square root, the outcome has integer basic dimensions. Thus the time period (T) for the swing of a simple pendulum is $T = \pi(L/g)^{1/2}$, where L is the length of the pendulum and g is gravitational acceleration toward the Earth. Dimensionally, T is $\{[L]/[L/T^2]\}^{1/2} = [T]$, as it should be.

In contrast, most quantities in social sciences are nondimensional, symbolized here as $[0]$, if needed. In the inverse square law of cabinet duration, $C = k/N^2$, the effective number of parties is a pure number: $N = [0]$. Since C has time dimension, the constant k also must be $k = [T]$. Money is the only widespread, uniquely social science quantity that might be dimensional. Like mass, it is a quasi-continuous variable that has a natural zero but lacks a natural unit. In contrast, in the expression for the number of seat-winning parties, $N_0 = (MS)^{1/4}$, all quantities are zero-dimensional, based on counting (however indirectly, in the case of the effective number of parties). In exponential growth or decay, $y = Ae^{kt}$, output y may stand for a dimensional measure or a pure number based on counting units, and the constant A must have the same units. Since exponent kt can only be a pure number—$kt = [0]$—it must be that $k = [1/T]$.

This brings us to the notion of uniformity in units: At analogous positions in the same equation, the same counting units must be used. For instance, effective number of legislative parties can be calculated from $N_2 = (\Sigma S_i)^2/\Sigma(S_i)^2$, using for S_i either numbers of seats for different parties or their percent shares or fractional shares—but the same measures must be used at the top and the bottom. While such a requirement may look self-evident in this simple example, it may be missed in more complex expressions.

If linear regression is used, it must be kept in mind that regression units may not be pure numbers even while they may look so in a computer printout. Suppose the output y is a pure number. If x_1 stands for GNP/capita [money], then its regression coefficient a_1 must have the compensatory dimension [1/money]. Its numerical value depends on whether euros or dollars are used.

Two measures of cabinet life presented in this chapter were observed to be related as Life II = $1.15(\text{Life I})^{0.45}$ when both are measured in years. When converted to months, it becomes Life II = 0.30(Life I)$^{0.45}$. It is bad enough that the constant depends on units used, even when the same unit is used for Life I and Life II, but dimensionally things become really awkward: $[T] = [c][T]^{0.45}$. It means that the constant (be it 1.15 or 0.30) must have the dimension of $[c] = [T]^{0.55}$! One might be better off in trying to fit the relationship with Life II = k(Life I), even if it makes R^2 much worse. At least the dimensions would be kept simple.

Sometimes it helps to divide a variable by a constant rather than multiply, because then the variable and the constant have the same dimensions (or quasi-dimensions—see below). For this reason the number of treaties in the Appendix to Chapter 8 was expressed as $T = T_0 (1 + B/b) (1 + L/l) (1 + R/r)$ rather than $T = T_0 (1 + b'B) (1 + l'L) (1 + r'R)$. This way, the constants b, l and, r can be characterized as the values of B, L, and R that double the output. The multiplicative constants (b', l', and r') offer no such simple interpretation. Remember: meaningful constants are better than anonymous. In the case of Life II above, however, this approach does not work either.

Let us return to the basic feature involved in dimensional analysis. Measured quantities of different types often can be multiplied or divided together to yield new meaningful quantities. Kilometers and hours combine to yield velocities in kilometers-per-hour. This property is not inherently restricted to measured quantities. Measured and counted quantities can combine in a similar way, such as GDP yielding "per capita GDP." Counted quantities can also combine among themselves. In some elections, each voter has more than one vote that he or she can use. The actual votes cast per person (v) can be expressed as $v = V/P$ where V is the number of votes and P the number of people participating. All these entities have zero dimension, yet they combine like dimensional quantities in velocity = distance/time. There is sort of quasi-dimensionality.

Such quasi-dimensionality just might become a useful notion in social sciences. It could bring some of the benefits Luce (1989: 262) has in mind in the quote above. Presently, however, dimensionality tends to set apart the basic building blocks in physics and in social sciences.

Part III

Synthesis of Predictive and Descriptive Approaches

14

From Descriptive to Predictive Approaches

- Routine statistical approaches are essentially descriptive, giving answers within a narrow range of questions. Quantitatively formulated logical models force us to ask further questions and are predictive in an explanatory way.
- Descriptive approaches are not conducive to detection of social laws, especially if one simultaneously feeds in variables which actually connect sequentially.
- Rather than a single sequence of "hypothesis testing," scientific procedure involves repeat cycles where predictive and descriptive approaches enter intermixed.
- Hopes of a unified "theory of everything" emerge mainly at dawn (philosophers' stone!) and at high noon of a discipline. In its late morning, scientists are too busy casting cumulative and interlocking knowledge into more limited theories of *something*.
- Directional models and reams of numbers ground out by canned computer programs must make room for quantitative models and sparse conceptually grounded constants.

Much quantitative work has been produced in social sciences during the last 50 years, adding to our qualitative understanding of social processes and data collection. Yet the payoff has been far from optimal, because of overemphasis on analysis in a narrowly statistical sense, often reduced to mindless ritual, and relative neglect of conceptual model building. We need both more thoughtful use of statistics and going beyond statistics.

Routine statistical approaches are essentially descriptive, giving answers within the range of questions we ask. They do not talk back to us. If we ask for linear regression, the program does not print out "You really should consider curvatures." When we analyze mean cabinet duration on the basis of district magnitude, the program does not whisper "Include assembly size too!" From where can we get the questions to be posed in the course of statistical analysis? This is where the conceptual "How *should* it be on logical grounds?" enters.

Quantitatively formulated logical models are essentially predictive in an explanatory way. They produce not only answers but also new questions. Expanding the predictive approaches by no means implies dumping the descriptive ones. There is nothing wrong with statistical methods. Plenty is wrong with the way these methods have been misused and overused in social sciences. Mixed strategies are often the most efficient. So let us see how to mix them.

Could Statistical Approaches Find Social Laws?

This book asked early on (Chapter 2) whether the present-day social science approaches could find the law of gravitation. The test presented could legitimately be criticized on two accounts: the use of blind data and asking social scientists to find something outside their realm. Well, Chapter 10 offers a set of empirically tested logical models that connect eminently social science variables—institutional inputs and political outputs. The corresponding data are widely available. Could these predictive results of logical modeling be obtained by descriptive methods?

We may have to specify what constitutes a worthwhile result. Potential for informed social intervention could be a major aspect. Various intermediary links in the sequence presented are of intellectual interest but cannot lead to action. It is nice to know that mean duration of cabinets is strongly connected to the number of parties, but this number cannot be changed by decree, even if there should be consensus that cabinet durations in the given country are too short. Institutional inputs such as assembly size (S) and district magnitude (M) are another matter. They can be altered by legislative decision, in principle, so as to alter outputs such as number of parties and mean duration of cabinets (C). The equation $C = 42 \, (MS)^{-1/3}$ in Table 10.1 enables the legislators to manipulate these institutions so as to alter the average output not only in the desired direction but also to a desired degree. This simple model has a considerable range of error, but measures to reduce it exist (Taagepera 2007c), and future refinements can be expected.

This potential for institutional engineering is a prime practical payoff in the given case. It opens ways for informed social intervention, something that would justify expenditures on political science in the eyes of decision-makers. Abstract studies of classical mechanics received a major boost when they could be applied to improve the accuracy of artillery. I hate to draw this analogy, and rulers may be more interested in guns than institutional reform, but practical payoff cannot be ignored. How well could the conventional social science approach serve this purpose in this particular instance?

Political scientists have tried to connect cabinet durability to a huge number of factors—see review by Grofman and van Roozendaal (1997). Among the variables that deal with the number and size of parties and electoral districts, it could have been noticed early on that mean duration of cabinets (C) seems to go

1. up with increasing seat share of the largest party (s_1);
2. down with increasing effective number of parties (N);
3. down with increasing district magnitude (M).

Faced with such a directional model, a conventional social scientist would automatically set up the regression equation $C = a + bs_1 + cN + dM$. This is precisely what Sørensen (1998) called the gas station approach (Chapter 10)—buying a little bit of extra duration with the largest share, a little bit of (negative) duration with number of parties, etc. Among the input variables, N is likely to emerge as statistically "significant," but so may one or even both of the other variables.

Note that no dependence on assembly size can be detected with raw empirical data, because of its limited range of variation (cf. Chapter 10). This impact, prominent in the conceptual model $C = k(MS)^{-1/3}$, cannot emerge until one starts looking for it on conceptual grounds and designs the inquiry accordingly. Hard-boiled empiricists may feel that what is hard to detect can be neglected, but this would be poor science. Ask physicists who have spent decades pinning down the elusive neutrino and gravitational waves.

No explanatory pattern in a conceptual sense could emerge from $C = a + bs_1 + cN + dM$, any more than it did from the regression analysis of gravity pseudo-data (Chapter 2). This is so not only because no conceptual explanation is sought in the first place but also because the regression approach is hardly conducive to it. Beyond straight regression, a competent statistician would inquire into correlations between s_1, N, and M. These correlations are of course strong, but they are nonlinear: $s_1 = (MS)^{-1/8}$, $N = (MS)^{1/6}$, and $N = s_1^{-4/3}$, respectively (cf. Table 10.1). If only linear correlations are looked for, they may or may not appear significant. The following outcomes may materialize.

If two of the inputs are eliminated through linear autocorrelation, these would be M and s_1, given the much more direct connection of C with N. The outcome would be $C = a' - c' N$, with positive c' and a quite satisfactory R^2. Such regression would misinterpret the inverse relationship as a subtractive one. The conventional researcher would not discover the inverse square relationship of C to N, unless exposure to physics models has conditioned him or her to taking logarithms of *all* variables. Statistical data configuration alone would not call for it. It may suggest "logging" C but not N, because the range of N is quite limited. Logging C would lead to $\ln C = a'' - c''N$ and hence $C = Ae^{-c''N}$. In the absence of full logarithmic transformation of data, the inverse relationship would be misinterpreted as a decreasing exponential. Either way, no hope for informed social intervention emerges, because the number of parties cannot be altered by fiat.

Now suppose that linear autocorrelation eliminates only one of the inputs. The casualty would most likely be s_1, as the logical connection between N and M is more remote in the causal chain, thus reducing autocorrelation. The outcome may have the form $C = a - cN - dM$ (where elimination of s_1 alters all coefficients). If the wide range of M is noticed, one might shift to its logarithm: $C = a - cN - d \ln M$. If the range of C is also deemed wide, one may use $\ln C = a - cN - d \ln M$ and hence $C = Ae^{-cN}/M^d$.

Either way, the actual *sequential* relationships $C = k/N^2$ and $N = (MS)^{-1/6}$, which combine to $C = k(MS)^{-1/3}$, are scrambled into a single "gas station" equation. The term in M could offer some institutional engineering ability, but success would be severely limited, because interaction of M with assembly size is ignored and changes in M would also alter N in a way not specified in the regression equation.

However, it may turn out that increasing district magnitude might seem to *increase* cabinet duration. This is so because the logical impact of M through $M \to N \to C$ is preempted by inclusion of N. The residue is mostly random effect of secondary factors which could add up to a positive or negative d in $C = Ae^{-cN}/M^d$. Such random residues should not look statistically "significant," but sometimes they do—cf. Kittel's

Logical sequence

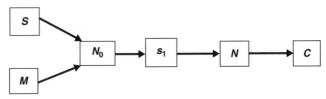

Regressional gas station: Pumps s_1 and M feed only random noise

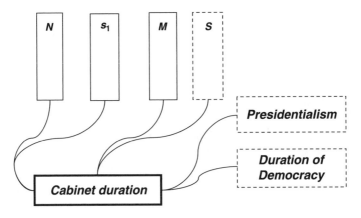

Figure 14.1. Logical sequence and "gas station approach" for mean duration of cabinets

(2006) experiment in Chapter 7 and discussion of statistical significance in Chapter 6.

So as to improve the fit, the conventional researcher might add more ingredients to the gazpacho. One may introduce further variables that might have some impact. Not only assembly size but also duration of the democratic regime, and a dummy for presidentialism might come to mind. In Sørensen's (1998) terms, more pumps are added to the gas station—see Figure 14.1. The R^2 may increase marginally, leaving the impression that one is "explaining" ever more, while actually the picture is muddled up even further.

The conclusion is that descriptive approaches alone are not conducive to detection of social laws that follow the multiplicative pattern frequent in physics. More broadly, they are not conducive to detection of any sequential connections, by definition, because they mistakenly replace sequence by simultaneous combination.

Could Statistical Approaches Distinguish between Multiple Modes of Causation?

Previous section has shown that multivariate regression alone cannot figure out social laws when sequential processes are involved. Replacing $A \rightarrow B \rightarrow C$ with simultaneous inputs $A \rightarrow C \leftarrow B$ royally confuses the issue. In Sørensen's gas station analogy, one would try to buy gasoline from pumps A and B, without realizing that pump B merely transmits what it gets from pump A. There is another situation where the gas station analogy enters. When pumps A and B are distinct, your car engine might work as well on gas purchased from either of them alone. In other words, it might be that $A \rightarrow C$ under some circumstances and $B \rightarrow C$ under some others. Once again, $A \rightarrow C \leftarrow B$ would confuse the issue. When an outcome sometimes results from one cause and sometimes from another, multivariate regression duly parcels it out among them, as if they acted together.

Multiple roads can lead to the same endpoint. Sometimes called *equifinality* in social science literature (Ragin 1987; Schneider and Grofman 2006), it is taken as obvious by chemists. Different chemical reactions can lead to the same final products. Water is a byproduct in a multiplicity of reactions. Chemists would be concerned only about the opposite—when the same starting materials lead to different reaction products, under apparently identical conditions. They would then look for what is different in the conditions, rather than call it "path dependence" and let it be. Once more, dependence on computer programs will not do. One has to think and build predictive models.

What Is Theory?

Given the extreme contrast between the physics approach and such a gas station approach, how come that the physicists' notion of a unified "theory of everything" (TOE) has struck a chord among some social scientists? What does it tell us? We have to specify what theory means.

My high school philosophy of science course in Marrakech taught me that "theory" has a quite opposite meaning in science, compared to everyday speech (Figure 14.2). In science, theory is the combination of many interlocking laws, themselves conceptually grounded and empirically tested. It is the endpoint, the ultimate roof. In everyday speech, in contrast, "It's just a theory" means it is just a hunch, even less firm than

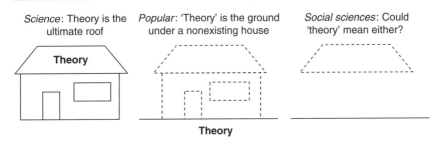

Figure 14.2. The opposite meanings of "theory"

a well-worded hypothesis. What I later encountered in physics agreed with this lesson in philosophy. *Webster's New Collegiate Dictionary* (1981) covers the range, from "an unproved assumption" to "a plausible or scientifically acceptable general principle or body of principles offered to explain phenomena."

But what does "theory" mean in social sciences? The following example from political science may be indicative. For understandable reasons (complexity and fluidity of the subject, plus limited ability to experiment), the achievements of political science are more reminiscent of physics before than after Newton. (If this is not so, then who is the Newton of political science?) Yet, "Does Comparative Politics Need a TOE?" (Wallerstein 2001) was a lead essay in the newsletter of the Comparative Politics section of the American Political Science Association. In that essay, "theory" seems synonymous to "paradigm" or "conceptual framework." Its comparisons with relativity and quantum mechanics happily overlook the respective stages of development. How could the thought of a TOE emerge?

Hopes for a unified "theory of everything" emerge mainly at dawn and high noon of a discipline. In its late morning, scientists are too busy turning cumulative and interlocking knowledge into more limited theories of *something*. The quest for a TOE began with the alchemists' notion of philosophers' stone. A single chunk of it could produce gold, youth, etc. Such a quest faded as physical sciences began to produce more modest but usable predictions. After the advent of not only Newton and Maxwell but also Einstein, Bohr, and Schrödinger with their theories of something, physicists began to look for a unified theory for all physical phenomena, semi-jokingly dubbed the "theory of everything." In contrast, biologists have little time left for a "theory of life," busy as they are with exciting studies of *something*, such as the human genome.

When their "something" does not look predictive and cumulative, some social scientists are tempted to latch on to the label "TOE," given that the more fitting term, philosophers' stone, has lost its glamor. But at this stage, dreams of a unified theory sound like "alpolitics," something more analogous to alchemy than chemistry. To be more than a philosophers' stone, a unified theory presumes a basis in firmly established partial theories—and political science is as yet far from that stage. The interlocking predictive models for party sizes and cabinet duration come closest to a theory of something, but the single strand pattern (instead of a crisscrossing network) is a limitation.

Throughout social sciences, the term "theory" remains ambiguous. Sometimes, a mere directional model is presented as "theory" even before being tested. More often, it is so qualified after directional testing. Similarly, a "law" could mean either something conducive to quantitative prediction or merely a vague tendency expressed in a felicitous wording. Sometimes "theory" is presented as more diffuse than "law": It is "a very general set of propositions from which others, including 'laws', are derived" (Achen and Snidal 1989). It can be seen as even weaker than "hypothesis": "A theory is a set of interconnected assumptions....From the theory, we derive one or more hypotheses" (Souva 2007).

A hallmark of science at the level of partial theories is cumulativeness. Successive paradigms build on each other rather than replacing previous ones. Relativistic mechanics adds specifications to the Newtonian rather than refuting it. Wave and particle approaches to light combine in a synthesis that defies everyday common sense. The last major notion fully dumped in physics was ether, two centuries ago. In contrast, many social sciences offer a succession of fashions parading as paradigms. Cumulativeness proceeds chiefly at the data collection level. (It might correspond to the Tycho Brahe stage in astronomy.) There is one difference, compared to the quest for philosophers' stone: In social sciences the paradigm is not stable but may change every quarter-century or so.

Analogies with more developed sciences may offer a useful road map when the location of various social sciences within the general scheme of development of sciences is fixed realistically. Borrowing the term "unified theory" from the physicists' current quest and pretending that social sciences, too, have already several proven and stable theories in need of unification is *mania grandiosa*. Let us first establish reasonably firm quantitative laws (in a scientific sense), and with a sufficiently interlocking set of such laws, some theories of *something* will eventually emerge.

As for conceptual frameworks, they are inevitable at any stage. Any empirical inquiry is guided (or misguided) by some such framework, explicit or implicit. Empirical findings, in turn, affect the conceptual framework, but the latter may have appreciable inertia. Thus, the Ptolemaic framework in astronomy yielded to the Keplerian with great reluctance. This implies that major breakthroughs may come from researchers at the fringes of accepted paradigms. From this viewpoint, the frequent shifts in dominant frameworks, such as Wallerstein (2001) and Grofman (2007) observe in political science, may speed up the process. If one is out of fashion, one may only have to wait for 25 or twice 25 years to have one's findings seriously considered. It may also offer entry points to something more cumulative and hence lasting.

Cycles and Sub-Cycles in Scientific Procedure: At what Stages Do Predictive and Descriptive Approaches Enter?

In physical sciences, statistical approaches enter mainly in the applied phase. Engineers fine-tune the workings of natural laws for specific conditions. These laws are mostly nonlinear in form. Over sufficiently short distances, however, any curve can be treated as a straight line—even a circle! Here multi-variable linear regression makes sense, provided one understands what one is doing. This means being aware of the broad laws and the extent of the range over which they can or cannot be linearly approximated. These underlying laws themselves, however, cannot be discovered by statistical approaches alone. Trying to do so is a dead end, be it in physical or social sciences. Discovering natural or social laws requires thinking about how things might hang together. The sooner social scientists reach this insight, the sooner social sciences can become sciences with some ability to predict.

The scientific method includes creativity, which by definition cannot be reduced to a cookbook formula or a computer program. It may mean creation of new methods, but often it is a matter of creative choice among existing building blocks to pick and combine. The broad approach

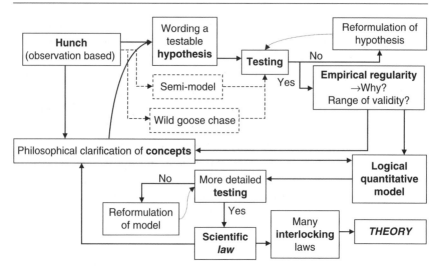

Figure 14.3. Cycles and sub-cycles in scientific procedure

that underlies the thinking in this book was briefly presented earlier (Chapter 6) as an ascending spiral:

> Initial hunch (qualitative hypothesis) → limited data collection →
> → quick testing → quantitative predictive model (quantitative hypothesis) → further data collection → testing → refined model → testing → further refining of model *or* data → testing...

Figure 14.3 fleshes it out, without claiming that this is the only way to see it. The scientific method may look somewhat different to different people.

We start with qualitative observations about apparent or possible relationships among phenomena. In a relaxed way, we try to find measurable features that express some hopefully essential aspects of these phenomena. We do not expect an operational measure to express the entire essence of notions like "literacy," "individualism" or "power." Humbly, we feel lucky if our measure has hopes to express *something* about such notions. It is an observation-based hunch.

Some quick and superficial data collection would follow, so as to get a "fingertip feel" for the data (*Fingerspitzengefühl*, as political scientist Harry Eckstein used to put it in our private conversations). This includes a feel for the range of occurrence of various variables and their possible interactions. Does *y* always decrease with increasing *x*, or is it messier than that? Could it first go up and then down? The more manual is this stage, the more one may get a feel for the data. Entering data into a table by hand might be preferable to typing them into a computer. The same goes for graphing.

At this stage, quantitatively predictive modeling could but need not begin. A testable hypothesis may be worded, or it could remain only a diffuse quasi-model. It might even be a wild goose chase with no more specific "hypothesis" than reconnoitering the terrain and hoping to gain further serendipitous insights. As a result, the initial hypothesis may be specified or reworded, leading to a repeat of the previous cycle. Or an empirical regularity may surface, leading to questions "Why?" and "Over which range is it valid?" It may lead to a philosophical clarification of the underlying concepts.

At the same time, broader data collection might take place. It may include further variables that might conceivably affect the outputs either directly or by modifying the direct inputs. Linear regression and other standard descriptive approaches could be applied at this stage of preliminary investigation, so as to sort out the most promising factors. Yet, one has to keep in mind that a low degree of linear relationship does not necessarily exclude a variable—it may be related strongly in a nonlinear form which is to be found by predictive modeling. Conversely, a strong showing by a variable that logically does not fit in suggests it might be a proxy for some other, more meaningful factor. The model may consist of several stages, each involving only a few variables. At this stage, statistical analysis is not an end in itself but a way to supply thinking material for a logical model.

Once a quantitatively predictive logical model has been devised, statistical methods enter again, this time for testing the model. However, now the testing is not done on raw input variables but on their transforms. This is why "model testing" is preferable to "hypothesis testing," a term which has been devalued in social sciences to mean nothing more precise than directional testing on raw inputs.

If linear regression is to be used in model testing, then the variables must first be transformed in the light of the model so that linear relationships could be expected. It is not always easy. When there are no free parameters, one can regress actual values against the predicted ones and vice versa, expecting both $y = 0 + 1.00x$ and $x = 0 + 1.00y$—which means that symmetrical regression (Chapter 12) must be used. But when the regression itself must be used to calculate the parameters, transformation may become difficult.

If testing does not confirm the model, not only the model may be reformulated but also the data may be revised. Either way, the testing cycle is repeated. Once testing is highly successful, a law in the scientific sense might result. Finally, combination of many interlocking laws may lead to a theory as a grand roof.

In sum, linear regression and other descriptive approaches have their place in preliminary investigation at the one end and in testing logically established quantitative models at the other. In between, descriptive approaches alone are disastrous when they substitute for logical modeling.

15

Recommendations for Better Regression

- Take seriously the introductory advice by most introductory texts of statistics: graph the data and look at the graph so as to make sure linear regression makes sense from a *statistical* viewpoint.
- Graph more than the data—graph the entire conceptually allowed area and anchor points so as to make sure linear regression makes sense from a *substantive* viewpoint.
- If using linear regression, report not only the regression coefficients and the intercept but also the ranges, mean values, and medians of all input variables.
- Symmetric regression has advantages over OLS. But fully reported and symmetric regression is still merely regression.
- Look up further recommendations in the Conclusions.

Establishing a quantitatively predictive logical model is never automatic. One has to understand the nature of the problem on hand. It is easy to give such general advice, but it is not very helpful. How does one start? What is the first practical step, for a person who knows the statistical methods to some extent but has no idea where to go beyond that? This chapter addresses the issue of starting from scratch, or almost so, and making the most of statistical approaches.

Data: Graph It!

This is the advice all good introductory statistics texts offer (e.g., King et al. 1994; Berry and Sanders 2000). Take them seriously! Once this advice is given, these texts assume that you have followed it, and they focus on

Table 15.1. Four data-sets that lead to the same linear fit and R^2 when linear regression is (mis)applied

X	y_1	y_2	y_3	y_4
4.00	4.26	3.10	5.39	6.00
5.00	5.68	4.74	5.73	5.75
6.00	7.24	6.13	6.08	5.50
7.00	4.82	7.26	6.42	5.25
8.00	6.95	8.14	6.77	5.00
9.00	8.81	8.77	7.11	7.50
10.00	8.04	9.14	7.46	10.00
11.00	8.33	9.26	7.81	9.75
12.00	10.84	9.13	8.15	9.50
13.00	7.58	8.74	12.74	9.25
14.00	9.96	8.10	8.84	9.00

Source for y_1 to y_3: Anscombe (1973); y_4 is my own addition.

All y_n vs. x have the same properties: mean $x = 9.00$; mean $y = 7.50$; $R = .82$; $R^2 = .67$; regression line y on x: $y = 3.00 + 0.50x$. Regression line x on y corresponds to $y = 0.75 + 0.75x$, and symmetric regression line is $y = 1.9 + 0.61x$.

data for which linear analysis is justified. The introductory text may later address the issue of fitting nonlinear data configurations, but it may do it so briefly as to leave the mistaken impression that linear configurations are the rule and curved configurations rare exceptions. The reverse is the case, once forbidden areas are taken into account.

Various patterns where linear analysis would ignore reality were presented in Figures 3.1 and 3.2. The matter is so important that it is worth offering further cautionary examples. Anscombe (1973) has published a splendid collection of four data-sets which look identical in standard linear regression. Three of them are shown in Table 15.1 (y_1, y_2, y_3), along with an addition of my own (y_4). They all have the same mean and range of the input variable, the same mean and approximately the same range of the output variable, the same respectable linear correlation coefficient ($R = .82$, $R^2 = .67$), the same OLS regression lines y-on-x and x-on-y, the same symmetric regression line, etc. Yet linear regression makes sense in only one of the four data-sets, as jumps to the eye the moment these data are graphed in Figure 15.1.

It can be seen that linear regression looks acceptable for y_1 because the data cloud is uniformly dispersed, with no visible curvature. In the case of y_2, the points fit neatly on a parabolic-looking curve, and a corresponding transformation should be applied before statistical testing. The transformation could be based on statistical considerations, but this is also prime time for asking *why* this is so that y first rises and then falls with

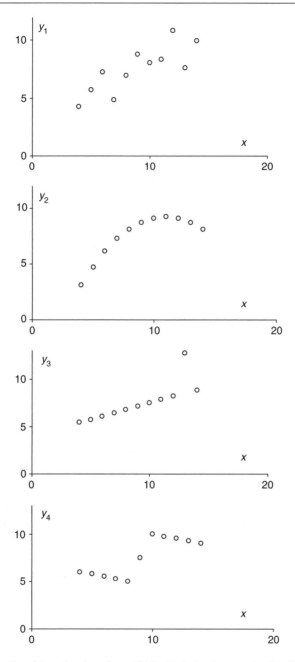

Figure 15.1. Graphing the data from Table 15.1 checks on whether linear regression makes sense

increasing x. Data-set y_3 has 10 points perfectly aligned, while one point is a blatant outlier which clearly does not belong and should be omitted. The statistical justification for deletion is that it deviates by more than 3 standard deviations. One should also try to figure out how it came to be included in the first place. Maybe there is a typo.

All these three data-sets have the same x values, ranging uniformly from 4 to 14. In contrast, Anscombe's (1973) fourth data-set (not shown) had 10 points with the same value of x and hence forming a vertical line, plus a single point elsewhere. I have replaced it in Table 15.1 and Figure 15.1 with another data-set (y_4) where x ranges from 4 to 14. This set, too, has the same mean x, mean y, regression equations, and R^2 as the rest. When graphed, a pattern emerges that is far from a rising straight line. We observe two distinct populations where y actually decreases with increasing x, plus an isolate. This pattern should make us wonder about the underlying structure.

Graph More than the Data!

Graphs should include not only the data but also boundary conditions, anchor points, and sometimes the equality lines. Only then can the data be seen in a wider perspective conducive to model building. In particular, when both x and y are in percentages, entire ranges from 0 to 100% should be shown.

This was effectively the case in Figure 12.1, which also illustrates two general features. First, linear regression oblivious of conceptual constraints can lead to viewing as deviant some data points that eminently do fit. Second, drawing in the equality line may offer a handy comparison level, even when there is no reason to expect equality of y and x. Some simple patterns that may make sense were discussed in Chapter 8.

Figure 15.2 (reproduced from Taagepera 2007c: 71) illustrates the need to graph more than the data. It shows the "proportionality profiles" for elections in two countries: advantage ratio (% seats/% votes) graphed versus the percentage of votes. As far as the data are concerned, the range beyond 60% could be omitted—and often mistakenly is. When graphing only the US data, the range below 30% would also seem superfluous, and the range of advantage ratio could be restricted to 0.7 to 1.2. Indeed, many computer programs impose the ranges 30 to 60 and 0.7 to 1.2. The empirical "best fit" OLS line would be calculated, along with R^2 and

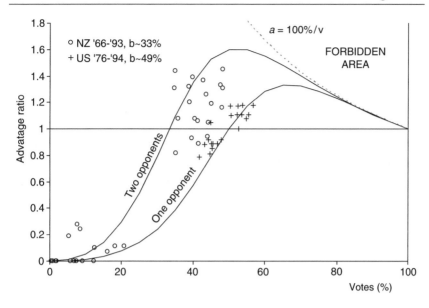

Figure 15.2. Proportionality profiles for elections in New Zealand and the United States: data and conceptual range (from Taagepera 2007c: 71)

some measure of significance. This line would extrapolate to a very high advantage ratio near 100% votes and a negative advantage ratio (implying negative number of seats) near 0% votes. However, much food for thought emerges the moment the entire allowed range is included in the graph—0 to 100% votes and 0 to much above 1 for the advantage ratio, as shown in Figure 15.2.

Once the full conceptual range is included in the graph, we are motivated to ask what the advantage ratio would be for zero votes. It would be expected to lead to zero seats. This may look like an indeterminate zero/zero, but consider the percentage of votes *tending toward* zero. At sufficiently few votes, any electoral system would allocate zero seats, so that the advantage ratio becomes zero. This is a lower anchor point.

We would also be motivated to ask what the advantage ratio would be for 100% votes. Such a party would be expected to win 100% of seats—but no more! This means an advantage ratio of only 1.00. This is an upper anchor point. It is then easy to establish that $a > 100\%/v$ is a conceptually forbidden area, as indicated in Figure 15.2.

In sum, the linear OLS fit becomes untenable. The curve must bend up toward the point (0; 0) at low values. It also must bend down toward

(100; 1) at high values of votes. One could draw in such a curve, free-hand, and one would not be far off from the curve shown, which is based on a logical model (see Taagepera 2007c: 201–11).

Consider Graphing by Hand

Figure 12.1 further illustrates some problematic features that canned graphing programs may present. When graphing on a computer, one may find that the program used imposes an autoformat mood that refuses to extend the scale beyond the range of actual data, or extends it excessively, and also refuses to enter the equality line.

The scales shown on the two axes in Figure 12.1 run from less than 0 to more than 10, although the ratings involved can go only from 0 to 10. Hence the borders shown are wider than the conceptual limits. In the given case the entire conceptually allowed space is filled with data points, however sparsely, so that the conceptual limits stand out visually despite not being shown. With fewer data points, however, visual impression can be quite misleading, by suggesting that extreme cases do not occur when they actually do. This is the case, for instance, with several graphs in Arend Lijphart's excellent *Patterns of Democracy* (1999: 193, 214, 229, and 241). The author tells me that his original graphs were restricted to the conceptual limits, but they were altered during the publishing process so as to look nicer by some nonscientific criteria. Thus, even those of us who know better have to struggle against the dictates of computerized graphing.

The autoformat of graphing programs usually can be overridden, but some overrides need fair computer skills. Small wonder then that students sometimes offer technical restrictions as something one has to yield to and accept. This is not so. Computers are supposed to help us do science, not hamper us. If a canned program restricts research, look for a more flexible one. If none can be found at the moment, do the graphs by hand. As an alternative, one may copy the computer graph in a sufficiently reduced form so that one can add by hand the conceptual limits (and the equality line, if it makes sense).

There are some broad advantages in doing graphs by hand, on paper with a square grid. My experience is that students who graph by hand understand graphs better and notice more detailed implications, compared to those who let the machine do the job. This understanding becomes crucial when graphing on logarithmic scales is required, as is the case whenever relationships have the form $y = ax^b$ or $y = ae^{kx}$. All too many social science students cannot take in the information contained in printed graphs of such format unless they have graphed data themselves on old-fashioned "fully log" or "semi-log" graph papers.

When the data involve more than one input variable, simple two-dimensional graphing can use only one input at a time. A second input variable can be introduced by color-coding data points as Low, Medium, or High for that variable. Approximate best fit curves for these sub-groups can yield some ideas on how this second input affects the output. Constraints imposed by the second input can be shown in a similar way.

One may run an exploratory multivariable linear regression (preferably the symmetric version) so as to get some rough idea of which variables matter the most. Then the output can be graphed against some of the inputs, to check that there is no curvature or some other odd feature akin to those in Figure 14.1. There are statistically more elegant ways to do it, but the power of eyeballing should not be undervalued. This is so even when one truly understands the statistical methods one uses, including their limitations—and even more so when this is not the case. The gravitation test in Chapter 2 serves as a warning: There is no guarantee that multifactor linear regression can pin down the underlying processes, but it is one way to proceed in exploratory research.

Turning the Pattern Linear

Once the pattern of data plus conceptual anchor points and boundary conditions has been established, one should look for an explanation in terms of a quantitatively predictive logical model. One may or may not succeed at the moment. Either way, the data should be transformed into a format where linear regression or some other standard statistical procedure (e.g., *logit* or *probit*) makes sense. If a logical model is proposed and it involves no free parameters, one could graph the actual values against the expected ones and run symmetric linear regression. If no model can be proposed, some empirical transformation may be found, such as the ones in Chapter 8, which transforms the data cloud *and the anchor points* into something not outrageously far from linear shape.

Many statistical approaches go beyond linear regression, but I will focus on the latter, because a fair share of quantitative publications in social sciences uses something based on or closely related to OLS version of linear regression. Thus any issues raised in this context have wider implications. Preferably, OLS should be replaced by symmetric linear regression (Chapter 12), but either way, regression results should be reported in such a way that other researchers can make the most of them. This is not so self-evident.

How to Publish Regression Results

Why do we publish regression coefficients? What is the purpose of getting into print tables that sometimes fill an appreciable chunk of the total space in an article? We presumably want to let other scholars know about our research and enable them to make use of it (hopefully leading to entries to our benefit in their *citation index*). The eventual overall outcome of such joint effort should be some cumulative knowledge useful to society and/or decision-makers. If so, then how come that a statistician recently told me that many social science papers look qualitative, with statistical analysis added as an afterthought or decoration?

A colleague once told me that the purpose of publishing statistical stuff is to satisfy grant-giving outfits, even while "everyone knows that it is meaningless." Most of us do not play such a cynical game, but many may respectfully follow a mysterious tradition. Publishing regression coefficients is just what we are supposed to do, so as to fit the commonly accepted norm. Trouble is that the game earns us little respect outside the profession, if it produces no useful results. We can do better than that.

When we publish regression coefficients, then why do we do it? There might be goals less demanding than quantitative prediction (precise or imprecise) or at least postdiction. This issue is discussed in the Appendix to Chapter 15. What is certain is that publishing of regression coefficients becomes mandatory if we want to give our colleagues (and ourselves) some predictive/postdictive capability beyond the direction of impact. "When a, b, ... are the given numerical values of variables A, B, ... our best guess for the numerical value of y would be $y = b_0 + b_A a + b_B b + \ldots$, where b_0 is the intercept, and the other b_i are the regression coefficients for A, B, ..." This is predictive in an explanatory way, if there is a logical model, and at least postdictive (cf. Chapter 1), if no logical model can be found. Moreover, regression coefficients can sometimes supply a starting point toward a quantitatively predictive logical model (see Chapter 16).

Enabling predictions is a major intellectually supportable reason for spending printed space on numerical values of regression coefficients. If

Table 15.2. A typical table of regression results

Independent variables	N_V	N_S
Effective threshold (T)	−0.03**	−0.05**
Log assembly size (log S)	0.12	0.12
Intercept	4.07	3.66
R^2	.11	.30
Adjusted R^2	.08	.28

*Statistically significant at the 5% level.
**Statistically significant at the 1% level.

we publish them, we might as well do so in the most fruitful way. It will be seen that even a little upgrade of present practices would go a long way. The advice has been around at least since Gary King's *Unifying Political Methodology: The Likelihood Theory of Statistical Inference* (1989).

The example in Table 15.2 is excerpted from a case (Lijphart 1994: 108) that already is among the better ones, as it does include all the regression coefficients, intercept included. Standardized coefficients, *t*-values and some output variables have been omitted here, and the labels for variables have been modified. Only two input variables have been kept: effective threshold of representation (T), and the logarithm of assembly size (log$S$). The output variables are the effective numbers of parties (as defined in Chapter 4), based respectively on votes (for N_V) and on seats (for N_S). The database can be inferred from other tables in Lijphart (1994), and this comes in handy in the course of the following discussion.

This table means that the average outputs for given inputs can be calculated from $N_V = 4.07 + 0.12 \log S - 0.03T$ and $N_S = 3.66 + 0.12 \log S - 0.05T$, respectively. For a given electoral system, one could look up the actual values of T and S, and calculate the best estimates for N from these equations. But Table 15.2 indicates that S is not statistically significant. Then why should we have to look up its specific values when we want to calculate N_V and N_S? The values of S are random and could as well be replaced by the *mean value* of S for the cases used in regression (King 1989: 105)—if we knew this mean value. The problem is that Table 15.2 does *not* report the mean values of the input variables. Despite King's (1989) advice to include them, this has not been part of general practice—and this is precisely my point. *The way regression coefficients are customarily published, one cannot use them for prediction, short of looking up lots of input data which the author has found to be nonsignificant.*

The present example was chosen because in this case the data in other tables in Lijphart (1994) enables me to estimate the geometric mean of

S. It is around 148 seats. (The median is 158.) With substitution $\log S = \log 148 = 2.17$, the previous equations become $N_V = 4.07 + 0.12 \times 2.17 - 0.03T = 4.33 - 0.03T$ and $N_S = 3.66 + 0.12 \times 2.17 - 0.05T = 3.92 - 0.05T$. If one graphs N versus T, these are the best fit equations.

It is extremely important to note that one can no longer use the intercept values listed in Table 15.2, once one omits variable S. This would be akin to assuming $0.12 \log S = 0$ for the average assembly, which is the case when the assembly has only one seat—an obvious underestimate. When one omits nonsignificant variables, the new intercept must include the average effect of the omitted variables. All linear (and similar) regression results worth publishing should report not only the regression coefficients and the intercept but also the mean values of all input variables.

Why require also the mean values of significant factors? There are four reasons. The first is uniformity of reporting. Second, when there are several statistically significant factors, we may wish to focus on only one, using the mean values of the others. This is what we would do, in particular, when graphing the output against one of the inputs, so as to detect possible nonlinear relationships (King 1989: 105). Third, reporting the y-on-x regression equation plus R^2 enables one to calculate the x-on-y and symmetric regression lines (Chapter 12), provided that the means are also given.

The fourth reason is that all too often there are many ways to assign a measure to a conceptual variable (cf. Chapter 13). Social science authors are not very good at specifying which measure they are using, especially when they personally are used to one of them, to the exclusion of all others. Thus, an author may describe a variable as party system "fractionalization" while actually reporting the effective number of parties (N) rather than the Rae-Taylor fractionalization index (F). Since F varies from 0 to 1 while N varies from 1 upwards, reporting the mean value helps to clarify which measure was used in the given regression equation.

But even more should be reported. In response to a draft of this section, Steve Coleman suggests that the domain (range) of all input variables should be reported. This is indeed desirable, as it would tell us over what range the model can reasonably be used to estimate outputs. In the present case, S ranges from 60 to 630 ($\log S$ ranging from 1.8 to 2.8) and T (in percent) from 0.1 to 35.

A zero value may be well outside these domains, as is the case here for $\log S$. If so, then minor changes in data may cause large fluctuations in the value of the intercept. As a result, the intercept may look statistically "not significant" even at the 5% level. This is the case in Table 15.2. I have

Table 15.3. A typical table of regression results, with suggested complements

Independent variables	Domain (Range)	Mean	Median	Coefficients for	
				N_V	N_S
Effective threshold (T)	0.1 to 35	11.6	7.0	−0.03**	−0.05**
Log assembly size (log$S$)	1.8 to 2.8	2.2	2.2	0.12	0.12
Intercept				4.07	3.66
R^2				0.11	0.30
Adjusted R^2				0.08	0.28

*Statistically significant at the 5% level.
**Statistically significant at the 1% level.

encountered arguments that such a "nonsignificant" intercept should be omitted from estimates of outputs, but this would mean assigning a zero value to the intercept, which often makes no sense at all. Intercepts 4.07 and 3.66 in Table 15.2 might conceivably be off by ±0.1 or even ±1, but assuming them to be 0 would lead to practically all estimates of the number of parties to be negative. We must avoid absurdities.

In addition to arithmetic mean, the median should be reported, because a disagreement between mean and median serves as a simple warning light to show that the actual relationship is not linear. In the case of Table 15.2, data in Lijphart (1994) confirm that mean and median of log$S$ are both 2.2, but for T the mean (11.6) strongly exceeds the median (7.0). The corresponding curvature appears when graphing N versus T (not shown here). It suggests that linear regression should be applied to log$T$ rather than T. This idea is reinforced when one notes that effective threshold cannot be negative.

Table 15.3 expands the previous table to include the suggested complements. In sum, we can easily improve on the customary format of reporting, so as to make the published results much more useful for estimates of outputs, for graphing the average patterns, for calculating reverse and symmetric regression lines, and for resulting comparison with analysis of other data-sets. It also helps in devising logical models, something not followed up in this example. The general recommendation is as follows.

All linear (and similar) regression results worth publishing should report not only the regression coefficients and the intercept but also the ranges, mean values, and medians of all input variables.

Steve Coleman raises one further point that goes back to Fisher (1956: 42): "Personally I find it annoying when people only report what is significant at certain p levels, usually $p < .05$, which is a not very helpful convention and more of a historical accident of statistics. I prefer the actual p value so I can make up my own mind" (Steven Coleman, personal communication, June 2007). It might take little extra room to add this information too.

Conclusion: Ten Recommendations for Running and Reporting Linear Regression

Statistical analysis and regression in particular can be done better than it often has been done in social sciences, by following a few simple recommendations. For those based on arguments presented in other chapters, these chapters are briefly indicated.

1. *Use regression only for exploratory research and for testing quantitatively predictive logical models.* These are the early and the late phases in research process. Do not even think of using regression for model construction itself (cf. Chapter 14).

2. *Graph possibly meaningful relationships, so as to avoid running linear regression on inappropriate data configurations.* First, this means taking seriously the introductory advice by most statistics texts: graph the data and look at the graph so as to make sure linear regression makes sense from a *statistical* viewpoint. Second, graph more than the data—graph the entire conceptually allowed area and anchor points so as to make sure linear regression makes sense from a *substantive* viewpoint.

3. *Replace the practice of profusion of variables by the principle of parsimony.* Having more than two or three input variables in a regression disregards Occam's razor (cf. Chapters 3 and 5). Use sequential equations rather a single melting pot. Avoid dummy variables.

4. *When regression makes sense at all, replace unidirectional by symmetric regression* (cf. Chapter 12).

5. *Distinguish between statistical significance and substantive meaningfulness* (cf. Chapter 6).

6. *Avoid "asterisk syndrome"*—report actual significance levels rather than $p < .01$ and $p < .05$.

7. *Report not only regression coefficients and the intercept but also the ranges, means, and medians for all input variables.*

8. *Report only one of the many regressions you might run,* the one you deem the most meaningful (cf. Chapter 5 and 7).

9. *Run separate regressions for low, median, and high thirds of those "control variables" you really deem meaningful*, not just statistically "significant." This is a loophole for item 8, an afterthought that may be debatable.

10. *Do not use these recommendations blindly.* Think. There can be exceptions. Know what you do and do what you know.

It should not be concluded that following this advice would make indiscriminate application of statistics acceptable. When linear regression amounts to unjustified data crunching, it remains so even when the results are fully reported, symmetric regression is used, etc.

Appendix to Chapter 15

How NOT to Publish Regression Results

One rarely encounters articles that show only the correlation coefficient R^2, omitting the regression coefficients. Rather frequently, however, intercept is omitted. I will first address the information value (or lack thereof) of such presentations, followed by more general discussion.

I Have a Well-Fitting Relationship but Will Not Tell You What It Is

In his study of volatility (as reported in Chapter 4), Heath (2005) observes that earlier studies (Pedersen 1983; Bartolini and Mair 1990) also obtain a positive relationship with the number of parties but his has a higher R^2. He could not compare his best-fit equation to previous ones, because these earlier studies only reported correlation coefficients, without giving the substantive equation relative to which the R^2 is calculated. Now imagine Galileo reporting the R^2 for speeds of falling bodies, while omitting the equation to which it relates! If this had been the practice in physics, we would not have computers in the first place, with which even those averse to mathematics can calculate the R^2.

It may be argued that one might want to see if a set of variables "explains" an outcome better than another set, by comparing their R^2, without aiming at prediction. But what does an "explanation" stand for, if devoid of ability to predict? In the case above, if all authors obtained roughly the same intercept and slope in $V = a + bN$, we would have a solid empirical regularity even if all of them found low values of R^2. The numerical values of a and b would still look reproducible. On the other hand, if they all got high R^2 but for wildly different regression lines, then we would have nothing, unless we could introduce some other factor to explain the discrepancy. In such a case, high values of R^2 would actually enhance the confusion (cf. Chapter 4, section "Can data with low R^2 confirm a model?").

Correlation coefficients are pointless in the absence of equations. It should be realized that even the worst-quality data fit equation is worth more than an excellent value of R^2, reported devoid of the substantive equation to which it applies. If a physicist reported R^2 alone, he would meet blank stares: You say you have good quality results, but what *are* the results? The practice of reporting R^2 without the equation to which it refers has fortunately become rare. The cult of R^2 carried to that point would pull any journal down to the level of pseudo-scientific formalism.

What Can One Predict Without Intercept?

The argument can be made that some types of predictions can be made without the intercept. In many applied situations one is concerned with the change in output variable (y) when an input variable (x) is changed marginally (by an amount Δx). For any given starting position (x_0; y_0), if we know the regression slope b, we supposedly can infer that at $x_1 = x_0 + \Delta x$ we would have $y_1 = y_0 + b\Delta x$. No knowledge of intercept seems needed. To what extent does it hold?

Consider a regression line with positive slope, as shown in Figure 15.3. The regression slope is the property of the data-set as a whole. As such, it is likely to apply to *typical* points, those at or close to the regression line, such as point A in Figure 15.3. Starting from A, a marginal increase in x is likely to move us to a point A_1, on the regression line.

But what about an outlier, such as point B? How sure can we be that a movement parallel to the regression line would take place, to point B_1, as application of slope b would lead to? The location of B could result from a random disturbance off the general pattern, which represents a sort of equilibrium. If so, then an increase in x

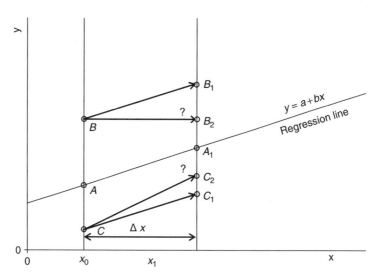

Figure 15.3. Will outliers follow the regression slope?

212

may exert no pressure at all on B to move further upwards, and the outcome might be point B_2. In the absence of any further information, our best guess would be that the actual slope would be somewhat less than b. Conversely, an outlier in the opposite direction, such as C, might move parallel to the regression line, to point C_1, but it might also move with a steeper slope than b, to a point such as C_2, if its outlier position was due to a random disturbance off the general pattern.

In sum, the more the starting point is off the regression line, the more the slope of a marginal change is likely to deviate from regression slope b. The likely direction of deviation, downwards or upwards, is such as to have the point approach the regression line. We are safe to use b only when the starting point is reasonably close to the regression line. (I will not go into the mathematics of what is "reasonable.") How do we know that the point we start from is not a marked outlier? We have to compare it to the regression line—which means we have to know intercept a.

Estimating the change in y for a marginal change in x on the basis of regression slope alone is based on the tacit assumption that the starting point is close to the regression line. Even in the absence of intercept, we can of course try to do our best. When not knowing whether our starting point deviates upwards or downwards from the regression line, our best guess is indeed that it is on this line. But why omit reporting the intercept, when this information is readily available and would enable the users of one's results to avoid the risk of predicting on the basis of an outlier?

Why do We Publish Regression Coefficients?

When we publish regression coefficients, then why do we do it? If the purpose is merely to report which factors have a "significant" effect on the output and in which direction, then it can be done in briefer form. No reporting of regression coefficients is needed for rejecting the null hypothesis or confirming a directional hypothesis—except for proving that one has actually carried out the statistical analysis. Beyond such reasons of transparency of analysis, one may just report which factors have a statistically "significant" positive effect, and in which direction. Printing regression coefficients would be superfluous for these purposes. These coefficients are needed only when one wants to make predictions.

This claim of mine has raised many hackles. Goals are asserted to exist that do not involve quantitative prediction but still need presentation of numerical values of coefficients. One may highlight a specific relation in a way that falls short of a strong quantitative interpretation, yet could not easily be summarized with only significance and direction. The objective may be to describe the general shape of causal relationships, rather than precise point estimates, so I am told.

All right, I can backtrack a little. There might be goals that fall between directionality and quantitative prediction. I might even think of examples in physics where such goals served a purpose—but only a temporary purpose while looking for predictability. It would be surprising if a large part of social sciences remained in that stage of development without need or possibility to proceed toward prediction.

Even purely empirical regressions equation could be predictive at least in a limited sense. If one plugged into it values of input variables for a case not included in the original regression, then the predictions could be compared to the actual values of the output variable—and deviations could occur. Calculation of predicted output values for new cases is the simplest to visualize and to carry out when the regression equation $y = a + \sum b_i x_i$ is written out, with the actual numerical values of coefficients inserted. Then it is easy to plug in the values of input variables for a new case. (The procedure is most direct for OLS, while requiring a standard conversion of variables in the case of *logit* and *probit*.) But this is not the usual format in social sciences. Most authors present coefficients b_i in a table, not within an equation.

Now suppose one asked the author of such an article: "OK, when for a given country we have $x_1 = 30$, $x_2 = 0.7$ and $x_3 = 273$, what is your best guess for the value of y for this country, on the basis of your table?" One may have doubts about some social scientists' ability to answer such a question, because in quite a few cases the constant (a) is omitted from their table (cf. Chapter 7), so that no answer is possible.

When such omissions can occur in published social science work, it strongly suggests that neither authors nor reviewers have prediction in mind. If an article includes several different "empirical models" for the same output variable, each would produce a somewhat different answer. Take your pick. Offering many competing answers amounts to offering none. For physics students, plugging values into a given formula is the lowest type of exercise, devoid of much thinking. But to what extent have social science practices reached even that stage?

16

Converting from Descriptive Analysis to Predictive Models

- The results of existing statistical analysis can sometimes be used to estimate the parameters in quantitatively predictive logical models. This is important, because it expands the value of previously published work in social sciences.
- Inferring logical model parameters in this way may require more involved mathematics than direct testing.

Suppose one already has analyzed the problem extensively from the statistical angle. When one wants to proceed to logical model building, how much can one extract from published statistical data analysis rather than start from scratch? Echoing Freedman (1987), Hedström (2004) feels that "estimating parameters of models that do not mirror substantive causal processes can only rarely be expected to yield valuable insights into causal process." Directly, this looks so, indeed. Indirectly, something might be scavenged. This applies foremost to quantities with a natural zero, implying a ratio scale. Conversion is more difficult for opinion polls and ratings, where the zero is set arbitrarily. The importance of this difference will emerge in Chapter 17.

The following example from recent literature shows that sometimes descriptive analysis already does include the ingredients for a predictive model. Here constants of the predictive model can be inferred from the regression coefficients, and the outcome casts new light on the meaning of these regression coefficients. The example also shows that a predictive model of a multiplicative format can sometimes be constructed even when this seems precluded at first glance by lack of a natural zero for some variables.

Votes for the Incumbent

The study of presidentialism and accountability by Samuels (2004) is a good example of competent linear regression analysis. It posits the following baseline model for gain or loss of votes for the incumbent president's party:

$$s = V_1 - V_0 = a + b_1 V_0 + b_2 E + b_3[I].$$

Here s is "vote swing" for the incumbent's party, defined as the difference between percent votes shares in initial and later elections (V_0 and V_1, respectively). Impact of economy, E, is operationalized as percent change in GDP/capita, and I is a dummy variable: $I = 0$ when the incumbent president's party presents a new candidate, while $I = 1$ when the incumbent runs for reelection.

A total of 13 different regressions result when Samuels (2004) distinguishes between concurrent and nonconcurrent executive and legislative elections, introduces further input variables, and adds multiplicative interaction terms. Out of these 13 equations, 8 have $I = 1$. The values of R^2 range from .12 to .39. Each regression involves 2 to 4 input variables and 1.33 to 1.67 constants/coefficients per input variable. It adds up to a total listing of 64 numerical values of freely adjustable constants/coefficients. Their numerical values cover a wide range. Depending on the inputs, a ranges from 3.0 to 18.2, b_1 from -0.18 to -0.56, b_2 from -0.5 to $+1.3$, and b_3 from 4.9 to 9.6.

Are these profligate and widely disparate values another instance of numbers dead on arrival in printed journal (Chapter 7)? It will be seen that quite a lot can be converted into something more stable. The "crazy methodology" can lead to something that makes sense.

Constructing a Predictive Model

How could we build a predictive model for the loss of votes? Since s and E can take positive or negative values, a multiplicative format (as highlighted in Chapter 5) may seem precluded. A shift in variables, however, makes it possible. Samuels (2004) observes that

1. the incumbent president's party tends to lose votes even when economy remains stable (i.e., when $E = 0$);

2. running the incumbent president improves the party's chances; and

3. an expanding economy improves the chances of the incumbent's party. Let us try to express these observations quantitatively, as simply as possible.

Consider first the simplified situation where economy is stable and there is no reelection of incumbent president. The subsequent vote share can be expected to depend on the initial vote share: $V_1 = f(V_0)$. The simplest way to specify this function is to assume that subsequent vote is proportional to the initial vote: $V_1 = V_0/p$, where the *penalty* constant (p) must be larger than 1.

If the party runs the incumbent, this outcome is multiplied by a *reelection* bonus (r), which must be larger than 1. Then $V_1 = V_0(r/p)$. Here r/p represents the total penalty-bonus constant in the case of reelection at constant economy.

Addition-oriented social scientists may point out that it is even simpler to subtract a penalty p' and add a reelection bonus r', leading to $V_1 = V_0 - p' + r'$. The difficulty is that it could lead to a negative V_1 at sufficiently low V_0. Extremely low initial votes for a presidential party certainly are rare, although presidents at times do emerge from quite small parties when two-round elections are used. More important, logically grounded models must not predict absurdities even at unrealistically extreme values. The same observation supports a multiplicative approach as we next address the impact of economy.

The impact of economy can be entered by comparing GDP/capita (g) before and after, that is, multiplying the previous outcome by g_1/g_0. This ratio exceeds 1 for an expanding economy and falls short of 1 for a shrinking one. Its impact on votes need not be proportional, so it should be entered with an exponent, n, which must be positive. The overall multiplicative model then is

$$V_1 = V_0(g_1/g_0)^n(r/p).$$

Taking logarithms reduces this model to a linear format suitable for linear regression, so as to determine the numerical values of the constants:

$$\ln V_1 = \ln V_0 + n\ln(g_1/g_0) + \ln r - \ln p.$$

Note that, despite my skepticism regarding dummy variables (Chapter 5), $\ln r$ effectively amounts to the coefficient of a dummy variable.

217

Guessing at the Values of Constants in the Model

This model has three adjustable constants (n, r, and p), compared to four in Samuels's baseline linear regression equation (2004). Moreover, here the constants have specific meanings and none are quite freely adjustable. Indeed, the penalty constant in the case of a new presidential candidate (p) cannot be less than 1—otherwise it would become a bonus. We would also be surprised, if more than one-half of the votes were lost ($p > 2$), although this is by no means a firm conceptual boundary (cf. Chapter 4). We could express it as

$$1 < p <\sim 2.$$

If forced to offer a specific value, I might offer the geometric mean: $p \approx 1.4$. The reelection bonus (r), when an incumbent president runs again, must also be more than 1, if it is to be a bonus, but it would surprise us, if reelection of the incumbent added 50% to the votes for the party. Hence

$$1 < r <\sim 1.5.$$

If forced to offer a specific value, I might offer $r \approx 1.2$, so that $r/p \approx 0.86$. But a further concern enters. The limits above would suggest that the vague limits on r/p are $\sim 1/2 < r/p <\sim 1.5$. Yet we may feel surprised if running the incumbent president fully abolishes the general incumbency penalty, hence we may feel that the upper limit on r/p is 1. If so, then $\sim 1/2 < r/p < 1$ would lower my average guess to $r/p \approx 0.70$.

The exponent n expresses whether a given change (g_1/g_0) in economy affects the change in votes (V_1/V_0) more than proportionately or less. It certainly must be positive—otherwise the incumbent party would get a bonus for poor economy. In the other direction, it would be surprising if economy entered with a very high exponent, so we might surmise that

$$0 < n <\sim 2.$$

In the absence of any knowledge about the direction of deviation from proportional effect, the average guess would be $n = 1$.

The attentive reader may have noticed another restriction. When the highest non-surprising values of r and n and the lowest non-surprising value of p are introduced in the model, V_1 could surpass 1 (100%) even for a fairly modest value of V_0. Building avoidance of this possibility into the model would complicate it, so I will neglect it in first approximation. Once the empirical values of the constants are determined, however, we must check that they do not lead to $V_1 > 1$ even for $V_0 = 1$.

In sum, the multiplicative model predicts not only a functional relationship but also the limits on acceptable values of the constants. While some of these limits are flexible, deviations far beyond the expectations would motivate a reexamination of the model. In contrast to the freely adjustable coefficients and intercept in regression equations, the present model has not a single completely freely adjustable constant—which makes the model eminently falsifiable.

One further prediction enters. Samuels's study (2004) includes both presidential and legislative elections. The presidential elections should be more sensitive than the legislative ones to the performance of the incumbent president. Hence one would expect the values of all constants to be equal or higher in executive elections. This merely directional prediction can also be tested.

Inferring Predictive Model Constants from Regression Coefficients

The best-fitting values of constants in the previous model should be calculated directly from data such as used by Samuels (2004), using linear regression of logarithms, as shown above. However, it can be shown (see the Appendix to Chapter 16), that in the present case the additive format

$$s = V_1 - V_0 = a + b_1 V_0 + b_2 E + b_3 [I]$$

used by Samuels (2004) can be connected to the predictive model when some simplifying assumptions are made. Then the numerical values of regression coefficients reported by Samuels can be used to estimate the constants in the predictive model, as shown in Table 16.1.

The exponent n for impact of economy is quite erratic in executive elections and exceeds the expected range. All other constants have values well within the expected acceptable ranges. They are more conservative (i.e., closer to 1) than my guestimates based on the geometric means of non-surprising ranges.

The observed ranges of numerical values for incumbent penalty (p) and reelection bonus (r) and their combined effect (r/p) are remarkably

Table 16.1. Approximate values of constants in predictive model for vote loss by incumbent's party, calculated from regression coefficients in Samuels (2004)

	Approximate incumbency penalty (p)	Approximate re-election bonus (r)	Approximate ratio r/p	Approximate GNP/ capita exponent (n)
Acceptable range	1 to ~2	1 to ~1.5	~0.5 to 1	0 to ~2
Geometric mean	1.4	1.2	0.70 to 0.86	1 (arithmetic)
All regressions in Samuels (2004)				
Range	1.07 to 1.25	1.10 to 1.21	0.92 to 1.01	−1.04 to +2.56
Median, executive	1.22	1.19	0.96	2.32
Median, legislative	1.16	1.11	0.93	1.38
Median, overall	1.19	1.17	0.95	1.6

limited, in contrast to the disparate regression coefficient values reported in Samuels (2004). How can widely dispersed values of regression constants lead to less dispersed values of constants in the predictive model? The Appendix to Chapter 16 shows how it happens that conversion to regression constants magnifies small variations in constants of the predictive model.

As expected, executive elections do have values of constants that exceed those for legislative elections, but these small differences can be due to random error. If so, then the overall median values of the constants may have broader validity. For instance, they might fit the loss of votes by the incumbent prime minister's party in parliamentary regimes—something that remains to be tested. The generalized model would then be approximately

$$V_1 = V_0(g_1/g_0)^{1.6}[1.17]/(1.19),$$

where "[1.17]" applies only in case of reelection of the incumbent.

What does this expression tell us? When economy remains stable and the incumbent does not run again, her or his party tends to bag only $1/1.19 = 86\%$ of its previous votes. When the incumbent does run, her or his party tends to lose only 2 to 5% (see below). When GDP/capita changes by a certain ratio, it affects votes with a higher ratio. The coefficients in regression equation such as Samuels's (2004) Baseline Model, $s = 12.906 - 0.477V_0 + 1.172E + 8.680[I]$, do not offer such direct interpretation (except arguably for E).

The vagueness "2 to 5%" above has the following reason. The ratio of median r and median p in Table 16.1 is $1.17/1.19 = 0.98$, while the median of r/p derived from individual regressions is 0.95. The model fails at very high V_0 and economic growth, leading to V_1 larger than 100%. It is possible to guard against such possibility, but it would make the model somewhat more complex.

The numerical values in Table 16.1 are approximations based on simplifying assumptions applied to the regression coefficient values reported in Samuels (2004). The actual best-fitting values of constants would have to be calculated directly from linear regression of logarithms, $\ln V_1 = \ln V_0 + n\ln (g_1/g_0) + \ln r - \ln p$. This is of course the proper course to follow, if one designed the project from scratch. The present exercise shows that something may be salvageable even later on, with some loss of precision.

Would such a fit of logarithms yield higher R^2 than those based on regression of $s = V_1 - V_0 = a + b_1 V_0 + b_2 E + b_3 [I]$ as used by Samuels (2004)? It should, if the predictive model applies and the linear format is only an approximation for it. The difference may not be appreciable, however. The payoff is not in precision of fit to particular data-sets. It is in developing average constant values that (a) have a substantive interpretation and (b) might apply to many data-sets, yet yielding an R^2 not much inferior to that of the best fit for a particular set.

Conclusions

The results of existing statistical analysis can sometimes be used to estimate the parameters in quantitatively predictive logical models, once these are constructed. This should keep at bay the specter that an expanded methodological scope could mean junking much of what has been done up to now, making published work and entire careers obsolete. This would be an unfounded concern.

An unusually simple example was presented earlier, in Chapter 4. The one presented here is more realistic, in terms of complexity. Setting up the predictive model was fairly straightforward, and so would be testing it with linear regression of logarithms of variables. Inferring its constants or parameters from those of published linear regression required more involved mathematics—but it could be done. This is important, because it expands the value of previously published work in social sciences.

The reader may see a contradiction with Chapter 14. Here descriptive results could be reinterpreted in terms of a predictive model, however indirectly. The difference is that the predictive model used here happens to involve no sequential stages. All variables considered act directly on the output. In contrast, district magnitude acts on cabinet duration through the intermediary of number of parties.

So let us qualify the previous assertion. Descriptive approaches can be conducive to detection of social laws, if these laws introduce all variables simultaneously. In contrast, descriptive approaches are not conducive to detection of social laws, if these laws introduce variables sequentially, while the descriptive approach feeds them in simultaneously. One would not know whether this is the case unless one builds a logical model.

Appendix to Chapter 16

Connection Between the Regression Coefficients in Samuels (2004) and the Constants in the Predictive Model

How does the model $V_1 = V_0(g_1/g_0)^n(r/p)$ fit in with the linear regression equation $s = V_1 - V_0 = a + b_1 V_0 + b_2 E + b_3[I]$? The logarithmic form of the model can be transposed to

$$\ln(V_1/V_0) = n\ln(g_1/g_0) + \ln r - \ln p.$$

Recall the well known mathematical approximation $\ln(1 + x) \approx x$ when $-1 <<$ $x << 1$. When the vote swing $s = (V_1 - V_0)$ is small, then $\ln(V_1/V_0) = \ln(1 + s/V_0) \approx$ s/V_0. Also, when the percent change (E) in GDP/capita is small, $\ln(g_1/g_0) = \ln[1 + (g_1 - g_0)/g_0] = \ln(1 + E/100) \approx E/100$. The result is

$$s/V_0 = \ln r + nE/100 - \ln p,$$

and hence

$$s = V_0 \ln r + V_0 nE/100 - V_0 \ln p.$$

Compare this expression with the linear regression equation by Samuels (2004):

$$s = a + b_1 V_0 + b_2 E + b_3[I].$$

They would be identical, if $b_2 E = V_0 nE/100$; $b_3[I] = V_0 \ln r$; and $a + b_1 V_0 = -V_0 \ln p$. Assume that the first two components are relatively minor, so that we can approximate the actual value of V_0 in those components by its median value, which is around 50% for an average presidential party. Then

$$n = 2b_2$$

and

$$r = \exp(b_3/50).$$

Assume further that the relatively small intercept a_0 is due to random error and replace $(a + b_1 V_0)$ by the line with zero intercept that yields the same fit at $V_0 = 50\%$. This leads to

$$p = \exp(-b_1 - a/50).$$

Plugging in the regression coefficients values from Samuels (2004) yields the values shown in Table 16.1.

How can widely dispersed values of regression constants in the linear fit correspond to less dispersed values of constants in the predictive model? The correspondences above are not linear. This is why small variations in the constants of the predictive model can be magnified in conversion to regression constants. As for the regression intercept a, it is extremely unstable because most data are around $V_0 = 50\%$ and even a slight random tilt alters the intercept appreciably.

17

Are Electoral Studies a Rosetta Stone for Parts of Social Sciences?

- Fully developed scientific disciplines tend to be explained in terms of other sciences, which hence may be considered more fundamental.
- The degree of quantitative formalism has tended to increase over time in all sciences, with physics and biology ahead of social sciences, and history behind.
- Whether social sciences can eventually achieve the predictive precision of natural sciences is a moot question. What matters is whether *some* aspects of social sciences can be made *more* predictive and, in this sense, *more* like natural sciences.
- Electoral studies look akin to natural sciences in having many variables with a natural zero (ratio variables). This makes them amenable to certain types of logical model building, setting them apart from other social sciences.
- Still, plenty of ratio variables occur in other social sciences too, and here electoral studies may offer valuable methodological tips.
- From temperature to political involvement, looser scales sometimes have a way to turn into ratio scales, if we dare to play with them.

Rosetta stone, unearthed in 1799, made deciphering of Egyptian hiero-glyphic script possible, because it featured the same text in hieroglyphic, simplified demotic, and Greek scripts. It did not solve all the problems of Egyptology, but it represented a major breakthrough, sort of a key to hieroglyphs. Could some aspects of predictive methodology developed in electoral systems offer vaguely analogous openings for some other parts of social sciences?

How come I see precisely my own subfield as having special qualities worthy of emulation? It may look self-aggrandizing. The sequence in time, however, was the reverse. I was motivated to switch from physics to institution-oriented electoral studies, rather than some other aspects of social sciences, because it offered a wealth of ratio variables on which one could build. Elsewhere, I could develop a number of individual models—for the number of polities, trade/GNP ratio, etc. (cf. Chapter 11)—but they remained isolated. Only in electoral and party studies did an interlocking network begin to take shape.

Trouble is, this in itself makes electoral studies an atypical subfield. The more it looks like physics, the less it may look like typical social science. To address such issues, we have to start with a much broader framework.

Interconnections of Scientific Disciplines

Full-fledged sciences are connected in a logical order. While they may initially develop in isolation, they eventually begin to be explained in terms of some other sciences, which hence may be considered more fundamental. Mathematics may do without physics, but physics cannot do without mathematics. Chemistry and physics separated two centuries ago, but nowadays application of quantum physics makes it possible to calculate the probability of getting chemical reactions and select their products for interesting properties, without having to produce and test all these products in the laboratory. Molecular biology, in turn, is increasingly grounded in chemistry, and the likely biological properties of potential pharmaceutical products can be calculated. Thus a third approach—*in calculo*—is added to the traditional *in vivo* and *in vitro*.

The chain extends toward social sciences. Neurobiology offers deeper understanding of cognitive processes. A fully developed cognitive science (psychology) may eventually supply a more solid foundation to anthropology, sociology, economics, political science, and even history. In which order these disciplines may explain each other remains to be seen.

Figure 17.1 shows these direct connections. Each successive discipline is shown with a larger script and a wider box, to reflect increasing complexity. The box sizes also roughly coincide with the current number of publications, which expands as we go from mathematics to chemistry, with biology rapidly catching up. This expansion may extend to cognitive and social sciences, shown as dashed boxes because they are still far

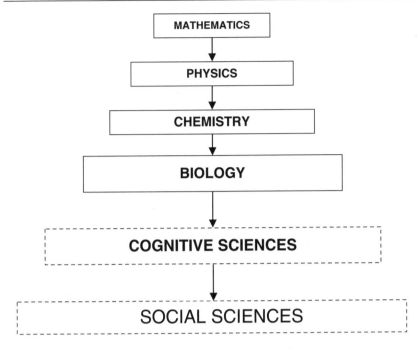

Figure 17.1. Direct interconnections of scientific disciplines

from maturation. Figure 17.1 might be redrawn as a cactus with roots in mathematics and each successive segment larger than the previous one.

Remote inputs, not shown in Figure 17.1, complement the direct connections. Every discipline uses mathematics, sometimes in a form different from its antecedent discipline. Biophysics complements chemistry's input into biology. Physics and chemistry might enter cognitive processes in a way that bypasses biology as such. Such remote influences extend to social sciences in the form of analogies, common dimensionalities, and specific methods. The notions of velocity and acceleration were developed in physics, with x in dx/dt and d^2x/dt^2 meaning length, but they can be applied with other meanings of x. The effects of size are especially prone to inspiration from physics, even when the size considered is not physical. Thus the observed decrease of the trade/GNP ratio with increasing country size could be predicted quantitatively by a model of absorption of commodities by customers. This is in analogy with absorption of physical particles in a nuclear reactor (Chapter 11).

Not to be excluded are influences in the other direction. Infinite matrices were first used by quantum physicists, who needed them, despite their mathematically questionable nature. This successful application induced mathematicians to regularize the status of infinite matrices. Understanding cancerogenous mechanisms has also led to new challenges in mathematics. Such feedback may arise among any disciplines. It may be hard to imagine how biology might affect physics or cognitive sciences chemistry, but it is too early to discount such possibilities completely.

Evolution of Quantitative Formalism

Each discipline has tended to proceed from description and directional prediction toward more quantitative approaches and predictive ability. A coarse index of quantitative formalism illustrates such a shift toward quantitative approaches (Taagepera and Shugart 1989: 240–1). The first step is to determine the percentages of articles in major journals that include at least one data-based table, data-based graph, or any type of mathematical equation. The index of quantitative formalism is the mean of these three percentages.

Physics and chemistry (which were not clearly distinguished) started with an index value of less than 10% in 1800 and surpassed 70% in 1980. Biology, psychology, and economics all took off from about 20% in 1900, but then they diverged. While biology surpassed 60% in 1980, psychology leveled off around 45%, and economics only slowly reached that level. In political science, the index remained around 10% as late as in 1960, but then it rose sharply before leveling off at 40%. Since 1920, history has moved slowly from 5% to 20%. (See graphs in Taagepera and Shugart 1989: 240–1.)

Historically, tables came first, equations followed, and graphs came last, partly due to technical difficulties in printing. It may come as a surprise that, as late as the early 1800s, such formats were still little used in physics and chemistry. Each new discipline entering the quantitative phase of its development has tended to adopt quantitative formalism faster than the preceding disciplines, but exceptions and even reversals occur.

The three components enter the index of quantitative formalism to different degrees. In political science around 1980, for instance, the index was propelled upwards by the use of tables (65% incidence) and held down by equations (35%) and graphs (under 30%). This difference reflected an emphasis on reporting results of data analysis in the form of tables of correlation coefficients rather than full regression equations, not to mention predictive models. The use of graphs remained rare, compared to natural and cognitive sciences. The use of equations was less frequent in political science than in physical sciences and economics but actually more frequent than in some biology and psychology journals.

The type of equations used differs. In physics, they often express theoretical models to be tested against data, and economics approaches this pattern. In sociology and political science statistical expressions predominate. Here the dearth of model-based equations contributes to low incidence of graphs, given that graphs are often used to compare theoretical predictions and data.

A minimal use of quantitative formalism does not indicate, of course, its extent and sophistication. Sometimes, an advance in quantitativeness can actually lower the formal index. Thus, the equation for the effective number of parties used to be presented whenever this number was invoked. It is now considered so standard that the formula is often not spelled out—which would contribute to a decrease in the incidence of "equations." Nonetheless, the index of quantitative formalism offers some idea of when the various disciplines started to pay attention to quantitative approaches and what the comparative levels have been. In this light, Figure 17.1 may reflect adequately the sequence of scientific development or maturity of various disciplines.

Can Social Sciences Achieve the Degree of Predictive Ability of Natural Sciences, and Does It Matter?

While conceivably expanding as outlined at the bottom of Figure 17.1, it remains to be seen whether social sciences can eventually match natural sciences in predictive theory. It may seem that physics laws are "true for all times," while economics and other social sciences depend on a socioeconomic context that keeps changing. If so, then each historical or contemporary episode should be "interpreted as the application of general principles to unique contexts" (Arrow 1985). To which Colomer (2007) replies: "Actually, physics laws do not predict the future in an unconditional sense. They merely say that if certain conditions are fulfilled, then certain outcomes can be expected."

Physicists themselves are the first to wonder why anything like "laws of nature" exists and why we are able to discover them (Schrödinger

1932). Eugene Wigner (1960) anchors this phenomenon in the property of invariance, applied in two senses. First, laws such as those initiated by Galileo and leading to the universal law of gravitation are valid everywhere. Second, these laws include only a small number of factors, regardless of many other factors that also *could* have an effect.

Wigner (1960) argues that physics would be impossible if the relevant factors were not small in number. In his view, the scientist's skillfulness and inventiveness expresses itself largely in ferreting out which factors are essential to the process and which are marginal. Gravity does not ignore feathers rising in the air, but Wigner admires Galileo's ingenious ability to focus first on relatively heavy bodies. Such exclusion may look self-evident only in retrospect. Physical world in Galileo's time looked as multifactorial as social world may look to us. Even in the absence of multivariable regression, he could have spent his time expressing the "richness" of the world in erudite classifications, but he opted for Occam's razor instead.

Physicists are cautious about the range of application of their laws. In cosmology, the permanence of even the most basic laws of physics is not taken for granted. Time and space frames are narrower in biology, and still more so in social sciences, but this may be a question of degree rather than kind.

The influence of the observer on the observed is arguably stronger in social than in natural phenomena. It enters deepest in quantum physics. How does this compare with people using their knowledge of law of gravity to circumvent its impact and start flying "like birds"? Our awareness of laws of biology has enabled us to develop antibiotics, to which microorganisms respond with tactics of their own, changing the biosphere in ways that cannot always be anticipated. When people become aware of laws that govern social interactions, they may find ways to circumvent them. The fading of the "cube law" of Anglo-Saxon elections in UK may be one example (Taagepera 2007c: 214). In this respect, the difference between social and natural sciences is fuzzy.

Asserting that social sciences can eventually achieve the predictive precision of natural sciences represents an act of faith—as does the opposite assertion. We need not present the issue in such an either/or way. What matters is whether *some* aspects of social sciences can be made *more* predictive than they are now and, in this sense, *more* like natural sciences. It is the direction of development that matters, not the eventual parity or non-parity of outcomes. As far as electoral and party studies are concerned, considerable advances have been made during the last

20 years, as partly reviewed in Chapter 10. The usual rules of thumb for extrapolation suggest further advances during the next 10 years.

Are electoral studies typical of social sciences, or are they bound to remain a marked exception? They are both. I will start with "electoral exceptionalism" and then reconnect the electoral studies to broader social sciences.

How Electoral Studies Look More Akin to Natural Sciences

Within social sciences, descriptive "empirical models" (statistical data fits) have predominated over predictive "formal models" to a larger degree than is the case in more developed disciplines. Even when formal models do occur they can take different forms. Thus, in political science they come mostly as rational choice models on the one hand and as institutional models in electoral and party systems on the other. The two rarely meet.

Rational choice depends on preference orderings, where the strength of preferences is hard to measure ahead of the time. I will not try to disentangle what is postdiction and prediction in that field. In contrast, electoral studies deal with quantities more recognizably similar to those in natural sciences. This makes it possible to develop vaguely similar methodological approaches, but it also may put electoral studies somewhat apart from the rest of social sciences.

Natural sciences largely deal with variables with defined intervals. This means that the differences $a - b$ can be uniquely defined. Most often these variables also have defined ratios, which means that the ratio a/b can be defined. Such ratio variables imply the existence of a natural zero. Time, length, and voltage have no natural zero points, but time, length, and voltage *intervals* do. In social sciences, utility and psychophysical theories also use ratios of differences of the form $(z - r)/(x - r)$.

Electoral systems largely deal with counting variables—votes and seats—which do have natural zeroes. They even have a *natural unit*: one vote or one seat. This is something few physical variables have, until one proceeds to count elementary particles. The number of parties has a natural zero, but interval presents problems, because parties differ in size and other properties of interest, in contrast to electrons and seats. The effective number of parties has defined intervals and zero point, but its inability to take values between zero and one leads to special difficulties.

Some differences between variables used in natural sciences and institution-oriented electoral studies are considerable. They pale, however, when compared to the differences that enter when one considers the types of variables used in opinion measurements, power relations, and preference rankings common in sociology as well as the rest of political science. People could be asked to indicate their ideological location or their country's degree of corruption on a scale ranging from 0 to 7 or from -10 to $+10$. Both scales are arbitrary. There is no natural zero. The interval is also doubtful, because people may distinguish between fine details of ideology in the center while they may lump different degrees of extremism together—or vice versa. Who is to tell which intervals are properly equal? (Actually, there may be ways, but this is a subtler issue to be considered in the next section.) Social sciences methodology has developed largely with such softer scales in mind.

Thus, as far as the nature of data is concerned, the dividing line between natural and social sciences may seem to put electoral studies on the side of natural sciences. This means that various model-building approaches reminiscent of natural sciences are possible in electoral studies—those based on logical constraints, in particular. These methods have been slower to develop in electoral studies than they could have been, because by habit, political scientists have applied methodology devised for soft scales, without noticing further opportunities offered by firmer scales.

This book—and Chapter 8 in particular—has presented some of the predictive methods that apply in electoral studies, thanks to the existence of ratio variables. Pointing out the nature of variables helps to explain why such predictive models came about in electoral studies rather than somewhere else in social sciences. But it also builds an apparent barrier to the spread of such methods elsewhere. This is the gist of a panel discussion in *European Political Science*, where Taagepera (2007*a*, *b*), Coleman (2007), and Colomer (2007) take a rather optimistic view, while Grofman (2007) stresses the marked difference in the nature of variables. What may work in institution-oriented electoral studies arguably could not spread beyond.

How Temperature Became a Ratio Variable

Actually, ratio scales do occur in social sciences rather frequently, even outside electoral studies. In opinion studies, people are often asked yes/no questions, and the percentage of affirmative answers is reported. Here we have a scale with a well-defined zero and the maximum, analogous to percentages of votes or seats, and the same broad model-building approaches apply. We even have a well-defined midpoint between zero and the maximum. Electoral data may not be utterly different from other social data.

Moreover, scales sometimes have a way to turn themselves firmer. Take temperature. The various scales used by Fahrenheit, Reaumur, and Celsius bear witness to the absence of an obvious zero in early studies. Measurement of temperature started with determination of the extent to which fluids like alcohol or mercury expand when heated. There was no fixed zero, and even the interval was doubtful. Ice-cold water shrinks rather than expand when heated, up to 4°C. Hence, one could not be certain about uniformity of expansion in other liquids. It took tenacity and optimism to work with such an ill-defined quantity as temperature. Gradually, the existence of an interval scale was confirmed.

But this was not the end of it. When temperature (t) relative to an arbitrary zero was compared to the product of gas pressure (P) and volume (V) in a closed system, a linear relationship was observed: $PV = Rt + a$, where R and a are constants. It could also be expressed as $PV = R(t + b)$, where b is another constant, with dimensions of temperature (for dimensionality, see the Appendix to Chapter 13). Empirically, b was found to be +273°C. It pointed to −273°C as the temperature at which $PV = 0$, so that either pressure or volume would become zero. This conceptual limit defined the absolute zero below which temperature could not fall. Measuring temperature based on this zero point turned it into a ratio variable (T), so that the ideal gas law was simplified to $PV = RT$. Later interpretation of temperature as measure of vibration of molecules gave it a deeper meaning, far beyond the understanding of Celsius and Fahrenheit.

Note that the initial formulation followed a linear form reminiscent of linear regression approach, but with a crucial difference: Pressure and volume were not entered in an additive way. When pressure was observed to increase with increasing temperature but decrease when volume is allowed to increase, it was *not* automatically formulated as $P = a + bt − cV$ or $P + cV = a + bt$. This would have led to a dead end. More thought was given to how the variables connected. Once $PV = Rt + a$ was established, the partly additive format could be changed into purely multiplicative by shifting the arbitrary zero in temperature to a more meaningful location.

How Electoral Studies Could Still Be a Rosetta Stone for Some Parts of Social Sciences

Some soft scales used in social sciences could eventually turn firmer, vaguely analogous with the evolution of temperature. Is affirming it a mere declaration of faith, or do we have examples? Here recent work by Lorenzo De Sio (2006a, b, 2008) may be path-breaking.

Campaign gimmicks and personal appeal of candidates may sometimes induce a socialist to vote for a rightist candidate, and vice versa. De Sio posits and tests the hypothesis that less involved voters are easier to nudge into voting contrary to their ideology. Political science has developed "spatial models of voting" which express various dimensions of an "interest space." In contrast, De Sio considers a two-dimensional "political space" where the ideological left–right dimension is complemented by a dimension of political involvement (both using an arbitrary scale converted to 0 to 1). It matters that he tests not a merely directional but a quantitative prediction. The result is a set of parameters that characterize various electorates in Italian regions (De Sio 2006a, 2008) and the United States (De Sio 2006b). These parameters can be used for comparisons with further electorates.

De Sio proceeds as if he dealt with quantities that have a natural zero and a maximum. Such quantities can always be converted to the interval 0 to 1. He applies the simplest family of curves that join 3 anchor points, complementing them with a bias factor (cf. Chapter 8). Regarding substantive research, this is an excellent example of predictive modeling that applies conceptual constraints. But the methodical implications reach much further.

The point is that the quantities De Sio (2006a, 2008) uses are actually measured on eminently soft scales. The ideological self-positioning on the left–right dimension was originally done on the standard 10-position L–R ruler. A true zero could correspond to a perfectly extreme leftist stand beyond which one cannot go. This is different from the lowest category into which one can place oneself. As for political involvement, a composite index was constructed, based on political knowledge and self-declared interest. The possible answers for frequency of political discussion were "never, a few times a year, a few times a month, a few times a week, every day"—and similarly for the other components. It is hard to claim that such intervals are equal on any scale.

Treating such scales as if they were not only interval scales but also ratio scales represents an act of faith comparable to that of physicists who began to measure temperature. It may be condemned by purists of measurement theory as unwarranted—and rightly so, from their viewpoint. But venturing into messy terrain is part of advancing science. If the type of work done by De Sio should show a consistent deviation from predictions, it might or might not suggest a rescaling of the Left–Right scale or a revision of the compound scale for political involvement. Either way, the validity of the resulting scale would be reinforced.

There may not be right or wrong ways to measure something, but some ways are more conducive to predictions about relations among variables—which makes them more useful (Chapter 13). De Sio's work suggests that some predictive modeling approaches that apply in principle only to ratio variables can, with a mix of caution and optimism, be applied to variables measured on softer scales. If so, then the predictive approaches developed for electoral systems could indeed be a Rosetta Stone for some other parts of social sciences.

Conclusions

Institution-oriented electoral and party studies are unusual in social sciences by dealing with a large number of ratio variables. This is why an interlocking network of logical models has begun to form there rather than elsewhere. On the other hand, these studies are part of social inquiry and face the common problems of non-laboratory sciences, plus a social scene that keeps changing. This is why they may offer more insights, compared to natural sciences, of what approaches could be transferable to social sciences. There remains, however, the issue of dimensionality (see the Appendix to Chapter 13). It tends to set apart the basic building blocks in physics and in most of social sciences, electoral studies included.

18

Beyond Regression: The Need for Predictive Models

- Society needs more from social sciences than they have delivered. More can be done, and this book offers openings.
- To the society at large, quantitative social scientists presently seem no better at prediction than qualitative historians, philosophers, and journalists—they just look more boring.
- Computers could be a boon to social sciences, but they have turned out a curse in disguise, by enabling people with insufficient understanding of scientific process to misuse canned computer programs to grind out reams of numbers parading as "results," to be printed—and hardly ever used again.
- One may discard this book on the basis of errors of detail, but the problems it points out will still be there. Unless corrected, they will lead social sciences to a Ptolemaic dead end.

The ruling emperor of social sciences has no clothes. His quantitative garb is largely make-believe. The Foreword by Duncan Luce calls it "a form of mass deception."

Our qualitative understanding of social phenomena has expanded beyond recognition, during the last 100 years. It has produced durable results. Yet, social sciences have not become as scientific as this basis would allow them to be, because they have overemphasized descriptive statistical analysis to the detriment of conceptual model building. They must rethink their understanding of the scientific process and what constitutes "results." At the moment, all too many social science publications end where Galileo began, satisfied with proving a directional model and not proceeding to quantitative models.

Science combines the empirical "What is?" with the conceptual "How *should* it be on logical grounds?" Describing the world is not enough. It also must be *explained*. Quantitatively predictive logical models are at the core of science, and a discipline that ignores this core is not science. A better balance of methods is possible and will make social sciences more relevant to society.

The scientific process does not consist of a single chain going from a simplistic "hypothesis" to purely statistical testing. It involves interplay between models and data, a rising spiral where both data and models may be modified. These evolving models must be substantive or broadly logical. They should be quantitative, not merely directional. Statistical data fits should not masquerade as "empirical models." This misleading term should be forgotten.

In natural sciences, quantitative prediction is a major criterion of meaningful results. The very meaning of "results" has been corrupted in social sciences, as quantitative prediction is discounted in favor of merely directional prediction. To be usable for sociopolitical decision-making or as basis for further research, results should offer specific averages and ranges of error. King et al. (2000) offer two contrasting examples (cf. Chapter 5). Expressions like "the coefficient on education was statistically significant at the 0.05 level" most often hide the absence of usable results. As an alternative that makes sense, they offer "Other things being equal, an additional year of education would increase your annual income by $1,500 on the average, plus or minus about $500."

This is good description that makes some sense to decision-makers and to the public at large, in contrast to the jargon in the earlier expression. But it still involves no explanation of how education brings about such an outcome, and why it does so to the given degree and not much less or much more. As far as theorizing is concerned, it still is what Aage Sørensen called the "gas station" approach (cf. Chapter 10). Without conceptual models, we cannot know how the advantages of education would translate to other countries or remain valid in the country where the empirical data were collected. We should not restrict ourselves to

mindless hypothesis testing in lieu of doing good research: measuring effects, constructive substantive theories of some depth, and developing probability models and statistical procedures suited to these theories. (Luce 1988)

We must distinguish between the roles of scientist and statistician in the course of research (cf. Chapter 1):

> The proper division [of labor] should be one in which sociological theory suggests a mathematical model of a social process and statistics provides the tools to estimate the model, not, as is common today, that statistics provides models that sociologists use as ad hoc models of social processes. (Hedström 2004)

Otherwise we are reduced to a "crazy methodology" (Kittel 2006) of statistical games which clumsily tries to mimic natural sciences and ends in a caricature of science (cf. Chapter 7).

Computers could have been a boon to social sciences, but they have turned out a curse in disguise, by enabling people with insufficient understanding of scientific process to misuse canned computers programs. They ditch Occam's razor in favor of "garbage can regression" and grind out reams of numbers parading as "results," to be printed—and never used again.

Social sciences depend heavily on methods unable to detect not only the law of gravitation (Chapter 2) but also the determinants of mean cabinet duration (Chapter 14). Can we continue to depend on methods unable to detect such regularities? Of course we can. Bad money can drive out the good, but at a price. Why should sociopolitical decision-makers and the public at large pay any attention to such games? Society still values predictive ability. Presently, it gives quantitative social scientists even less credence than to qualitative historians, philosophers, and journalists. Compared to the latter, much of present quantitative work in social science seems no better at prediction—it is just more boring.

Unease about the trends of recent decades in social sciences has been voiced by many thoughtful people, as illustrated by the quotes above. Whenever such concerns go beyond observing the limits and dead ends of the presently prevailing practices, they point toward more emphasis on theorizing, in contrast to statistical analysis. The specific expressions may differ. I add my voice, trying to offer some specifics that do no exclude various others.

There are ways to widen our methodological scope, both for tackling new problems and for reworking previous findings. Whenever the nature of variables suggests it, logarithms of all input and output variables should be taken before linear regression is run (Chapter 8)—and it should be symmetric regression (Chapter 12). This approach corresponds to testing the multiplication–division format so frequent in natural sciences (Chapter 5). But this would still be mechanical. It is essential that more effort be directed to constructing detailed logical quantitative models, with their types indicated by the nature of the problem on hand (Chapters 3, 4, and 8–11).

Our logical models must go beyond predicting the *direction* of effect—they must specify its quantitative extent (Chapter 6). Quantitatively predictive logical models need not involve more complex mathematics, compared to regression analysis. But they do require active thinking about how things connect. The major intellectual challenge is in daring to make outrageously simple assumptions, out of which systematic logical conclusions can be drawn in a quantitative way (Chapter 8).

Expanding quantitatively predictive logical modeling by no means implies dumping the descriptive approaches. One can build on their achievements and go beyond them (Chapters 15 and 16). Mixed strategies are often the most efficient. However, "mixed" does not mean gazpacho but judicious sequential insertion of various factors. Regression and other statistical approaches enter mainly in preliminary investigation and in final testing (Chapter 14). In between, quantitatively predictive logical models must take over.

One reason why some methods of natural sciences find it hard to diffuse to social sciences is dearth of people with training in both. Compared to physics students, graduate students in social sciences tend to have less facility in basic algebra, of the type often needed for building simple logical models. Maybe it is time to introduce some undergraduate level interdisciplinary programs, where students get a good two year's worth of physics training, are at the same time introduced to social sciences, and—this is essential—are encouraged to apply their physics skills to social phenomena. I have described (Chapter 3) how some engineering freshmen were taken aback when introduced to the ludicrously naïve-looking model for ideal gas law. Two years later, such approaches would look natural to them. Some aspects of basic methodology are not explicitly taught to students of natural sciences, nor could they. Rather, they are instilled indirectly. It is harder to do it with social science graduate students who already are set in their statistics-oriented ways.

This book goes beyond a critique of the existing dominant approach. Most of it deals with constructive complements that have yielded specific predictions in some aspects of social sciences and could do so in some others. While this approach is not new, it certainly has been neglected.

As this book covers extensive ground, it can most likely be charged with a number of acts of omission and commission. Its mathematical terminology may not always be orthodox—this is the wording of an experimental physicist who switched to social science. Further examples of well-tested quantitative models exist in social sciences, mainly in economics and psychology—many empirical ones and some with a logical foundation. I have not tried to cover the entire terrain. I would be delighted if further sequentially connected models could be pointed out, to offer company to the seat product-cabinet duration sequence (Chapter 10).

It may be claimed that I have exaggerated the overdependence on statistical analysis in social sciences and the predominance of simple linear regression. One may also detect errors of detail and clumsy expressions that may be interpreted as erroneous. On such basis, one may discard this book, if one so chooses. But the problems it points out will still be there. Society needs more from social sciences than they have delivered. More can be done, at the present stage of factual knowledge. The alternative is a Ptolemaic dead end.

References

Achen, Christopher and Snidal, Duncan (1989). "Rational Deterrence Theory and Comparative Case Studies," *World Politics*, 41: 143–69.

Ahn, Woo-kyoung, Kalish, Charles W., Medin, Douglas L., and Gelman, Susan A. (1995). "The Role of Covariation Versus Mechanism Information in Causal Attribution," *Cognition*, 54: 299–352.

Anscombe, Francis J. (1973). "Graphs in Statistical Analysis," *American Statistician*, 27: 17–21.

Arbuthnot, John (1710). "An Argument for Divine Providence, Taken from the Constant Regularity Observ'd in the Births of Both Sexes," *Philosophical Transactions of the Royal Society*, 27: 186–90.

Arrow, Kenneth (1985). "Economic History: A Necessary though not Sufficient Condition for an Economist," *American Economic Review*, 75: 320–3.

Bartolini, Stefano and Mair, Peter (1990). *Identity, Competition and Electoral Availability: The Stabilization of European Electorates 1885–1985*. Cambridge: University of Cambridge Press.

Berry, William D. and Sanders, Mitchell S. (2000). *Understanding Multivariate Research*. Boulder, CO: Westview Press.

Bochsler, Daniel (2006). "Quantitative Analyse der Konkordate: Abkommen unter Nachbarn oder unter Freunden," Working Paper, University of Geneva.

Brambor, Thomas, Clark, William R., and Golder, Matthew (2006). "Understanding Interaction Models: Improving Empirical Analyses," *Political Analysis*, 14: 63–82.

Braumoeller, Bear F. (2004). "Hypothesis Testing and Multiplicative Interaction Terms," *International Organization*, 58: 807–20.

Cartwright, Nancy (2002). "The Limits of Causal Order, from Economics to Physics," in U. Mäki (ed.), *Fact and Fiction in Economics: Models, Realism, and Social Construction*. Cambridge: Cambridge University Press, pp. 137–51.

Coleman, James S. (1964). *Introduction to Mathematical Sociology*. New York, NY: Free Press.

—— (1981). *Longitudinal Data Analysis*. New York, NY: Basic Books.

Coleman, Stephen (2004). "The Effect of Social Conformity on Collective Voting Behavior," *Political Analysis*, 12: 76–96.

References

Coleman, Stephen (2005). "Testing Theories with Qualitative and Quantitative Predictions," Third Conference of the European Consortium for Political Research, Budapest, 8–10 September.

—— (2007). "Testing Theories with Qualitative and Quantitative Predictions," *European Political Science*, 6: 124–33.

Colomer, Josep M. (2007). "What Other Sciences Look Like," *European Political Science*, 6: 134–42.

—— and Riba, Clara (2005). "Mathematical Models: From Physics to Economics, and to Political Science?," Third Conference of the European Consortium for Political Research, Budapest, 8–10 September.

Crease, Robert P. (2004). "The Greatest Equations Ever," *Physics World*, October: 19–23.

De Sio, Lorenzo (2006a). "Political Involvement and Electoral Competition," Center for the Study of Democracy, University of California, Irvine. Research Monograph CSD 06-02, www.democ.uci.edu

—— (2006b). "A Matter of Attraction: Voting Behavior of Heterogeneous Voters," ECPR Annual Joint Workshops, Nicosia, April 20.

—— (2008). "Are Less Involved Voters the Key to Win Elections?," *Comparative Political Studies*, 41: 217–41.

Diwakar, Rekha (2007). "Duverger's Law and the Size of the Indian Party System," *Party Politics*, 13: 539–61.

Dodd, Lawrence C. (1976). *Coalitions in Parliamentary Government*. Princeton, NJ: Princeton University Press.

Finifter, Ada W., ed. (1993). *Political Science: The State of the Discipline II*. Washington, DC: The American Political Science Association.

Fishburn, Peter C. (1977). "Multiattribute Utilities in Expected Utility Theory," in D. E. Bell, R. L. Keeney, and H. Raiffa (eds.), *Conflicting Objectives in Decisions*. New York, NY: Wiley, pp. 172–96.

Fisher, Ronald A. (1935). *The Design of Experiments*. Edinburgh, UK: Oliver & Boyd.

—— (1956). *Statistical Methods and Scientific Inference*. Edinburgh, UK: Oliver & Boyd.

Flanagan-Hyde, Peter (2006). "The Least-Squares Regression Line Is Not a Trend Line," *STATS: The Magazine for Students of Statistics*, No. 45, pp. 18–20.

Folk, Mark D. and Luce, R. Duncan (1987). "Effects of Stimulus Complexity on Mental Rotation Rate of Polygons," *Journal of Experimental Psychology*, 87: 395–404.

Freedman, David (1987). "As Others See Us: A Case Study in Path Analysis," *Journal of Educational Statistics*, 12: 101–28.

Gelman, Andrew and Hill, Jennifer (2007). *Data Analysis Using Regression and Multilevel/Hierarchical Models*. Cambridge: Cambridge University Press.

Gigerenzer, Gerd (2004). "Mindless Statistics," *Journal of Socio-Economics*, 33: 587–606.

—— Krauss, Stefan, and Vitouch, Oliver (2004). "The Null Ritual: What You Always Wanted to Know About Significance Testing but Were Afraid to Ask," in David Kaplan (ed.), *The Sage Handbook of Quantitative Methodology for the Social Sciences.* Thousand Oaks, CA: Sage, pp. 391–408.

Grofman, Bernard (2004). "Rein Taagepera's Approach to the Study of Electoral Systems," *Journal of Baltic Studies*, 35: 167–85.

—— (2007). "Toward a Science of Politics?," *European Political Science*, 6: 143–55.

—— and van Roozendaal, Peter (1997). "Review Article: Modelling Cabinet Durability and Termination," *British Journal of Political Science*, 27: 419–51.

Hamming, Richard W. (1980). "The Unreasonable Effectiveness of Mathematics," *American Mathematical Monthly*, 87/2: 81–90.

Harlow, Lisa L., Mulaik, Stanley A., and Steiger, James H., eds. (1997). *What if There Were No Significance Tests?* Mahwah, NJ: Erlbaum.

Heath, Oliver (2005). "Party Systems, Political Cleavages and Electoral Volatility in India: A State-wise Analysis, 1998–1999," *Electoral Studies*, 24: 177–99.

Hedström, Peter (2004). "Generative Models and Explanatory Research: On the Sociology of Aage B. Sørensen," *Research in Social Stratification and Mobility*, 21: 13–25.

Helmke, Gretchen (2002). "The Logic of Strategic Defection: Court-Executive Relations in Argentina under Dictatorship and Democracy," *American Political Science Review*, 96: 291–303.

Herrnstein, Richard R. and Murray, Charles (1994). *The Bell Curve: Intelligence and Class Structure in American Life.* New York, NY: The Free Press.

Hill, Kim Quaile (2004). "Myths about the Physical Sciences and their Implications for Teaching Political Science," *PS: Political Science & Politics*, 37: 467–71.

—— (2005). "Science and Political Science Redux," *PS: Political Science & Politics*, 38: 6–7.

Huck, Schuyler W. and Sandler, Howard M. (1984). *Statistical Illusions: Problems.* New York, NY: Harper & Row.

Hyde, Earl K., Pearlman, Isadore, and Seaborg, Glenn T. (1964). *Nuclear Properties of the Heavy Elements, 1.* Englewood Cliffs, NJ: Prentice Hall.

Keeney, Ralph L. and Raiffa, Howard (1976). *Decisions with Multiple Objectives: Preferences and Value Tradeoffs.* New York, NY: Wiley.

Kennedy, Peter (1998). *A Guide to Econometrics.* Cambridge, MA: MIT Press.

Kermak, K. A. and Haldane, John B. S. (1950). "Organic Correlation and Allometry," *Biometrika*, 37: 30–41.

King, Gary (1989). *Unifying Political Methodology: The Likelihood Theory of Statistical Inference.* New York, NY: Cambridge University Press.

—— (1997). *A Solution to the Ecological Inference Problem.* Princeton, NJ: Princeton University Press.

—— Keohane, Robert, and Verba, Sidney (1994). *Designing Social Inquiry.* Princeton, NJ: Princeton University Press.

References

King, Gary, Tomz, Michael, and Wittenberg, Jason (2000). "Making the Most of Statistical Analysis: Improving Interpretation and Presentation," *American Journal of Politics*, 44: 341–55.

Kittel, Bernhard (2006). "A Crazy Methodology? On the Limits of Macro-Quantitative Social Science Research," *International Sociology*, 21: 647–77.

—— and Winner, Hannes (2005). "How Reliable is Pooled Analysis in Political Economy? The Globalization-Welfare Nexus Revisited," *European Journal of Political Research*, 44: 269–93.

Kochen, Manfred and Deutsch, Karl W. (1969). "Toward a Rational Theory of Decentralization," *American Political Science Review*, 63: 734–49.

Krantz, David H., Luce, R. Duncan, Suppes, Patrick, and Tversky, Amos (1971). *Foundations of Measurement I: Additive and Polynomial Representations*. San Diego, CA, and London: Academic Press. Dover reprint 2007.

Laakso, Markku and Taagepera, Rein (1979). "Effective Number of Parties: A Measure with Application to West Europe," *Comparative Political Studies*, 23: 3–27.

Lanchester, Frederick L. (1956). "Mathematics in Warfare," in James R. Newman (ed.), *The World of Mathematics*. New York, NY: Simon & Schuster, 4: 2136 ff.

Lijphart, Arend (1984). *Democracies: Patterns of Majoritarianism and Consensus Government*. New Haven, CT: Yale University Press.

—— (1994). *Electoral Systems and Party Systems*. Oxford: Oxford University Press.

—— (1999). *Patterns of Democracy: Government Forms and Performance in Thirty-Six Countries*. New Haven, CT: Yale University Press.

Limpert, Eckhard, Stahel, Werner A., and Abbt, Markus (2001). "Log-Normal Distributions across the Sciences: Keys and Clues," *BioScience*, 51: 341–52.

Loftus, Geoffrey R. (1991). "On the Tyranny of Hypothesis Testing in the Social Sciences," *Contemporary Psychology*, 36: 102–5.

—— (1993). "Editorial Comment," *Memory & Cognition*, 21: 1–3.

Longford, Nicholas T. (2005). "Editorial: Model Selection and Efficiency—Is 'Which Model . . . ?' the Right Question," *Journal of the Royal Statistical Society, Series A*, 168: 469–72.

Luce, R. Duncan (1988). "The Tools-to-Theory Hypothesis: Review of G. Gigerenzer and D. J. Murray, 'Cognition as Intuitive Statistics,' " *Contemporary Psychology*, 33: 582–3.

—— (1989). "R. Duncan Luce," in G. Lindzey (ed.), *Psychology in Autobiography*, vol. VII. Palo Alto, CA: Stanford University Press, pp. 247–89.

—— (2005). "Measurement Analogies: Comparisons of Behavioral and Physical Measures," *Psychometrika*, 70: 227–51.

—— Krantz, David H., Suppes, Patrick, and Tversky, Amos (1990). *Foundations of Measurement III: Representation, Axiomatization, and Invariance*. San Diego, CA, and London: Academic Press. Dover reprint 2007.

Lühiste, Maarja (2007). "Rahulolu demokraatia toimimisega" [Satisfaction with the functioning of democracy]. B.A. thesis, University of Tartu, Estonia.

McGregor, James P. (1993). "Procrustus and the Regression Model: On the Misuse of the Regression Model," *PS: Political Science & Politics*, 26: 801–4.

Mainwaring, Scott and Torcal, Mariano (2006). "Party System Institutionalization and Party System Theory After the Third Wave of Democratization," in Richard S. Katz and William Crotty (eds.), *Handbook of Party Politics*. London: Sage, pp. 204–27.

Maslow, Abraham H. (1966). *The Psychology of Science*. New York, NY: Harper & Row.

Melton, Arthur W. (1962). "Editorial," *Journal of Experimental Psychology*, 64: 553–7.

Misiunas, Romuald and Taagepera, Rein (1993). *The Baltic States: Years of Dependence 1940–1990*. London: Hurst; Berkeley: University of California Press.

Oakes, Michael (1986). *Statistical Inference: A Commentary for the Social and Behavioral Sciences*. Chichester, UK: Wiley.

Oren, Ido (2005). "Is Political Science Really Young?," *PS: Political Science & Politics*, 38: 3.

Ozminkowski, Mariuzs (2005). "A Reply to 'Myths about the Physical Sciences and Their Implications for Teaching Political Science,'" *PS: Political Science & Politics*, 38: 3–5.

Pearson, Karl (1901). "On Lines and Planes of Closest Fit to Systems of Points in Space," *Philosophical Magazine*, 2: 559–72.

Pedersen, Mogens N. (1983). "Changing Patterns of Electoral Volatility in European Party Systems, 1948–1977: Explorations in Explanation," in Hans Daalder and Peter Mair (eds.), *Western European Party Systems: Continuity and Change*. London: Sage, pp: 29–66.

Phillips, Alban W. (1958). "The Relationship between Unemployment and the Rate of Change of Money in the United Kingdom, 1861–1957," *Economica*, 25: 283–99.

Prachowny, Martin F. J. (1993). "Okun's Law: Theoretical Foundations and Revised Estimates," *The Annals of Mathematical Statistics*, 75: 331–6.

Ragin, Charles (1987). *The Comparative Method: Moving Beyond Qualitative and Quantitative Strategies*. Berkeley: University of California Press.

Richards, James A., Sears, Francis W., Wehr, M. Russell, and Zemansky, Mark W. (1960). *Modern University Physics*. Reading, MA: Addison-Wesley.

Richardson, Lewis F. (1960). *Arms and Insecurity*. Pittsburgh, PA: Boxwood.

Samuels, David (2004). "Presidentialism and Accountability for the Economy in Comparative Perspective," *American Political Science Review*, 98: 425–36.

Sargent, Thomas J. (1999). *The Conquest of American Inflation*. Princeton, NJ: Princeton University Press.

Schrödinger, Erwin (1932). *Über Indeterminismus in der Physik*. Leipzig: J. A. Barth.

Scientific American (1973). "Newton Fudged," *Scientific American*, 228/4: 44–5.

Segré, Emilio (1964). *Nuclei and Particles*. New York, NY: Benjamin.

Schneider, Carsten and Grofman, Bernard (2006). "It Might Look Like a Regression Equation... But It's Not! An Intuitive Approach to the Presentation of QCA and

FS/QCA Results," Conference on "Comparative Politics: Empirical Applications of Methodological Innovations," Sophia University, Tokyo, 15–17 July.

Sørensen, Aage B. (1998). "Theoretical Mechanisms and the Empirical Study of Social Processes," in P. Hedström and R. Swedberg (eds.), *Social Mechanisms: An Analytical Approach to Social Theory*. Cambridge: Cambridge University Press, pp. 238–66.

Souva, Mark (2007). "Fostering Theoretical Thinking in Undergraduate Classes," *PS: Political Science & Politics*, 40: 557–61.

Stevens, Stanley S. (1946). "On the Theory of Scales of Measurement," *Science*, 103: 677–80.

Strakes, Jason E. (2005). "In Response to 'Myths about... Political Science,'" *PS: Political Science & Politics*, 38: 5.

Strömberg, Gustaf (1940). "Accidental and Systematic Errors in Spectroscopic Absolute Magnitudes for Dwarf Go-K2 Stars," *Astrophysics Journal*, 92: 156–69.

Studenmund, A. H. (2001). *Using Econometrics: A Practical Guide*. Boston, MA: Addison Wesley Longman.

Taagepera, Rein (1973). "Fractional Iteration of exp x, and Fractional Arithmetic Operations," Social Science Working Paper 44c, Irvine: University of California.

——(1976a). "Crisis around 2005 A.D.? A Technology-Population Interaction Model," *General Systems*, 21: 137–8.

——(1976b). "Why the Trade/GNP Ratio Decreases with Country Size," *Social Science Research*, 5: 385–404.

——(1979). "People, Skills and Resources: An Interaction Model for World Population Growth," *Technological Forecasting and Social Change*, 13: 13–30.

——(1984). *Softening without Liberalization in the Soviet Union: The case of Jüri Kukk*. Lanham, MD: University Press of America.

——(1993). *Estonia: Return to Independence*. Boulder, CO: Westview Press.

——(1997). "Expansion and Contraction Patterns of Large Polities: Context for Russia," *International Studies Quarterly*, 41: 475–504.

——(1999a). *The Finno-Ugric Republics and the Russian State*. London: Hurst.

——(1999b). "Ignorance-Based Quantitative Models and Their Practical Implications," *Journal of Theoretical Politics*, 11: 421–31.

——(2002). "The Logical Underpinnings of the Hyperbolic Rank-Size Rule," unpublished.

——(2005a). "Beyond Regression: The Need for Logical Models," Yearly Conference of the Belgian Political Science Association (French), Liège, 29–30 April.

——(2005b). "Predictive vs. Postdictive Models," Third Conference of the European Consortium for Political Research, Budapest, 8–10 September.

——(2007a). "Why Political Science is not Scientific Enough: A Symposium," *European Political Science*, 6: 111–13.

——(2007b). "Predictive Versus Postdictive Models," *European Political Science*, 6: 114–23.

——(2007c). *Predicting Party Sizes: The Logic of Simple Electoral Systems*. Oxford: Oxford University Press.

——and Ensch, John (2006). "Institutional Determinants of the Largest Seat Share," *Electoral Systems*, 25: 760–75.

——and Grofman, Bernard (1985). "Rethinking Duverger's Law: Predicting the Effective Number of Parties in Plurality and PR Systems—Parties Minus Issues Equals One," *European Journal of Political Research*, 13: 341–52.

——and Hayes, James P. (1977). "How Trade/GNP Ratio Decreases with Country Size," *Social Science Research*, 6: 108–32.

——and Hosli, Madeleine O. (2006). "National Representation in International Organizations: The Seat Allocation Model Implicit in the EU Council and Parliament," *Political Studies*, 54: 370–98.

——and Kaskla, Edgar (2001). "The City-Country Rule: An Extension of the Rank-Size Rule," *Journal of World-Systems Research*, 7: 157–74.

——and Nurmia, Matti (1961). "On the Relations between Half-Life and Energy Release in Alpha-Decay," *Ann. Acad. Sci. Fennicae A.*, VI: 78.

——and Shugart, Matthew S. (1989). *Seats and Votes: The Effects and Determinants of Electoral Systems*. New Haven, CT: Yale University Press.

——and Sikk, Allan (2007). "Institutional Determinants of Mean Cabinet Duration," unpublished.

——and Williams, Ferd (1966). "Photoelectroluminescence of Single Crystals of Manganese-Activated Zinc Sulfide," *Journal of Applied Physics*, 13: 3085–91.

——Storey, Robert S., and McNeill, Keith G. (1961). "Breakdown Strength of Caesium Iodide," *Nature*, 190: 994.

von Eye, Alexander and Schuster, Christof (1998). *Regression Analysis for Social Sciences*. San Diego, CA: Academic Press.

Wallerstein, Michael (2001). "Does Comparative Politics Need a TOE?," *apsa-cp* (Newsletter of the Organized Section in Comparative Politics of the APSA) 12/1: 1.

Webster's New Collegiate Dictionary (1981). Springfield, MA: Merriam.

Wigner, Eugen P. (1960). "The Unreasonable Effectiveness of Mathematics in Natural Sciences," *Communications in Pure and Applied Mathematics*, 13: 1–14.

World Almanac and Book of Facts (2002). New York, NY: World Almanac Books.

Index

absurdities, avoidance of predicting 29, 112, 217
  conceptual inconsistency 62, 68, 113, 139, 148–9, 152
  contradictions 30–1, 48
  even under extreme circumstances 23, 52
  impossible negative values 26–7, 97, 100, 209
Achen, Christopher 194
Ahn, Woo-kyoung 9, 83
American Political Science Review 89–90
annihilative vs. enhancing factors 112–14
Anscombe, Francis J. 202–4
alchemy 11, 193–4
anchor points, conceptual 34, 37–9, 44–5, 49
  respect for 47–8, 155, 169
  for typical constraints 95–111, 203, 234
approximations, first and second 24, 34–5
arms races 144–53
assembly sizes 130–8, 139, 142–3, 153, 189
Arbuthnot, John 73, 78
Arrow, Kenneth 229

Bartolini, Stefano 211
Berry, William D. 199
biology 7, 162, 193, 230
  connections to other sciences 12, 226–9
Bochsler, Daniel 113
boundary conditions 45, 48, 95, 131, 145, 205
Boyle's law, *see* gas laws
Brahe, Tycho 6, 7, 194
Brambor, Thomas 55
Braumoeller, Bear F. 55

cabinet duration 153
  choice of index 176–81, 182–3
  connection to institutional inputs 130–8
  failure of statistics approach 188–91
  inverse square law 141–2, 158

Cartwright, Nancy 84
Casablanca riots 122
causal direction 31, 50, 135
causation, multiple 192
ceilings, conceptual 49–50, 107, 147
  exponential approach to 41, 104, 106, 137
ceteris paribus 28, 76
chemistry 12, 192, 226–9
citation frequency 150–1
city–country rule, *see* rank–size rule
coefficients/constants in equations:
  number of 52, 58–60, 68, 87–90, 112, 150
  guessing at values of 38, 218–19
cognitive sciences 226–8
Coleman, James S. 4, 111
Coleman, Stephen vii–ix, 7, 9, 78, 83, 105–6, 152, 208, 209, 210, 232
Colomer, Josep M. viii–ix, 53, 164, 165, 229, 232
communication channels 139, 140–3, 153
Compte, Auguste 12
computers, canned programs for 33, 195, 204
  excessive use, without understanding vii, viii, 11, 14, 30, 187, 238
  not possible for logical model building ix, 3, 29, 152
conceptual inconsistencies, *see* absurdities
conserved quantities 62, 139, 152
constraints, conceptual 10, 96, 111
  absence of 96–7
  core part of explanatory models 8, 29, 34, 45, 48–9, 95
  one 104–6
  two 97–100
  three 106–7
  four 107–10
continuity 49, 96, 114, 137
contradictions, *see* absurdities
correlation coefficient (R^2):